The Wilderness Coast

*Adventures of a
Gulf Coast Naturalist*

The Wilderness Coast
Adventures of a Gulf Coast Naturalist

Jack Rudloe

*Line Drawings and Map
by Julia Damon Hanway*

A Great Outdoors Book

*Great Outdoors Publishing Co.
St. Petersburg, Florida*

Published by Great Outdoors Publishing Co.
4747 28th Street North, St. Petersburg, FL 33714
(727)525-6609 / www.floridabooks.com

Publisher's Cataloging in Publication Data:
(Provided by Quality Books, Inc.)

Rudloe, Jack.
  The wilderness coast : adventures of a Gulf Coast
naturalist / Jack Rudloe ; line drawings and map by
Julia Damon Hanway.
    p. cm.
    Includes index.
    1. Marine biology—Gulf Coast (U.S.) 2. Marine
biology—Mexico, Gulf of. 3. Rudloe, Jack. 4. Marine biologists—United
States—Biography. I. Title.

QH104.5G84R83 2004   578.77'0976   2004112635

ISBN 0-8200-1207-6

Printed in the United States of America

Contents

Introduction:
The Marsh Monsters

Slowly but perceptibly the tide rose, a thin sheet of water moving inexorably through the marsh. It soaked into the barren white sands of the salt flats, changing them to gray, percolating down into fiddler crab burrows, and bubbling up air. My wife, Anne, and I had witnessed the rise a thousand times and always it was exciting.

We were hiking in the upper reaches of northwest Florida's wetlands, searching for a lost freshwater spring and collecting sea creatures. A strong south wind blew, pushing the water through the dense strands of needlerush that fringes much of the northern Gulf of Mexico. Far out in the bay whitecaps rolled. The tide had already covered the last of the mud flats and oyster bars, but here, far up in the protective marshes, muffled from any wave action, the rising water hardly rippled.

I stopped, put down my buckets, and looked about the great wilderness of spongy golden marshes that seemed to go on forever. Occasional hammocks of pines and palms marked slight elevations in the land rising from the flatness. Bubbling out of the marsh was the spring. "We can head that way," I said, pointing uncertainly toward the big hammock, "but there's a good chance the tide will catch us and we'll have to swim the creek."

Anne shrugged, "'So we'll swim the creek. It's a nice day. The way the tide is coming in, the water will be too deep to catch the grass shrimp in the seine if we don't get a move on."

We plunged forward, deeper into the soft boggy ground. Salt marshes must be taken on their own terms. They are glorious places, bugs and all. With their green and brown grasses producing nutrients for the sea, they are among, the richest and most productive environments on earth. Able to withstand salt water, the grasses stand eternally as a buffer between the murky estuaries and bays and the high green forests, exud-

Marshes are glorious places, bugs and all.

ing life and energy. Bubbling, splashing sounds of crawling, swimming creatures hint at the vast abundance of life that dwells in the wetlands.

Chances are we could catch the creatures we needed in any creek, but we had hoped that we might find something different, something interesting and rare around the spring. There is something magical about a spring that bubbles fresh water up from the ground. Back in the 1920s the commercial fishermen who built their camps in the tree hammocks at the edge of the shore used to hike out into the marsh to fill their water bottles. The sulfur-rich mineral springs that boil up from the cavities in the limestone bedrock beneath the marshy sediments were believed to have great medicinal value.

All the old-timers had passed on, and it was up to us to rediscover the springs. It had become a quest, adding spice to our day-to-day existence making a living on the wilderness coast, collecting marine organisms for the Gulf Specimen Company, our small commercial biological supply house.

Only from the air is it clear how vast the wilderness coast is.

The Florida peninsula reaches down into the Caribbean, and the coastal shallows of the Gulf Coast encompass 60 million acres of submerged sea grass meadows, sand bottom, limestone outcroppings, and coral reefs. Below Cedar Keys the shoreline is covered with dense,

impenetrable mangrove forests that whine into the night with mosquitoes. Northward are great open marshes, like the ones we were walking through. Flying above the land you can see sinkholes with tannin-stained water gleaming up from the earth amid a sea of grass.

The eastern Gulf of Mexico, which extends from the Florida Keys north and west to Mobile Bay, has some of the richest and most diverse wild coastline left in the continental United States.

Between the Mississippi Delta and the Dry Tortugas there are some fifty-thousand square miles of continental shelf, making this one of the shallowest large bodies of water in the world. All but five thousand square miles of the fifty thousand lie inside the fifty fathom curve, and there is no telling how much of the area is only neck-high on normal high tide, like the interminable tideflats of Tampa Bay and Crystal River that go on and on out to sea.

Where the west Florida shelf narrows greatly, near Destin, extending to Pensacola, and on to Alabama, a veritable "boom" city has sprung up, exuding glittering neon carscapes, bikinis on the beaches, glistening suntan-oiled bodies, and giant purple plastic dinosaurs hovering over innumerable putt-putt golf courses. With deep water so close to shore, the waves polish the sands until they gleam, scouring away the mud and silt and leaving white sands and blue tropical water.

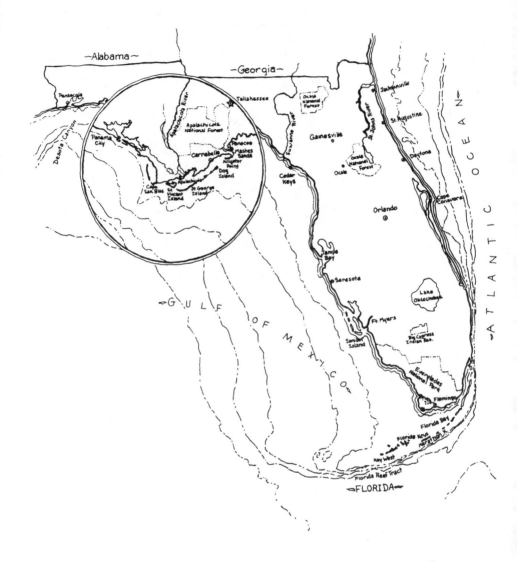

Map of Florida. Circled detail shows "wilderness coast."

Save for occasional sudden storms, the waters along the shelf are placid, not like the North Atlantic or Pacific, where the deep ocean slips into the depths a little way off shore. Here the submerged shelf drops off at the rate of only one foot per mile. Fifty fathoms is at least seventy miles from most Gulf shores except off Destin, and then miles beyond that lies the one-hundred-fathom curve. Snapper fishermen accurately enough call it the "Edge of the Earth." There the continental shelf plunges into the depths, down, down, down, until the line runs completely off the average depth recorder two or three thousand fathoms. The West Florida escarpment, as oceanographers call it, is one of the steepest slopes in the ocean. With angles of up to fifty-five degrees, this giant limestone cliff rises some six thousand feet above the ten-thousand-foot-deep sea floor.

For the most part, the bottoms and the waters remain largely unexplored. Out here is a vast, unspoiled blue panorama. This area, with its endless submarine sea grass meadows and sand flats, is generally one of Florida's best-kept secrets. Spotted sea trout, redfish, drum, and bluefish concentrate in the mud holes and creeks. Sometimes acres of mullet move along the shallows, in two feet of water, throwing a wake, and commercial fishermen strike their gill nets hauling them in. Meanwhile sports fishermen traveling in small boats cast four-pound test lines around oyster bars and are often rewarded with a big catch of redfish.

It was a glorious day; the warm sun and blue skies beamed down on Anne and me as we hiked along. At the edge of a salt flat we found a game trail, a narrow passage through the tall marsh grass. The black mud was packed with deer tracks but was firm enough to bear our weight. As we got deeper into the marsh, other game trails split off and joined us, always staying on relatively firm ground. Suddenly the previously impenetrable marsh was open before us and we made rapid progress.

Despite its prickliness, its uniform long thin reedy stalks, needlerush is extremely fragile. Deer and raccoon leave permanent trails snaking through the wet grasslands. At one point we crossed a freshly flattened wide line of grass, an alligator trail—a big, fresh alligator's trail. It was a strange feeling being out there in the world of the prehistoric reptile. As we followed along the already trampled animal trails, the ground squished beneath our feet, leaving our imprint in the muddy sands, atop the cloven hooves of deer, and the fingerlike impressions of raccoon that left behind their scats of red yaupon berries and chewed-up fiddler crabs.

When we traveled into any coastal environment, we always had a shopping list of creatures to collect. Much of the time we were on natural tideflats, hiking out over the horizon of emerging sand and grass, picking up starfish and sea cucumbers with benumbed fingers on the winter low tides. Like blue herons stalking the shallows, our eyes roved the sand for telltale keyhole slits of quahog clams and the impressions of water droplets where they spurted out water. These clams will bring a touch of the real world to a classroom miles from the ocean.

We dove along the rock jetties, located at either side of the ship's channel in Panama City and Destin, and checked out the immense Skyway Bridge spanning Tampa Bay. Oil rigs around the mouth of the Mississippi were good places to see concentrations of red snapper, black sea bass, and other fish. And when sport fishing clubs dumped car bodies, tires, construction rubble, and sunken ships on the bottom to create fish habitat, we partook of the riches of glistening chunks of pink and green sea pork that grew on them. The creatures we gathered were put on jets and whisked away to research or teaching laboratories, leaving us behind. We dragged our seines through the man-made drainage ditches in the marshes, as well as the natural winding creeks, to catch the grass shrimp, killifish, juvenile redfish, and mullet for public aquariums and schools.

It took ingenuity and adaptability to exist on a wilderness coast. Sometimes we were commercial collectors digging brachiopods, or lampshells, on tidal flats; other times teachers with a class explaining how they were seeing some of the oldest species of creatures on earth, dating back to the Paleozoic Era. With an occasional grant, we were scientists investigating phenomena such as the movements and migrations of horseshoe crabs or mariculture of slipper lobsters.

Needlerush, *Juncus roemerianus*, is not the most pleasant stuff to walk through. The tips of its spiky blades came up to our waists and continually pricked our fingers. And in *Juncus*, one doesn't dare bend over for fear of getting stabbed in the eyes. Although wetter, it was easier to walk through the creek beds, following the winding watercourses that wove in and out through the marshes. Somewhere in that matrix there was the lost spring, welling up fresh water from the honeycomb of buried limestone. Although finding the spring kept our sense of discovery alive, it had a practical side as well. Anne had a Ph.D. in marine biology, which she used occasionally to augment the meager income we received from collecting creatures and writing about them. She taught environmental education courses, and being able to direct a group of college students to an artesian spring out in the wilderness was part of our stock-in-trade.

"It's time to face reality," I said, wiping the sweat out of my eyes. "Trying to combine exploration with a collecting trip during a weekday when there are orders to pack just isn't going to work. It's two o'clock now; we still need to seine the ditch for grass shrimp and put them on this afternoon's flight. Besides, the tide is rising, and if we don't get a move on, the shrimp will be all up in the marsh grass, and we won't be able to catch them."

"I know, I know," Anne conceded, "but it's such a lovely afternoon. Let's at least hike over to the Indian midden for a few minutes; then we'll go."

Several hundred yards away a tree hammock loomed above the golden sea of grass. We struggled through the mud, until the vegetation thinned and we ascended the incline of shell and dirt. There we perched enjoying the elevation and the breeze, ten feet above the marsh, next to prickly pears, cabbage palms, pines, and toothache bushes. Mankind has been on this wilderness coast for at least ten thousand years, and some archaeologists say twenty. Stone Age projectile points and tools are common almost everywhere in the pine palmetto flatwoods and salt marshes. Beneath our rumps were all sorts of secrets. Amidst the shells and fish bones archaeologists have unearthed copper bracelets, pottery, beads, and human bones. They were storehouses of information on the fauna and flora of the coast and what people ate. Creatures long extinct from north Florida, like the ivorybill woodpecker, were once part of the Indians' diet. The remains of Florida panthers and manatees were part of the record.

Unfortunately, many of those secrets and records were destroyed. Once there was a gigantic complex of middens on Fiddler's Point at the head of Dickerson Bay in Panacea, but they were lost to the bulldozer when the road that gave us access into the marshes was built. The shell mounds, with all their secrets, were scooped up and leveled out into the wetlands.

There is something magical about these middens. Elevated above the marsh, they afford an expansive view of the vast wilderness coast. And there we sat, overlooking the cosmic blending of water, land, and sky, mystics in search of an answer. When our minds cleared, we turned back into being businesspeople in search of an income, collectors in search of animals, writers and consultants in search of a contract.

Gazing across the great expanse of marsh, we could see our truck parked up on the road shoulder, which destroyed the mystical mood. It was a reminder that time was pressing, and we started back toward it. Going in a straight line was not the easiest way to travel. We followed the game trails and the creeks. Moving along at a less than leisurely pace, marsh rabbits occasionally bolted ahead of us and melted into the grass, standing still as death until we passed by. From the dense grass came angry loud squawks of the marsh hens, reminding us that we were intruders. Only now and then, if we paused at the edge of one of the many creeks that wound through the marsh and stood perfectly still, could we catch a glimpse of these ugly brown, nearly flightless little birds. Occasionally one would emerge from the wall of grass, hurry over to the herd of fiddler crabs at the edge of the creek, snatch one up, and fade back into the grass. Once a mother hen darted in front of us with four homely, drab baby chicks. They were masters of camouflage. Then seeing us, she blared a raucous caterwauling protest. The message from all these creatures was clear: we were in their world, and they left little doubt in our minds that they preferred to be left alone.

It was easier to walk along the creek bed than fight the grass. So when we reached the edge where the tannin-brown waters meandered their way through the carpet of cheerful green marsh grass we plunged in.

The bottom was sandy, almost hard-packed. Small blue crabs and minnows scurried ahead of us, darting into the protective foliage of marsh grass. The water was alive with fish. Everywhere there were ripples and splashes.

Along the steep banks where *Spartina afterniflora*, or cordgrass, sank its dense roots into the mud, ribbed mussels protruded, anchored with a network of byssus threads. Male fiddler crabs waved their large single claws, forever beckoning the small-clawed females into their burrows. All of this exists amid the green cordgrasses that flourish at the edge of the sea from Maine to Texas.

Along the Atlantic seaboard *Spartina* is the dominant marsh, but here on the west Florida shelf it only fringes the needlerush. Each of the broad beautiful dark-green blades of grass secretes salt crystals through special tubes, or vesicles, and deposits them on the leaf's surface, where the tidewaters wash them away. All the marsh plants have their own special mechanisms of coping with salt. In the nearby salt flats, where the salt buildup is so concentrated that almost nothing grows, saltworts and pickleweeds hang on by storing fresh water in their tissues like cacti.

The ability to withstand this harsh environment has its rewards. If any seed of an upland or freshwater plant blown in by the winds dared to sprout, it would quickly wither and die. Without competition the salt marshes can flourish as a monoculture, one endless grassy plain free from shading by invading shrubs and trees, limited only by water depth as they reach out to sea. The closer to the creek, the taller the *Spartina* marsh grows. Unlike the abundant needlerush, *Spartina* has to receive regular inundations of the tide to flourish.

The creek meandered and wound into another creek, and that one ran into still another larger one that ran through a concrete culvert under the road. Because it was such a rich area, we often took school groups there. The grass was matted down on the shore where busloads of schoolchildren waited as we dragged the net before them to demonstrate the incredibly wide diversity of life that could live and thrive in such a narrow stretch of water. We did this to instill an environmental awareness in young people, to help them share our love of nature, and to enlist their future aid in our endless battles to save the wetlands from mindless and irresponsible development along the Gulf Coast.

Yet it was ironic that we preached environmental protection from the banks of a man-made ditch. It was dug during the 1920s by prison labor, right through mosquito- and fly-infested boggy marsh in the scorching sun. Men in striped uniforms worked with the chain-gang bosses standing over them with a ten-gauge shotgun. It was a study in good old Southern prison torture, but the old-timers said it kept everyone honest.

We waded across the ditch, and all about us the water boiled and flurried with life. Unseen creatures streaked and splashed and broke the flat surface into concentric circles. On the other side we hiked up the shell midden embankment where the truck was parked. "We better make it quick," I said, grabbing the minnow seine and buckets. "It took longer to get here than I thought."

"If we miss the flight, can't we ship tomorrow?" asked Anne.

"No, this is for the Environmental Protection Agency. They have an experiment planned in the morning."

The shrimp and fish would be used to monitor water quality. Live animals would be subjected to various concentrations of contaminants, such as pesticides or some industrial discharge. Some biologists referred to it as "kill 'em and count 'em," but I felt good about dragging our seines to catch these creatures. Somewhere, some toxic material might be stopped from spewing into a marsh because the regulatory agency had the data that said it was lethal.

But there were no factories or oil rigs here yet, no major housing developments, only a quiet marshy bay and a paved road. Nothing is more adaptable than nature. When the marsh grass was originally scooped out and water flowed in, the ditch became a superhighway for estuarine life that swarmed in on high tides. When the water receded, many of the small fish became trapped in the borrow pits that retained a foot or two of water to the absolute delight of the wood storks, herons, and other wading birds that promptly began feasting on the fish in them.

As the tide flooded into the creeks, organisms of all kinds moved in among the forests of stems and roots, spreading out into the protective jungle of grasses. Hastily we spread the net across the creek and started pulling it.

The water rippled ahead of our feet as hordes of small, and not so small, torpedo-shaped bodies rocketed ahead trying to flee the approaching wall of webbing. Small grass shrimp hiding down in the mucky sediments jumped as the lead line rooted them out, only to be engulfed by the nylon webbing. With Anne on one side of the ditch and me on the other, we moved inexorably on, holding the lead line on the bottom with our feet. The bobbing corks kept the top suspended above the water so that nothing could swim over the wall of quarter-inch webbing, and for most life in the ditch there was no escape. Soon the wings of the net, now bent into a U between us, were showing small silvery bodies of killifish pressed up against the webbing. Some frantic fish darted into the fringes of the marsh, at the edge of the ditch, as their instinct told them to, and succeeded in escaping. A large blue crab moved past my feet into the safety of the shallow marsh behind me. Like other predators, we were only partially efficient catching the slower and less cautious fish.

"Whatever you do, keep the lead line down," I cautioned Anne, as we pulled the net along. "We haven't got time to do this twice."

"That may not be easy with all the lugworm eggs," she called back across the ditch.

As we trudged along dragging the minnow seine, gelatinous pink muddy blobs of lugworm eggs broke off and packed into the middle of the net. Sometimes, when the worms were spawning on the full and new moons, the eggs were so copious that dragging became impossible. But they soon hatched, the jellylike egg masses disappeared, and the shrimp and fish feasted on the tiny worms.

Grass shrimp, tiny transparent things, exploded out of the mud like popcorn as our feet churned up the bottom. "I don't think we'll have any trouble filling an order for a mere two thousand," I said optimistically; "even with the lugworms, I'll bet there's thirty or forty thousand in the net right now. If these were juvenile peneid shrimp, we could take them back and grow them to maturity and get rich."

"I know, my students always are so disappointed when I tell them this is as big as they get, and they're not the commercial shrimp," said Anne.

Grass shrimp never grow very large, certainly not large enough to eat (although the Japanese consider them a delicacy), but they are tremendously important to the sport and commercial fishermen because all the larger fish eat them. Virtually everything with a mouth goes crazy when it meets schools of transparent crustaceans. Perhaps that's why the shrimp prefer to hide in the uppermost reaches of the marsh and in the shallowest of water.

The shrimp become enormously abundant in the late fall when the water temperatures begin to drop. Then starting around May they become scarce, and by July we have to work to find a few hundred. We suspect that all the larger hungry fish crowding in the marsh in warm weather have something to do with their vanishing.

Grass shrimp, *Palaemonetes pugio*, were much in demand as live food for the aquarium. All we had to do was introduce a batch of living grass shrimp into our tanks, and even the most finicky fish would go berserk and start lunging at the shrimp as they desperately flounced, jumped, and tried to get away. Curators at some of the large public aquariums around the nation have told me that living, or even frozen, grass shrimp will turn a frail rare African or Asian marine tropical fish into a healthy, voracious feeder overnight.

As I reached the end of the ditch, I felt no inordinate amount of strain. Although there were a few lugworm eggs, we hadn't jellied down to the point where it was gut-busting to haul the net in.

I waded back across to join Anne on the other side. Herds of fiddler crabs scurried away from the water's edge as I drew near. This was a critical time: we had to keep our lead lines pressed tightly down or everything would escape.

I crouched down, pressing the lead line all the tighter to the bottom, hauling back on the webbing, shrinking the semicircle space within the net, steadily concentrating the mass of life in the middle until we could heave it up on the broad bank.

As the wings of our minnow seine were piling up on the edge of the ditch, I glanced at the diminished water space within the half circle and noticed with some irritation that there was something large, black, and heavy being dragged along. It moved like dead weight , inert. Obvious-ly it was a log that could mess up our strike. Usually the big expanse of needlerush marsh alongside the creek system managed to filter out logs. I didn't recall any recent storms strong enough to send anything that large far up into the ditch. Maybe someone threw it there. In any case, it would have to be hauled out.

I turned my attention back to the net. It was the critical time when we began to draw the webbing up on shore. To keep the lead line down, I crouched down on my knees, bending way over and steadily pulling the lead and cork lines in together, hand over hand. If we didn't keep a steady, fast-moving tension on the wall of webbing, straining the water and packing the shrimp and fish together, they could get away. Escape lay either over the floating cork line or down beneath the lead line.

I glanced back at the obstruction in the net and cursed to myself. If the log became all balled up in our net, we could lose the entire catch. I wished we had a third person present to wade out and drag it up on the bank. But neither of us could turn the moving net loose to do so.

Vaguely I thought that something wasn't quite right. The log was shiny, almost leathery, I dismissed my concern and focused my atten-tion on the lead line. If I could keep it pressed down tight enough, I could perhaps drag the log and the catch up on the beach without balling up the net and letting everything get out.

I looked up again and, suddenly, came face to face with a pair of large cold yellow eyes staring back at me, no more than four feet away.

"What's the matter?" Anne cried, jumping up from her crouching position on the other end when she heard me yell, "God, God, an alliga-tor! Get away from that thing!"

For a few dangerous seconds I froze, mesmerized by those eyes. My whole body shook with fear as I looked at that dark leathery skin stretched tightly over the bony head. The coldness of the gaze, the ter-rible alien focus—it mattered not that it was only five-and-a-half feet long. It could still do plenty of damage.

Over the years there have been a growing number of attacks on humans, not so much by female alligators protecting their nests as by predatory males. Most are maulings, but there have been a few fatalities.

Comprising bone and muscle and less than one percent brain, the males can reach sixteen feet or larger. The females seldom grow more than eight or nine feet, and together they fill the night with terrifying mating roars and bellows that shake the swamp with thunder.

Alligators are among the closest things to monsters we have left on earth, the very essence of prehistoric life, remaining virtually unchanged for 60 million years.

People have mistakenly lost their fear of these ancient reptiles. Alligators have become the symbol of Florida tourism, plastered on billboards amid the neon and claptrap of tourist attractions. They appear ubiquitously on postcards, in animated cartoons, and as smiling mascots of the University of Florida's football team. But I had learned through bitter experience to take them seriously. They are not friendly stuffed dolls, or inflated green floats in swimming pools. They are throwbacks to the Age of Reptiles, surviving for more than 60 million years, and among the last true monsters left on earth.

In that fraction of a second, looking into those eyes staring up from the roadside ditch, atavism took over. True, it was only a five-footer, maybe six, but as the years vanished, terrible memories returned, when I battled another, far larger alligator than this trying to save my dog. It happened at Otter Lake, which was only a couple of miles away on the St. Marks National Wildlife Refuge. It used to be our favorite swimming hole. Anne and I would take our eight-month-old baby, Sky, and soak in the warm tannin waters beneath the towering cypress trees with their gnarled roots and buttresses that rose high above that water. What happened that morning on June 8, 1980, could have been much worse.

I had just finished jogging along the sand roads with Megan, my three-year-old Airedale, and went in for our usual swim. Then it happened. Even though it was eight years ago, I could still hear myself screaming, "Megan... Come, Megan... Meegaan!" My fright burst through the still morning air in desperation and disbelief.

An enormous alligator had rounded the curve of the lake shore and was bearing down on my Airedale. The cold, gold eyes, gliding just above the opaque water of Otter Lake, were fixed on Megan, my companion, my friend for the past three years.

Never had I seen a living creature move so fast, with such overtly grim determination. As the beast sped into the shallows, I could see ugly white spikes of teeth protruding from its crooked, wavy jaws.

Megan was almost out of the water, swimming to me with a bewildered expression, unaware of the danger closing in behind her in the lake where she swam almost every morning after a three-mile run with me.

Megan's feet hit the bottom.

She's going to escape!

I felt hope, joy. But the black, plated animal put on a horrible burst of speed. More and more of the knobby, black body emerged from the tannin-brown water. There seemed to be no end to it.

"No! No! No!" I screamed and rushed forward, somehow hoping to frighten it away, but the reptile couldn't have cared less. Its attention was fixed on Megan with cold-blooded intensity. With an explosion of water, it lunged upward, rearing above my dog almost as tall as a man, its front webbed claws spread menacingly apart. Time seemed to freeze. *Tyrannosaurus rex* had come to life.

Megan's confusion was transformed to terror that froze her to the spot. From somewhere inside the reptilian nightmare came a hissing like a steam boiler. The hissing became an unearthly roar as it struck, clamping its jaws on my pet. Crashing back into the water, it twisted and rolled, driving her down into the mud and weeds.

Something snapped in my brain. I had to do something. Adrenalin surged through me. With a cry of rage, of fear, of instinct, I found myself running and leaping through the air, onto the back of the thing attacking my Airedale.

Now the dark water exploded and cascaded, as the alligator slapped its tail. I slid over its plates and bumps, groping for a hold on its great back. I felt numbing pain in my chest, as my chin jammed into its ridged back.

My brain flooded with messages. It was bony to the touch, almost dry, not slimy. There wasn't an inch of give. As I struggled with every bit of muscle to throw it off Megan, it swelled with air, making the hard plated scales that normally lay flat rise upward like a spiny blowfish. The thing was suddenly bristling with spikes.

Ignoring me, the alligator surged forward and got an even better grip on Megan, who all but disappeared inside the horrid maw. My hands groped the soft underside of the monster's throat, feeling the alien beaded leather and scales. It was almost flabby.

The tail slapped again. Water exploded.

Keep clear of the tail, it can break your leg!

I hung on, desperately clinging, and tried with all my strength to turn the animal, to keep it from returning to the sunless, deep waters.

I've got to force it up on land.

My hands groped up to its mouth, right where its toothy smile hinged. At least here was a handle of sorts. But still, it was no more than a skull covered with leather. There was no flesh, no give.

I got a good grip, dug my knees into the sand, and yanked upward. The steel-trap jaws wouldn't yield. I sensed them shutting down harder, squeezing life and breath out of my Megan. I saw a flowing trail of bubbles.

If only I had a weapon. A knife!

She's drowning… I'm running out of time!

Again and again I dug in and pulled up on its upper jaw, but nothing I could do distracted it from its single awesome purpose. Fortunately for me, the saurian's only intent was to drag its prey down into the lake and drown it. Its small brain was able to focus on that and that only. I was only a hindrance, not an alternative. Maybe it thought I was another alligator trying to steal its meal away.

I felt my knees dragging through the weeds in the sandy bottom as it pushed inexorably back into the water.

With all my might, I slammed my fist down between its eyes, again and again. The only result was pain in my hands. It was like pounding a fence post. Time, depth, and distance worked against me as the alligator dragged Megan farther out into the water. I was losing the battle.

Desperately I threw my one-hundred seventy pounds into manhandling it, trying to turn it back into my world. For a second, hope returned. I succeeded. The beast did turn. But just for a moment. Then it lifted me up, swung around, and continued on its course.

The eyes… go for the eyes, something commanded in my brain.

My fingers worked their way over the unyielding leather-clad skull. I found its eyes, but the two sets of eyelids, one membranous and the other a thick leathery cover, closed automatically, sealing off its only vulnerable spot. Tightly closed, they weren't what I imagined them to be, soft and yielding. They felt like mechanical ball joints on a car. With all my might I jammed my thumbs down, but it was futile, as if I were jamming my thumbs against hard rubber handballs.

All my eye-gouging succeeded in doing was making the alligator swim faster. Black water closed over my head, the bottom was now sloping off quickly, and the beast had water beneath it. Any advantage I had was gone. Now it was rapidly entering its own world, and for me it was no longer a battle of land versus water; it was one of oxygen versus the depths.

I managed to force it up and get one hard gulp of air before it pulled me back down. Again I drove my thumbs into its eyes. By now, I knew that my efforts to save Megan were futile. Even if I could free her, and she weren't already dead, how could she survive having her bones crushed and her lungs punctured by eighty spiked teeth, each one an inch long.

Its long tail swept back and forth, sculling it forward. I was towed rapidly out toward the middle of the lake, no longer a problem to the powerful swimmer.

Once more I fought it to the surface long enough to grab another breath, and then we were going down, down, again. Down into the lightless swamp water. I was exhausted; my lungs were bursting. I could no longer see any sign of Megan. My vision was limited to inches—just enough to see the alligator's coat of mail.

Despairingly I let go and watched its plated trunk churning beneath me down into the gloom. It went on and on and on, like a freight train. I saw the rear webbed feet, churning one after the other, and then the narrow, undulating tail with its pale underside flashing. I could not see Megan. I would never see her again.

I boiled up to the surface, erupted into the air, swelling my lungs with oxygen. When I could breathe again, I let out the mindless despairing cry of a wounded animal. My arms and legs thrashed through the water, moving me toward the cypresses and the beautiful oaks with their long twisted branches. Finally hard sand grated beneath my knees as I scrambled up on the shoreline, crying and yelling incoherently.

In horror, I turned and looked at the empty lake—it had swallowed up all signs of disturbance. Its calm waters mirrored the blue sky, the stacks of white puffy clouds, and the moss-draped cypress trees. An osprey winged its way across the sky, calling its highpitched chirp. It was as if nothing had occurred.

For days I remained shaken and depressed. I had fought with everything I had and lost. I missed Megan terribly. I kept seeing her golden shaggy face looking at me in bewilderment as I urged her out of the lake. Over and over again, that big black head closed in on her. Slowly I reconstructed what happened from the bruises and scratches and pains in my body. The long linear scrapes on my chest had to have come from the alligator's dorsal bumps, the bruises on my ribs and belly from its thrashing back and forth. The aches in my thighs were from straddling it with a scissors grip.

Whenever I closed my eyes, the nightmares returned and so did the words of Walter Anderson, a hermit artist who renounced civilization and went to live on Horn Island, off the Mississippi coast.

What is man's relationship to nature? If he makes friends with it, does he lose the careless sowing of seeds? If nature becomes a god, will it not also become a demon and destroy him with that same careless brutality with which man destroys fish? If the brute is necessary, who is to be the brute?

Anne's agitated voice broke through my thoughts, "Forget the damn grass shrimp. Throw the net down and get away from it. Do you know what a severe infection you can get if it bites you, not to mention tearing your flesh to ribbons?"

"Just stay with the net," I barked back harshly. My fear turned to anger. "I can handle it. Keep your cork line up and your lead line down. I'll get him out."

"OK, but I hope you're not trying to prove something to yourself," she cautioned.

Anne was a safe distance away, and I wanted to keep her that way. But I was still in easy striking range. I knew how fast a frightened and angry alligator could move. I loosened the strain on the webbing but kept a grip on the lines, figuring that any minute the alligator would turn and bolt back into the water.

Instead, it just sat there, focusing on me with its reptilian eyes. Oh, those eyes! How they were burned into my nightmares. They were the last thing many creatures saw before they were dragged down into the depths of a dark water hole.

This was a dangerous situation. Instead of fleeing as it was supposed to, it just sat there regarding me with its sharp white teeth protruding from its upper jaw. I was still trembling to think that moments before I had pulled it up to within a couple of feet from my face, never suspecting anything. It seemed unbelievable that we had dragged that entire ditch, towed it along in the net, and never knew it was there. There was no struggle, no fight, no sign or warning.

Although we saw their trails through the marsh from time to time, the alligators were so secretive that we seldom encountered one. No doubt this one had swum up the tidal creeks, perhaps from the interior cypress swamps; crawled over the marsh; and moved into the ditch to feast on the concentration of grass shrimp.

I couldn't throw down the net and let all the shrimp swim out. We had a deadline to make at the airport, the day's shipments were packed and ready, and there was no time to make a second strike. The 'gator had to go!

"Get out; move," I shouted, giving the net a tug, and then letting off. The 'gator was pulled inertly toward me, but made no effort to move. That it sat there like a lump, just so much deadwood, ready to explode, was even more unnerving.

Ready to somersault backward at any sign of a forward lunge, I tugged the net again. That part I really didn't like. Every pull brought that placid time bomb of teeth, tail, and claws a little closer to me. But I jerked the webbing again, hard. The whole length of the alligator came up to the surface. I could see its entire body: it seemed to go on and on, the legs, the webbed feet, the front claws, and even some of its tail.

It let out a great hiss; opened its jaw, lined with white teeth; and gave me a view of its endless pink gullet. I reared backward, trembling, realizing how frightened I was of this animal, dropping the net and letting it go slack. Again memories of my last encounter with the one at Otter Lake returned with a rush. For several years it had been a legend in my mind, a demon, and now I was once again face to face with one of these big, flesh-and-blood predatory reptiles from a prehistoric past.

I just wanted the damn thing to leave, that's all. I shouted at it with fury, "Come on, damn it, get out." It responded by backing away, pulling farther into the minnow net, dragging some of the webbing back with it.

I was getting ready to give up and let him have the net and everything. An order of shrimp wasn't worth a maiming.

I had an idea. I waded out, getting dangerously close again; ignoring my wife's protests I grabbed the cork line and jerked it down beneath the surface. I knew I was proving something to myself, trying to conquer my fear. I watched many of the fish and shrimp swim over the top, but I didn't care.

No longer having the wall of corks blocking his escape, the 'gator backed over the net into the freedom of its own habitat. It turned and, with a great slap of its tail, bolted gratefully for open water. It disappeared beneath the murk, and in a moment the water was as placid as if the alligator had never been there.

Most of the shrimp had escaped, but that still left more than plenty for our order. Yet it was anticlimactic to be sitting there, casting glances at the empty water, picking out those little crustaceans and sorting them into buckets to take back to the lab. Any minute I half-expected to see the alligator pop up, and come forward hissing. Not the real one, but the alligator of my nightmares. I knew I would never recover from the time the alligator in the lake attacked my dog and I attacked it.

"I suppose it's only a matter of time before someone shoots that little 'gator," Anne pondered. "Probably the Fish and Game Commission will get a complaint and send a licensed hunter to blast it away. And its hide will be sold for belts and its meat to a restaurant. It won't be long before they're back on the endangered species list. How do you conserve a big reptile with teeth? I enjoy living on a wilderness coast where there are such creatures, but I don't want one to eat one of our children someday."

Still feeling the agitation, and fear, and excitement, I tossed the last handful of shrimp into the bucket and threw my pent-up energy into vigorously shaking the net to set the rest free. "There's no good answer. If they shoot too many, they'll become scarce, and we'll never see any. When I first moved to Florida thirty years ago, I never saw any 'gators, except at night with a spotlight. But if they're not hunted, and if too many people keep crowding in on their habitats, and they lose their fear of us, there's bound to be conflict."

As dredges suck up swamps and turn them into shopping centers and canals, the alligators are being driven from their sawgrass and river swamp homes. They take up new residence in golf course ponds, marina basins, and canals—and that's where accidents happen.

"Well," Anne said, grabbing the bucket and heading for the truck, "you have to admit, they do keep life interesting."

1. The Time of the Horseshoe Crab

Rain gusted down, and the car windshield was one continuous gray blur of water. Slowly we drove along the paved highway that ended at a narrow strip of sandy beach. I rolled down the window a fraction of an inch to get a look at the marsh. Nothing is more magnificent than a marsh when a squall brings the driving forces of wind and rain sweeping through the grasses. The wind gusts through the brown and green rushes, bending them low. Sea, air, and land all blend into a violent gray world.

It was the ferocious kind of weather that puts mankind in its place, the kind that could spawn a tornado. Lightning crackled, thunder rolled, and the air was rich in ozone.

"I wonder how all the grass shrimp and killifish are managing down in the creeks?" I ventured. "Do you suppose the marsh offers them any protection?"

"I doubt it," said Anne, wiping away the fog that was clouding the inside windshield. "I imagine they're taking the same punishment that everything on land takes." Her voice was a shade despairing, "And the same punishment we're going to take when we get to the beach. It sure would be nice if it stopped raining for a few minutes."

Perhaps the animals could burrow down into the mud where they would feel the vibrations of the incessant splattering of rain and the rolling thunder. Perhaps they could see the dark skies split by lightning. I thought of how shrimpers often complained that when lightning and thunder came, shrimp sixty feet down on the bottom disappeared into the mud.

I glanced at my watch. We had ten minutes until high tide to get out and drag a plankton net all the way down the beach. We could hardly see the beach as lightning and thunder again shook the very earth.

Yet this was the weather we wanted. When the summer squall had struck, we dropped other work to come right away to the shore, where the pounding waves were scouring layers of sand on the beach. We hoped to discover the mystery of how hatchling horseshoe crabs, buried deep in the sand, get to the surface and are liberated into the sea.

Every spring female horseshoe adults, with their large armored bodies and pointed tails, come ashore and bury themselves in the sand to lay eggs. Anne had been studying their movements and migrations for three years and she had learned that their arrival was precisely tuned to the hour of high tide. You could almost set your watch by it. On days and nights of the full and new moon, the large females come crawling up out of the surf, the smaller males clinging to their backs with grasping claws. Sometimes five or six males jostle each other, crowding around the female, spreading their white milt while she lays thousands of tiny gray-green eggs in sticky clumps several inches below the surface. Sometimes at night in calm weather we could hear the eerie sounds of creaking, copulating crabs on the empty beaches as thousands of horseshoes slowly flexed their armored bodies and dug down deeper.

The tiny eggs develop and hatch in about six weeks while buried a foot deep in the sand. Able to withstand rain and the broiling heat, the embryos develop safely.

By midsummer we could count on finding nests filled with hatchlings about an eighth of an inch wide waiting to be set free almost anywhere we dug along the high-tide line. As the season wore on, there were fewer and fewer of these trilobite larvae, named because of their close resemblance to those long-extinct animals.

And it was puzzling. We had never seen any sign of them pouring out of the sands, either on high or low tides. Day after day we walked the beaches, watching the big crabs come ashore, dug up nests, and found no clue to when the young ones emerged.

Maybe it took a violent storm like this one to scour away the foot or so of sand that covered them and scatter them into the waves. At that moment, there was a break in the weather and the deluge gave way to drizzle. Anne hastily put on her waders and headed out into the surf carrying her fine-mesh plankton net as she had done so many times before. Each time she dragged it through the waves about ten feet from the high-tide line, emptied it out, and looked for babies. Only once or twice were there one or two found in the floating grass—a long way

Nothing is more magnificent than a marsh when a squall brings the driving forces of wind and rain sweeping through the grasses.

from the millions and millions of tiny trilobite larvae that had saturated the sands.

I kept a watchful eye on her as she struggled into the heavy surf, trying to keep the waves from filling her chest waders and knocking her over. The waves thundered on shore, pushed by thirty-knot winds. Her progress was painfully slow along the same old path. Again thunder boomed and shook the sky, and from her expression I could tell her thoughts were changing from science to survival. She braced herself as a wave rolled in at eye level and tried to jump above it. The water flooded in, and she was soaked in a flash. It had all but wrenched the plankton net from her hands. I started forward, ready to wade in and help her out, but she waved me off and kept pulling the net.

Walking slowly, we reached the end of the beach, and she struggled ashore still towing her plankton net. Lightning struck a dead tree nearby, and we could smell ozone. In the sudden blinding flash we contemplated our mortality. "Did you see that!" she said, between chattering teeth. "We're making an excellent target. I must be nuts!"

The funneled end of the plankton net was heavy with sand, crammed with floating manatee grass, seaweed, and debris. With the rain beating in our faces, I inverted it and washed the contents out into a bucket of water. There, mixed in the marsh straw, were thousands of baby horseshoe crabs.

"We did it, we did it!" we cried, joined in that great feeling of elation that comes from making a discovery. Perhaps it wasn't a landing on the moon, the discovery of a new vaccine, or a breakthrough in computer technology, but it would piece together a missing gap in the life cycle of this still mysterious creature.

The raging waves were full of tiny horseshoe crabs, washed from their nests, riding the surf to life and growth and freedom. In the bucket they swarmed like bees, several thousand liberated hatchlings swimming in dizzying spirals. For a moment our excitement was so great we hardly felt the rain and the freezing wind as we made our way back to the car.

Paleontologists have long called horseshoe crabs "living fossils." They are virtually identical to horseshoe crabs chipped out of 200-million-year-old rocks in the Alps. Some 400 million years ago there were similar-looking horseshoe crabs roaming the earth with giant water scorpions and trilobites. They were old-timers when dinosaurs first roamed the earth. The heavy-shelled creatures existed when continents drew apart and when high mountain ranges rose and fell. With a few exceptions—the cockroach, perhaps the coelacanth, and an obscure deep-sea mollusk—these biological relics have outlasted every other species on earth. Once there were hundreds of species of horseshoe crabs, but today only four survive. By far the largest populations are found along the Atlantic and Gulf coasts of North America, the rest living on the shores of Southeast Asia from India to Japan. The American horseshoe crab is a master of adaptation and survival, ranging from the chilly rocky bays of Maine to the sweltering mangrove swamps of the Yucatán.

Adaptability is the secret. They will nest wherever there is a sandy shore with gentle waves. When one beach erodes, another accretes and builds up with the shifting sand. A creature that has outlasted mountain ranges knows in its genes how to live with change.

Horseshoe crabs have doubtless always moved with the tide, the sand, the sea level, and the cosmic flow of time. But they are not true crabs. Lacking antennae and having a depressed flattened shell with three distinct segments, they are more closely related to spiders, scorpions, and ticks. Like their cousins on land, they have two small feeding claws that are used to seize prey instead of the elaborate mouthparts of true crabs.

Back in the protection of our car, we gazed out over the angry sea. "They must get washed out and settle down a few yards from shore," Anne mused. That was where we had found the young ones, making tiny threadlike trails. Having molted for the first time, they no longer resemble a trilobite. They all acquire short telsons, or pointed tails, making them look more like the adults.

We drove off wet and victorious, but in the days that followed, Anne was troubled by the results. "You know, it's been bothering me. Storm release doesn't make sense; I don't think we've got the whole answer."

"You saw what you saw. What did we get, two thousand larvae in a five-minute plankton tow?"

"Yes, I know, but how could they have their entire reproductive effort dependent upon a storm? A storm is a random event, and it can't just be any storm; it has to be one at high tide, and one that's powerful enough to sweep the sand off the beach. Four hundred million years of waiting for a storm?"

"I don't know, slash pines wait until there's a fire before dropping their seeds. Parasitic barnacles that live on the gills of crabs throw their eggs into the water when the crab molts and they're about to die. So why not horseshoe crabs waiting until there's a storm brewing? This is a hurricane coast anyway; barrier islands are shaped by storms. Look at Texas. It's a good story."

"It's too good; I'm not satisfied," she insisted. "We're going to keep checking the beach until we see them emerge."

The problem remained perplexing. No matter how many times we went to Mashes Sands, and dug down a foot, we always found the larvae tightly packed, nestled in a bunch. There was no sign that they crawled up to the surface. Day, night, high tide, low tide—it didn't seem to make any difference.

The summer began to slip past. We watched hordes of copulating crabs come up on the beach to lay fresh eggs, and we watched them develop and hatch. And sure enough, as the days passed, there were fewer and fewer larvae in the sand, even though there hadn't been more storms. Somehow they were getting out beyond our scrutiny.

One afternoon in July we sat covered with sand and frustration on the beach. Behind us stretched a row of holes dug in the sand-it looked as if a dozen dogs had been at work all at once.

"This is pointless," my wife said. "All these months we've been doing it all wrong. Maybe the time frame is wrong."

"What do you mean, time frame?" I asked, watching the tide lap up on the shore. Each gentle wave dissipated its force and drained down into the sand.

"Well, we come and measure the depth every few days trying to see whether they work their way up over a period of weeks. They're always deep when we come, but there are fewer of them. The larvae are getting past us. They must come up fast and get out quick. We aren't checking it at short enough intervals to see that. Maybe we need to check every hour, not every few days."

"Anne, come on. You may have a point, but we can't live on the beach all summer. We have other things to do."

"I know, I know," she snapped. She sat still for a minute staring into the last hole. "Listen," she finally said, "what about this? The full moon is in a few days. The eggs are laid on a full-moon tide and it'd take another equally high tide to get the water back to them. Everything those crabs do seems to be according to the tides. Let's check it that night at least. We can camp on the beach. It'll be fun."

Many animals and plants not only withstand these drastic but regular and predictable lunar changes but use them to their advantage by timing their feeding, breeding, and other activities to peak tides, either high or low. Fiddler crabs remain in burrows beneath the mud at high tide, safe from predatory fish, and emerge to feed on the flats as the tide recedes. On the highest high tides at full and new moon, they release their young, and strong tidal currents carry them out into the ocean.

Oysters open their shells to pump in water and food at high tide, but by tightly sealing their heavy calcified shells, they withstand bitter winter winds and broiling summer heat at low tide. Crabs, fish, snails—virtually all residents of the intertidal zone time their lives according to the tide and the moon.

Horseshoe crabs are especially governed by the tides and the moon, their movements accurately and precisely timed by the ebb and flow. Most of the Gulf Coast adults come to the breeding beach precisely at the hour of high tide both day and night for a few days before and after the peak of full moon. The young, which live on intertidal sand flats, remain buried at high tide but rise to the surface to feed at low tide, making winding mazes of trails in the sand.

It seemed reasonable that the larvae would be released on a tidal rhythm at the extreme high tides of the full and new moons when the water reached the nests. High tide on the full moon, when the water reached its peak at three o'clock in the morning, might tell the tale.

The moon had just risen as we walked down the beach, several nights later. The tideflat next to the beach was dry, exposed, but the tide would be rising for the next six hours. In a few hours the surf would be pounding on the shore again. We pitched a small tent amid the sea oats in case of rain, tossed the alarm clock and other gear inside, and sat in the warm sands to wait.

The moon grew round, as it rose higher into the sky. Even though the sands were dry, when we excavated the nests moisture was seeping in through the sand grains, and there was an indication that the nests were rising up slowly. At nine o'clock they were around six inches deep, and by eleven they had risen to four inches. Would they break through the top layer and disperse into the waves and follow that bright moon above? We'd soon know.

Light is a primary guiding force in directing the movement of horseshoe crabs throughout their lives. The eyes are among the first organs to develop and respond to light. By inserting microelectrodes into the nearly microscopic larvae inside the egg, scientists have been able to prove they use their eyes in the earliest stages of development.

The tiny trilobite larva twirls about within the confines of the egg case and plays with its molted shell as it grows and sheds, passing the molt from claw to claw. It undergoes four molts inside the egg before it hatches.

Light stimulates hatching in the laboratory. Switching on ceiling lights inspires them to begin breaking out of the membranes. But this presents a puzzle.

Down in their dark world, a foot beneath the sand grains, there was no light. We did know that as soon as we scooped out a handful of larvae and dropped them into water they began their furious swimming, and if we shone a small flashlight beam on the surface of the water they followed it. But, as Anne had found out, after countless experiments, they mostly did so on the night of full moon. Other nights they swam randomly, or not at all.

Actually horseshoe crabs have seven different eyes: two large oval lateral eyes on each side of the carapace, two in the middle of the shell, and on the underside, three almost microscopic lightreceptive organs. Probably there is more known about the lateral eyes of horseshoe crabs than any sensory system in any animal. No eye is really simple, because of its very function of transposing light into images that are registered in the brain. But the more simple organization of a horseshoe crab eye, compared to that of a rat or human, makes recording the electrical signals with which the eye codes and transmits information to the brain easier.

A friend and customer of ours, Dr. Robert Barlow, was studying horseshoe crab vision at the microscopic level and explained his study on a visit to his laboratory at the Marine Biological Laboratory in Woods Hole, Massachusetts. His research provided important insights into the way the human eye perceives lines, borders, contrasts, and contours. In his dark laboratory a living horseshoe crab was bolted to a study apparatus, surrounded with space age technology of oscilloscopes, electrodes, and computers flashing digital readouts. A portion of the crab's shell was cut away to expose the white stringy optic nerve that fed into its large multifaceted eye. A dissecting scope was poised over the preparation, and as we peered through it, he explained, "We insert a microelectrode into the nerve trunk, suck a single nerve cell into a tube, and record the individual cell's responses to light." He adjusted a dial on the oscilloscope, and the impulse registered on the green screen, when the light pipe beamed on the eye. "These patterns of light sensitivity have given us clues to understanding genetic human eye diseases like retinitis pigmentosa, which causes tunnel vision and can eventually lead to total blindness."

It was a bizarre sight, this 200-million-year-old living fossil hooked up to space age technology. Here was our most sophisticated science struggling to fathom the visual nature of a creature older than the flowering plants, older than many amphibians, reptiles, and woolly mastodons, and far older than Florida itself.

Time seemed to dissolve as we sat on the beach watching the moon glittering on the Gulf of Mexico with a dark salt marsh at our backs. We could feel the pull of the moon in our blood, as the tidewaters swelled into the bay, soaking the sands with each lapping wave. There is a whole mythology about the moon and its effect on life. Never cut timber on the full of the moon because the sap rises in the wood and it will rot in years to come, the old-timers say. Shrimpers live by the moon. When it's full, they stay tied to the dock because no amount of dragging will produce any shrimp. And gill-netters say that fish get "moon burnt" when they catch them and rot, even on ice.

We were camped at the far end of a small undeveloped beach near an old Indian midden overgrown with live oaks and pines. It could have been a thousand years earlier and we the Indian people who had left only a few shells, potsherds and arrowheads to mark their nights beside the same sea, and the same moon. Did any of them ever sit here and wonder how little horseshoe crabs got to the surface? Probably they didn't need to wonder. Living close to nature without schedules, television, buildings, cars, and electric lights, they knew.

The remains of horseshoe crabs have been found in prehistoric Indian middens around the coasts of Florida dating back several thousand years. The Indians of Roanoke Island called them "Seekanauk," and used their sharp pointed tails for fish spears when English settlers established their ill-fated "lost colony" in 1587.

But the Europeans may have been only one of many groups of people to visit North America. Although there is no hard proof, many archaeologists believe that two thousand years ago seafaring travelers from Central America rode the Gulf Loop current—that great swirling arm of the Gulf Stream—up from Central America to Florida's west coast. It isn't a bad journey. Even today, when the winds and weather are right, people sail across the Gulf in small sloops and sailboats in a few days.

Mesoamerican influence is strongest in Crystal River, Florida, little more than a hundred sea miles south of where we were camped. The extensive earth and shell mounds were laid out in a fashion very similar to the thriving and awesome temples of Central America. Like the pyramids of Guatemala and Mexico, they were aligned to the summer and winter solstices. Many of the artifacts recovered from archaeological excavations have the same motifs and designs of the feathered serpent found everywhere in ruins on the Yucatán peninsula, across the Gulf of Mexico. Elaborate headdresses, ear spools, zoomorphic forms, and symbols are all similar.

Perhaps the ancient ones came to trade with the primitive Indian tribes along the Panhandle and central Florida Gulf Coast. Because they had deforested their own lands with their burgeoning civilizations and exploding populations, the Olmecs, Mayans, Toltecs, or whoever they were came in search of game. If they came to this coast looking for gold, silver, obsidian, or jade they found none. Like the Spanish later, all they found were vast endless swamps, and the bugs, seething dog flies, and mosquitoes that must have been truly awesome.

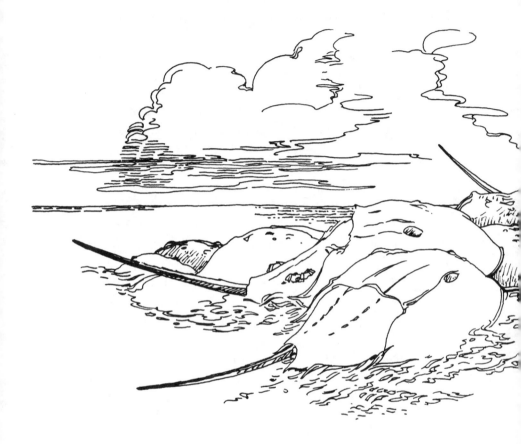

Soon the beach was covered with breeding horseshoe crabs. Moonlight gleamed on their ancient shapes as they performed their 400-million-year-old ritual of life.

They may have come as missionaries, to spread the word of Quetzalcóatl, the "feathered serpent," and taught the inhabitants how to lay out temple mounds aligning them to the solstices to worship the sungod. A primitive limestone stela still stands at the base of the great middens in Crystal River.

Those ancient temple mounds overlook the vast and endless marshes of central Florida's west coast. The wetlands there are far more extensive than those of the Panhandle. Instead of pine trees fringing the

marsh, there are dense forests of cabbage palms. Sometimes I stopped by to visit the little museum there, to climb up on the mounds and envision forty-foot dugout canoes paddled by dozens of bronze-skinned Indians, with a priest in a feather cloak standing at the bow, ready to set off and spread the word of the great feathered serpent.

Even though there is Central American influence in Georgia, Alabama, the Carolinas, and Ohio, it's doubtful that the travelers took off on foot through the forbidding Florida swamps. The Mississippi River was probably the gateway. The Crystal River itself extends only a short distance into the interior, winding with springs and manatees through the golden flat marshes. It was too shallow and remote for the Spanish explorers who followed a thousand years or more later. They sought deep harbors like Tampa, or St. Marks and Fort Walton Beach in the Panhandle.

For three hundred years the Spanish traveled the Gulf Stream, following the North Equatorial current west to the coast of South America, where they loaded their galleons with stolen Indian gold. The ships rendezvoused at Havana, Cuba, where they provisioned and set sail in the fabled treasure fleets bound for Spain. Today down beneath the mud, the sea grass, and the coral, there are still the remains of wrecks and doubtlessly chests still filled with gold. The conquistadores found most of the Gulf Coast abandoned. Yet the Crystal River ceremonial site and many of the middens around Panacea and St. Marks were used almost until the time of European contact. Was it because word had traveled that the devils were coming, spreading death with their fire sticks, diseases, and broken words?

The alarm clock rang. It was time to check the nests again—so much for Indians.

It was steady work there beneath the moon—ten minutes every hour was spent digging nests, measuring their depth in the sand, and then carefully re-covering the young crabs. Each time, new nests were excavated so we wouldn't remeasure already disturbed sites.

By now the tide had completely covered the once-exposed tidal flats, and one or two pairs of early horseshoe crabs were already at the water's edge, waiting to crawl up on the sloped beach when the tide reached its highest level. Soon there would be hundreds, perhaps several thousand copulating crabs.

We lit our lanterns and scooped out the sand, exposing more nests. Inserting the ruler to the level where the pack of motionless spiny little larvae lay, I called out, "Three inches on this one." Five more holes were scooped out, exposing the nests. "It looks like they're rising; I don't have to dig nearly so deep to uncover them."

"They are," Anne cried excitedly, "the little buggers are pushing their way up." Anne held them in her hand and spread the tiny immobile trilobites out on her fingers. "But they're still not moving. I guess the water table under the sand is pushing them up, but somehow they're not totally passive."

Our intellectual ruminations were interrupted by a solitary old man who waded up with a skiff, a light, and a flounder gig. "Howdy, what are you folks looking for?" he asked.

"Horseshoe crab larvae," Anne replied.

"Down there? They're coming in on the beach, lots of them. Don't they sting you?"

We explained that they were harmless, that the tail was used primarily as a levering device to enable the crabs to flip over when they were overturned by the waves on breeding beaches.

"What good are they?" the fisherman insisted, after we told him how we were studying them.

It was an all-too-common question. "The blood is turning out to be a valuable medical tool." Anne repeated wearily from rote, "It's used to diagnose endotoxemia-an often-fatal form of blood poisoning."

"Well, I hope it does some good. I'd better go before this tide drops and the flounder leave. Good night." Pushing his boat, he disappeared into the night.

The crabs now had justification. Why the presence of these ancient creatures emerging on the beach *en masse*, and not being edible, gnawed at people was beyond our comprehension.

The crabs have few natural predators. Big loggerhead sea turtles rip out their gills and chomp out chunks of their shells. *Limulus* has been found in the stomachs of eight- and ten-foot bull and tiger sharks.

Flocks of screaming sea gulls and willets gobble down their eggs, and the great schools of catfish and killifish that swarm along the edge of the sea to eat their eggs think they are very good indeed. Clam fishermen along the New England coast don't share that opinion. The crabs are constant and efficient eating machines, plowing trails in the mud, continuously churning small clams, worms, and tiny crabs along with grit into their hairy mouths, which are located between their legs. They use their spiny legs to grind up the food and shove it into their mouths with the two little pincers beneath the top of the shell, chewing with their elbows, as it were.

As the night passed on the Gulf beach, we began to be rewarded for our patience. Every few minutes the nests were a little higher up in the sand. It looked as if the level of the water table between the grains was rising slowly with the incoming tide and the nests were steadily moving upward, en masse, thousands of them perhaps actively, perhaps placidly coming up. For all we knew, they were frantically kicking their way up, perhaps oriented to moonlight or a microgravitational pull that made its way down into the sand.

Soon the beach was covered with breeding horseshoe crabs, and the moonlight gleamed on their ancient shapes as they once again performed their 400-million-year ritual of life.

The alarm clock rang again, and we lit our lanterns. It was three o'clock, high tide, and there in the sudden harsh light we had our answer. As the adults burrowed into the sand to lay their eggs, larvae were washing over them by the thousands. The nests had reached the surface, and each wave, as it washed back into the sea, carried the baby horseshoe crabs, in busy swarms, swimming upward toward the moon and the surface of the water.

We were elated, practically dancing in the moonlight, as we hurried up and down the beach photographing the phenomenon. The entire surf zone was filled with them, uncountable thousands of larvae. I waded out with the plankton net and towed it along. By the time we finished the transect, the net was clogged with *Limulus* larvae.

For the next half hour the eruption continued until the entire beach looked as if it were littered with coffee grains. Untold millions of the little black specks that were larvae boiled into the sea. Each wave washing back to the ocean carried them out, each creature swimming madly through the water, each orienting toward the big yellow moon above, as the water lapped on the shore and soaked gently into the sand.

The sea was alive with killifish now, darting in by the thousands, laterally banded little fish, scarcely four inches long. Swimming like sharks in a feeding frenzy, they dove down into the emerging nests, eager to eat the spiny little larvae even before they broke out of the sand. So obsessed were the killifish that from time to time we were able to reach down into a nest and grab three or four wriggling fish with our bare hands.

The tiny horseshoes spewed forth until the tide began to drop. An inch or two was all it took. Then all activity ceased. The copulating females plowed their way back out of the sands and moved into the surf. Males, clinging to the rear of the females with their tenacious hooks, half-crawled and were half-dragged along, and soon the beach was empty of all the big crabs.

But the sands were littered with windrows of young horseshoes. During the rest of the night, as the tide again receded, a drift line formed on the shore, a line of unlucky larvae that had washed out but failed to swim far enough and were now stranded by the receding waves.

But the nests that had not washed out completely were slowly moving back down into the sand, back to the level of the previous evening to await the next full moon and high tide. We continued our hourly watch, measuring them as they moved back down to their original depth.

The silver night slowly turned to dawn. Color began to reappear in the sky. For a few moments the full moon hung in a blue and pink dawn, and the planets shone brightly over the horizon, reflecting a slight glimmer on the water. Then the sun rose and the world was all red and golden. The tenuous beauty of the night was gone.

Suddenly a flock of willets and sandpipers swooped in and began racing up and down the shore feeding on the stranded larvae. Thousands of crabs died and birds were nourished, but many more young horseshoes were safely in the sea, beginning their immensely ancient life cycle anew.

We returned that afternoon, as the sun broiled down on the beach. It had done its work, baking the life away from the stranded larvae. The white ghost crabs, the sanitation engineers of the beach, were out of their burrows, scampering over the sands, feasting, and cleaning up the shoreline as well. The cycle was complete.

2. The Way of the Mullet

The sun was just rising, but it was already hot when we launched our canoe just below the Okefenokee Swamp in Georgia. We were beginning the 217-mile journey through Georgia and Florida to the Gulf of Mexico on the Suwannee River.

We paddled for days, with only the occasional splash of a bowfin or a garfish, or the bellow of an alligator, breaking the silence. Sometimes we ducked beneath the low-hanging branches bearing wasps' nests, watching for snakes among the contorted cypress tree roots. Day after day, Anne and I made camp on sandbars, listened to honeybees high in the branches of the oaks, and looked for river clams to fill our buckets for a tasty chowder. Like Huckleberry Finn, we moved with the river, heading south, watching it widen and flatten and lose speed. It was in the days before we had children, when there was more leisure time.

The Suwannee is one of the few large wild undammed rivers in the Southeast. As it leaves the sloughs and hammocks of the vast Okefenokee Swamp in Georgia it gradually coalesces, flowing through an eerie wilderness of stunted Ogeechee tupelo trees. Scattered cypresses rise above the swamps and give little shade from the blazing sun. We paddled along slowly, sometimes swimming behind the canoe as it sliced through Florida's sandhill and limestone cliffs and boiled over rapids.

Almost immediately after we left Fargo, Georgia, we started seeing garfish rise to the surface and gulp air.

"The first sign of the coast," I declared.

"How can you say that?" Anne asked. "Garfish are freshwater fish."

Then why have we caught them in the shrimp nets five miles off shore? Big ones, sometimes five feet long.

"I don't know," she said. "It's just typical of the whole situation. We know so little about nature's life histories. Ninety percent of the creatures we see, the millions of river clams and snails—all we have is the Latin name and maybe a distribution record. Beyond that, nothing."

Who could have thought that this peaceful river was capable of such violence? White water boiled over rocks and ledges.

"I wish we'd see a mullet up here and had a gill net to catch it. I'm getting tired of this freeze-dried backpacking food," I lamented. But I knew we wouldn't. Only a few miles downstream, where the acidic swamp water was mixed with springs, did mullet swim.

On hot days when there was little breeze and the river was flat calm, garfish rose all around us, coming to the surface, gulping air and rolling, probably because of the lower oxygen level in the water. Garfish were important to us. Running down that long, pointed, tooth-studded bill of theirs is one of the longest olfactory nerves to be found in nature. Neurophysiologists can easily excise the nerve from the rest of the tissues. In contrast to other systems, the garfish olfactory nerve is a virtual telephone cable that stretches on and on. It gives scientists plenty of membrane and material to work with. The biochemistry of olfactory nerve functions can be studied, and the electrophysiological impulses are simple to measure on oscilloscopes by hooking probes into the large tissues.

Like the hoary old brown bowfins, or mudfish, that abound in the Suwannee, the garfish have survived without change for 100 million years. They have an air-breathing lung and are among the most primitive and ancient of fishes. Paleontologists have chipped their fossilized remains out of sedimentary rocks that were formed long before the coming of the dinosaurs.

As we drifted on late one afternoon, we began looking for campsites on the dark white sandbars that rose abruptly along the river bends. Below Fargo, Georgia, the Suwannee loses its swampy character, cutting through sandhills covered with pine and oak scrub.

Entering Florida, white limestone outcrops rise from the bank and the Suwannee briefly roars over rapids. Even before the sign DANGER

SHOALS 500 FEET AHEAD came into view, we could hear the sound of it. We went ashore just above the rapids and made camp for the night. Only the thunderstorm and sky-splitting lightning that descended on us could obscure the noise of the rapids.

The next morning we awoke in sunshine and were treated to the magnificence of the shoals in the early morning light. Who could have thought that this peaceful river that filtered through tree roots and swamps a few miles to the north was capable of such violence, foaming, and churning? White water boiled over rocks and ledges. We searched among the crevices and grasses at the edge of the shoals, finding infinite numbers of caddis fly larvae and red-clawed crayfish hiding in the rushing white waters. Then it was time to move on. We portaged our gear around the rapids, pushed our empty canoes off the bank, and again were enveloped by the Suwannee. We were sucked up and swept along, fighting desperately to retain control as we approached the rocks we had been warned to avoid. Then we plunged nose-first into the water, swamped, paddled through air, and sank. Laughing and exhilarated, we dragged our canoes to shore to reload and press on to White Springs, well downstream.

"Do you suppose those rapids serve as some kind of natural barrier on the Suwannee?" I mused. "Surely alligators and turtles can't fight their way upstream. Maybe we'll start seeing mullet and sturgeon."

Anne paused thoughtfully from her paddling and let the quiet river take us past the tall pines on the bank. "Not when the water's high and the rapids are covered. I'm sure they can navigate easily then. And I don't think we'll be seeing any mullet up here; we're still too far inside northern Florida, much too far from the Gulf Coast."

My wife pointed out that it was the calcium content that determined how far, or even whether, sea life could penetrate up river. In alluvial muddy rivers where there is no limestone, blue crabs and mullet do not dwell. They must have a high mineral content to exist. But here we had limestone, untold amounts of it. We stopped along the shore and gathered fossils, coral, sea urchin casings, and mollusks, and near White Springs, we found fossil whale bones. All of it bespoke another era when this was all ocean.

With each day, the high sandbanks and levees gradually sank into endless freshwater swamps. We watched the river become marshy. Interminable swamps of red bay, river cypress, tupelo, and ash rose up from the mats of water lilies, wild rice, and maidencane along the shore. Our canoe glided through water hyacinths, lily pads, and quaking maiden-cane marshes. Scooping a dip net under the vegetation, we found it swarming with crayfish, snail insect larvae, transparent freshwater grass shrimp, and many more creatures than we had ever imagined finding in a freshwater environment.

Finally, we approached the town of Suwannee at the mouth of the river, where sawgrass blended naturally with the familiar coastal needlerush marsh, and islands of cabbage palms dotted the expanses of grass. And then through a number of channels, the river flowed out into the Gulf.

And it was there, at the very foot of the body of water we had called home for several weeks, that we ran into Jake Colson, a mullet fisher-man who hunted freshwater turtles and netted for sturgeon. His head was adorned with scars from innumerable barroom brawls and battles over the years. "I know every crook, bend, and log from here to Fannin Springs. I got turtle traps all up and down this part of the river. I got it right here." He tapped his grizzled head with a callused hand.

Just then something enormous leaped out of the water and landed with a giant splash. "Lord, I've got to get my sturgeon net and put some sets out," Jake said excitedly. "It's 'bout time for the season."

In just that instant, we could see a scaly brown body and great point-ed head rise out of the water. It was the first we'd seen on the trip, although sturgeon are reported as far up as Ellaville, nearly fifty miles inland.

"You see many of them?" Anne asked.

"They ain't as common as they used to be," Jake replied. "We see one now and then. Sturgeon sure is an ugly mother though. Seems to me like when an alligator mates with a garfish you get a sturgeon. I been fishing here all my life, and I ain't never seen one under this size." He spread his hands two feet across.

When Jake invited us to go mullet fishing with him, and camp on the wild offshore islands of the Suwannee, we quickly agreed. John L., his eighteen-year-old son, helped us pull our canoe up on the bank and piled our camping gear into their tunnel boat, a local craft built to fish gill nets in shallow water. He was less than enthusiastic about spending the night out there. But moments later we were speeding past the clut-ter of canals and trails and heading out into the open water. As we whirled down the creeks, the vegetation flattened down into marshlands, and soon the trees disappeared entirely. It was an exhilarating burst of freedom and speed, a completely different dimension from the green-walled river of the previous weeks. The vastness of the Gulf lay ahead.

Around us, fluttering through the air, were butterflies, hundreds of them. A cold front was moving through, there had been showers, and now the air was clear and crisp, causing them to move. All during the trip down we had seen sulphurs and monarchs, the latter moving in pulses and waves from Canada and New England south to central and south Florida, glittering black and orange.

Nor was it surprising to see them in open water, for during the fall they can often be seen many miles out in the Gulf, fluttering along, riding the air currents above the waves, adding color to the blue sea, heading for the mountains of central Mexico, where they winter. And now and then hundreds of them would land on a shrimp boat and perch there opening and closing their fiery wings and having a rest. Millions perish on their journey across the Gulf. More millions are blown and scattered with tropical storms and hurricanes, but the living, fluttering stream is inexhaustible. Each year around the time the mullet start running, the monarchs return.

What an exhilarating feeling of water, water, and more water, as the rolling swells splashed our faces, ahead of us the vast blending of sky and water, no vegetation, no confines, no sandbanks. Brown pelicans glided by, their bellies just clearing the chop. We passed terns and gulls, seeing bits of turtle grass floating on the surface. We had made it to the sea. Home! We now had a great feeling of the continuity of the land, with this magic artery of fresh water reaching far up into the interior, joined with the enormous eternal ocean. Now the idea of eels spawning in the Sargasso Sea and migrating across the ocean into freshwater streams made sense, and so did the mullet.

A streamlined, torpedo-shaped fish suddenly exploded through the water, sailed through the air almost in slow motion, and landed with a "plop" that shattered the silence. Jake had cut the motor, and we drifted across the tideflats, passing over oyster bars and grass beds. "They're too scattered out to strike," he said in a hushed voice, his hand over his eyes like a visor. "But it won't be long before we can strike 'em."

Another mullet jumped nearby. Some were serious jumpers, leaping two and three feet into the air. Suddenly one leaped even higher, splashed and disappeared beneath the water, erupting again and again, each leap extending in a straight line, a spectacular array of acrobatics. "It looks like you could strike 'em," Jake whispered almost as if he were afraid his voice would send them scurrying away, "but you can't. They ain't bunched up enough. We wouldn't catch a half a dozen, and there must be three or four hundred pounds in that school. We'll get 'em after dark."

Jake's son, John L., turned to us. "You study all this stuff, don't you? You got any idea why a mullet jumps?"

"No," I replied. "I've been asked that question a thousand times, and I still don't know."

"I think they use it to signal each other," Anne speculated. "They mostly jump in calm weather. We watch them near our dock all the time. The ripples they create by jumping might orient them to each other, so they can group together to form schools."

"I've always wondered about that," said Jake. "And I've fished all my life. You may have something there. Seems like they do kind of communicate with each other, now that I think about it. Don't let nobody fool you; a mullet's a smart fish. Has to be, with every shark, porpoise, and tarpon after him."

Another leaped, and another. As I watched them sailing through the air, I thought about seeing them a few days before in the crystal-clear springs that nourished the dark tannin-stained waters in the middle reach of the Suwannee. And down in cool, deep springwater near Branford we watched a school of mullet feeding. In the spring they were creatures of beauty, as their bluish-black saddles and white stomachs caught the sunlight. Slowly the school of several hundred fish had moved over the bottom, dipping down for mouthful after mouthful of mud, algae, and river swamp nutrients.

As the Suwannee herd consumed food, their curved toothless mouths worked constantly. We swam among them, and they showed little fear, unless we moved too close. Then, with a flick of the tail, they darted away.

It had seemed strange to meet our old friend of the coastal marshes and open sea so far from the ocean. During the fall, big Gulf mullet form huge schools, browsing through oyster bars and sandy reefs, grazing among the sea grasses, and feasting on the rich detritus of the marshes.

But we had seen them swimming in the limestone springs, many miles upriver. Some mullet wintered in the rivers, preferring the warm springwater that stayed at some seventy degrees year-round, substantially warmer than the bitter wintertime Gulf Coast flats that drop into the fifties.

All during our journey, from White Springs south, we had refreshed ourselves in the innumerable clear springs that gushed up from the limestone, pushing back the dark tannin waters. They created transparent fairy pools where fossils and shells gleamed twenty feet below the surface. Each spring varied in size, with its own characteristic life, and no two springs were alike. Some had turtles, others catfish, and still others bowfin. Farther down toward the coast, some had flounder and others saltwater fish.

Well below the confluence of the Santa Fe River, which feeds into the Suwannee, we paddled up Otter Springs Run, a small spring-fed creek that flows into the river, and saw saltwater needlefish, blue crabs and more mullet in the crystalline waters among the submerged meadows of aquatic grass. Golden-yellow sunlight filtered down through the overhanging Spanish moss-draped limbs of giant water oaks. Apple snails plastered the cypress knees with pinkish-white eggs, and the air was filled with the sounds of barking frogs and the calls of pileated woodpeckers. Inconspicuous green north Florida orchids bloomed on the massive tree limbs overhead, while gleaming emerald, blue, and black dragonflies landed on our canoe.

Because Florida is built on an immense outcropping of limestone, water flows underground through millions of holes and channels, sometimes hundreds of feet down. This is the Floridan Aquifer, and where it rises up to the surface, springs abound. One spring may be an underwater jungle, whereas another a few miles downriver results in gleaming sand and white limerock, free of vegetation. And fortunately they remain uncontaminated. Most are as pristine today as they were hundreds of years ago.

We spoke with Jake about it, and he said wistfully, "I always wanted to learn to scuba dive, but somehow I always had to get out and make a living. I just never got around to it." We told him we were on an assignment for *National Geographic* and that's how we were making our living. He shook his head.

We cruised around the shallow creeks and marshes of the offshore islands, looking for mullet, seeing a few jump here and there. Finally Jake cut the motor again. "They ain't a-gonna bunch; we'll just have to get 'em tonight. We can make camp on the island, like the old-timers used to do, and wait 'em out. That tide'll be rising around three in the morning, and then we'll slaughter 'em."

"Daddy, I don't want to stay out here all night!" John L. complained. "I was going into town to the movies. . . 'sides, we don't have nothing to eat."

"Nothing to eat!" Jake repeated, mocking, "Nothing to eat! Son, there's a whole world of things to eat. We got a net on board, don't we? I got a pocketknife, and you say there ain't nothing to eat." He turned to us and shook his head. "That's the trouble with this modern generation. All they want to do is hang out at the picture show, drink beer, and smoke dope. You can't get 'em to work."

"Aw, come on, Daddy, we're only thirty minutes from the dock," the young man pleaded.

Jake pointed accusingly to the shiny outboard motor mounted in the well of his tunnel boat. "You know what's caused it? It's this outboard motor. Everybody wants to go, go, go. It's the ruination of the world. It's hurt the fish more than anything else. Back in the old days my daddy used oars, and there was plenty of fish. Now they don't have anyplace to get away. These powerboats run them to death. They can talk about conservation laws and such, but if they ever want to save the fish, and bring the turtle and the sturgeon back, what they ought to do is outlaw the damn outboard." He paused, "I ain't being no hypocrite neither; I'd give this up in a second if everyone would give up theirs and go back to the way it was."

He snatched the starter cord on his motor, and the engine responded with a resounding roar. A few moments later we were coming up on the shore of Hog Island, a great block of wilderness, of hardwood forests and swamps. It was saved from developers by the Nature Conservancy and is now part of the National Wildlife Refuge system.

"We'll make camp here," Jake announced, after jumping out and pulling the bow up into the marsh grass. "Then we'll go get 'em tonight." John L. sat glumly in the stern. This had happened before, I suspected.

We made camp on a high berm above the marshes, watching the monarchs and fritillaries lighting on the saltbushes, opening and closing their wings, drinking the nectar from the asters and the goldenrods, and we talked a lot about the old mullet fishery that used to be here. There were still a few signs of the old fish camp in the woods, the frame of an abandoned shack, and some old bricks next to the two thousand old Indian middens where the ancient ones also fished for mullet once upon a time.

Mullet is as much a part of Florida's history as the decaying ribs of the Civil War steamer on the bottom of Fannin Springs in the middle of the Suwannee. Even before the Civil War, it was a traditional mainstay of west Florida; settlers tried to scratch a living out of the poor sandy soils in the pine flatwoods and augmented their diets and pocketbooks by commercial fishing. It was the food of the turpentine camps; it was used as barter. As Jake Colson said, "Long as you had a net, you didn't starve. Fishermen made good money back in the Depression."

In the late 1800s, fishermen stayed in primitive camps, usually just a shack where a few men had a fire to keep from being devoured by the clouds of mosquitoes, dog flies, and yellow flies. They were rough men, able to withstand the broiling heat and the freezing winds as they struck their nets and hauled in the mullet. Wild hogs and cattle roamed the marshes and woods, and game abounded everywhere. The fishermen had all the ducks, geese, and rabbits they wanted to eat. They stayed in isolation for weeks, waiting for the fish to run. There were no highways, only rutted sand roads that went down to the coast. And although some mullet were sold fresh, most were salted in wooden barrels and shipped by mule-drawn wagon or railroad.

The outboard motor and the automotive age changed everything. Rural counties along the boundless west Florida swamps and coastline started putting in roads with prison labor, though often it was a community effort. Everyone along the coastal villages worked, chopping trees, laying evenly cut logs side by side until they stretched for miles down to the coast. In some places along the Florida Panhandle, the remnants of the old corduroy roads still snake through the marshes. Access became easier, and the fishermen no longer had to live in total isolation. When word got out that the mullet were running, families arrived by mule-drawn wagons and Model A and Model T Fords. Women cooked for their men on the beach, while the children helped salt and pack fish and later played around the bonfire. Truckers and fish peddlers, who carried the catch back over dirt roads to Georgia and Alabama, eagerly awaited the fish.

The fishing took on an air of festivity that has lasted into the present. Everyone was excited when the mullet came streaking downshore, and the fishermen jumped into their boats and paddled out to encircle them. Tons upon tons of frantic, leaping, beating, frothing fish were hauled out on the marshy berm. The fishermen and their families worked into the night splitting and salting fish.

When the licks were big enough, the salted fish were loaded into boats and hauled to Cedar Keys, Apalachicola, Carrabelle, and other fishing villages that had a railroad spur, and their catches were shipped north by rail. When the mullet ran, they flowed along the Gulf shore in immense black rivers, with millions upon millions of fish carpeting the shallows for miles.

Before the turn of the century, places such as White Springs and Suwannee Springs were health spas, and mullet was consumed in quantity. People came to eat mullet with much the same fervor as they bathed in the mineral springs. Springwater was pumped into the hotels and heated. In some areas along the north Florida coast, like Panacea, it tasted like a combination of salt water and sulfur. No matter, people downed it like medicine, lauding its flavor, claiming it alleviated rheumatism, arthritis, and gout. They came from all over the United States. As the director of the Stephen Foster Center at White Springs told us, "People think there's something magic about the Suwannee. They come down here and want to touch it, cup it in their hand, or take it back in a jar."

The good times ended during the Depression. The money dried up and people stopped coming. Many of the old hotels mysteriously caught fire and burned to the ground. It was rumored that insurance payouts may have had something to do with it. After the Depression people lost their taste for mullet, perhaps because they ate so much of it during hard times. It was a cheap source of protein, and even the poorest people could afford it. Other seafood prices began to climb when times got better, but not mullet. The once-booming Panhandle towns began to dry up.

Only the fallen ruins of old buildings marked the thriving resort that was once Suwannee Springs, a hundred miles or so upriver from where we were camped. As we had paddled down the Suwannee in our canoe several weeks before, we could almost hear the ghost of the parties of the past, the music and laughter, and see people in long bathing suits splashing in pools. But now there were only unused stone steps leading down the riverbank from the hardwood forests, like jungle ruins. Little remained of the resorts except massive stone walls built around the clear springs to keep the dark waters from flooding them. We stopped and explored the concrete structures where minnows darted to and fro in the algae, and marshes grew where water once gushed from the ground in brick-lined pools.

Often during our journey, we passed areas of turbulence, where springwater boiled up into the tannin waters, and it was there that we often saw this peaceful, grazing fish the mullet gathering. No one netted for them upriver because it was illegal. But periodically we would see a few skillful cane-pole fishermen who had the knack and knowledge for catching mullet. They used a tiny hook, with dough or crab eggs as bait, and when the mullet mouthed it down, they could snatch them out of the water, with all the fight of a largemouth bass.

"It's just in the last few years that mullet's coming back as a market fish," Jake told us, as we set up our tents and opened our canned goods. "The Japanese are buying 'em."

They use the mullet roe, not the delicious flesh, in various sushi dishes. In Japan, roe is a gourmet delight.

"But I'll tell you something," Jake continued; "it plumb makes me sick to see what they do with the rest of the fish. They sell it for crab bait, yes sir, all that good eating. And no one wants it. I don't care what people say, there ain't no finer eating fish in the world."

After a light meal from our packs, we explored the island in the golden afternoon light that melted through the Spanish moss that draped down from the water oaks. We kept our eyes open for rattlesnakes and water moccasins. But far more dangerous was the chance of coming up on someone's stash of marijuana plants, or bales waiting to be offloaded. The mouth of the Suwannee and all the adjacent rural counties were a hotbed of smuggling.

We followed him toward the huge Indian mounds that rose up from the forest floor. Fossil oyster and clam shells stuck out from beneath the leaf litter as we climbed up through the tangle of junglelike grapevines that reached high into the canopy above.

After supper, I sat beside the campfire and filled my notebook with the day's impressions. In a few hours, when the tide came in, we would go fishing with Jake. Soon the mystery and magic of the island took over. Time was suspended. Surrounded by hardwood forests, the Indian midden behind us, and the sea before us was a moment frozen in time. It could have been fifty years ago, a hundred, or a thousand. Again I could feel the mythic aura of the Suwannee, the presence of something ancient and strange.

One of the oddest events in my life had happened early in our river journey, someplace just below the Florida state line. We had made camp

Suddenly, out of nowhere, I had a vision. A whole procession of forest spirits paraded before me.

on a bluff and had settled down for the night after a long swim in the cool waters of the Suwannee warmed by a fire of "fat-lighter" driftwood gathered from heart pine. Even on rainy nights, the resin-soaked branches blazed cheerfully. Outside our campfire the eyes of wild creatures gleamed, owls hooted, and bats swooped down above us while we lay beneath a wild bee tree and listened to the ominous buzzing that came from the monumental oak.

As the campfire died down, I stretched out in my sleeping bag. Suddenly, out of nowhere, I had a vision. A whole procession of forest spirits paraded before me. I had seen faces like this before in museums in the form of Indian masks, on totem poles, big horrible funny grins, intricate designs, and gleaming eyes. One face had yellow and black triangles rimming it; others were round with horns and big teeth.

I sat up and stared, my eyes wide open, thinking I had lost my mind. Anne was talking in a sleepy voice about logistics, when we should stop, where we could get some ice. I could see her, the tent, the sleeping bags, and the fire all very clearly.

And then these spirits were dancing before me. Some of them were horrible, yet I wasn't shocked. I wasn't worried. I was glad to see them. They gave me a joyful feeling, because even the terrible ones were smiling. In a way they were like children, all competing for my attention. One came forward in front of my outstretched legs, waved small infant hands

as if it were giving a casual "Hello!! Welcome to our forest," and then moved back. I felt at peace with the world, and yet, I was actually laughing, inspecting them one by one, smiling, and nodding back greetings.

"What are you laughing at?" Anne asked. And I didn't answer her; I didn't want to lose the image of the forest spirits for even a second. And then they were gone, leaving only darkness surrounding us.

"Did you see that!" I cried, after they had vanished and only the empty night remained.

"See what?" she asked sleepily.

"The spirits… I don't know what!" And I related what I had just seen.

"You've been sniffing too much deer's-tongue." Deer's-tongue is a medicinal herb that some of the people in the Okefenokee Swamp gathered for sale to pharmaceutical houses, and we had spent a considerable amount of time interviewing them and watching them picking the purple flower in the pine and palmetto flatwoods. "I didn't see a thing; it was just your imagination."

"My imagination!"

"You said they looked like totem poles. So you just conjured up an image you saw at the American Museum of Natural History or the Smithsonian or something," Anne suggested.

I didn't want to get into one of our endless arguments about fantasy versus reality. So, I closed my eyes, trying to recreate the vision from the shadows of my mind, but there was only darkness, and the orange glare of the fire burning through my eyelids. Were there really forest spirits? Maybe the Indians hadn't made them up. Perhaps they were carefully rendering the things they saw in their totemic visions.

I soon dropped off to sleep, still thinking about those pleasant friendly forest spirits, wishing that when my time comes to die I'll be received by something as friendly and joyful as they. Part of me longed to enter into the forest to look for them.

Although no visions came to me at the Indian mound, I definitely sensed a presence there of the people who lived long ago along the mouth of the Suwannee and on the coastal marshes and springs. Indians without names, cultures that have long vanished, people we now know only as "Deptford" or "Weeden Island" from the stampings of their ancient pottery sherds.

I climbed up to the top of one of the Indian middens, a hill of shell and dirt about fifteen feet high, and looked down at our campfire, listening to the tree frogs peeping all about us, and soaking in the night.

After a while Jake, carrying two beers, joined me. He seemed to sense my thoughts. "Sometimes I get the feeling there's all kinda ghosts running around on these islands, pirates, and the old Indians that lived here."

"There probably are," I agreed. "I'll bet whoever they were they spent a lot of time waiting for the tide to rise, and dark to come so they could go fishing for mullet just like us. The Indians ate a lot of mullet. Archaeologists have found bones and the remains of hemp nets and bone fishhooks in middens just like these."

"Is that a fact?" asked Jake, popping the top off his Budweiser and handing me the other one. "I figured they used some kinda net, build a weir or something to get 'em. Back then there must have been a few million tons of mullet, and all kinda other fish swimming around."

I told him how archaeologists had found the bones of sea trout, jack crevalle, black and red drum, toadfish, channel bass, shark, and many other fish. "They also knew how to fillet them."

"That a fact?" he asked again, taking another swallow of his beer, and letting out a belch of satisfaction. "And how'd they know that?"

When I told him how archaeologists excavated a number of middens at St. Marks, several hours north of where we were, and found piles of backbones but no heads or tails, he nodded with understanding.

"Mullet do make for good filleting, better than most other fish," he agreed. "Run a good sharp knife down the backbone, and you split the meat out in just a New York minute. But how do you reckon the Indians cut them up? They didn't have no metal."

"I guess they used sharpened bones, or maybe flint, like the arrowheads."

"I find plenty of arrowheads around here," Jake added. "We can look in the morning and we'll probably find two or three. But I ain't never seen no knives. Where did they get all that flint anyway?"

"The Indians did a lot of trading," I replied, sipping my beer, and related how archaeologists had found signs of trade with inland tribes. There wasn't much agriculture on the coast; it was mostly a hunting-gathering community. But by examining the soils microscopically scientists found pollen grains and fossil remains of farmed crops, including maize and grains, along with clay, which is rare in the sandy soils of the coastal plain. They also found copper bracelets and ear spools, which came from hundreds of miles to the north.

Likewise, in Indian middens in Georgia and the Carolinas, it was common to find seashells, like the left-handed whelk, which lives only in the Gulf of Mexico.

Food from the Gulf was dried, transported in dugout canoes up the river systems as far north as Ohio, and carried by backpacks. Today it is done by highways, refrigerated trucks, rail lines, and airplanes. But essentially little has changed. People still love seafood everywhere.

Jake took a final swallow of his beer and sent the can clattering down to the base of the midden. "I know one thing," he said with conviction, "if them archaeologists have any sense they'll quit digging in these mounds. Those old Indians will put a curse on anyone who messes with their burial place. I know one man who went to digging out here and found a human skull. He carried it back to town, showed it around, and sure enough he got killed in a car wreck the next day!" He stood up and stretched. "Well, we'd better go; tide ought to be about right now."

I followed behind him and picked up his beer can. There were lots of beer cans on Hog Island, peeking up from the leaf litter, some on top of the burial mounds. I wondered whether someday we'd be known by future archaeologists as the "aluminum can people." Some of the middens in central Florida date back to 9000 B.C., eleven thousand years of peoples' tossing their garbage. We were just one more.

We left the Suwannee River midden behind and, following the tradition of all those ancient fishermen, shoved our boat off the marsh grass and headed out to see what the sea would offer.

The stars blazed down on us with chilly magnificence as Jake's boat moved over the shallows. There is nothing more beautiful or eerie than standing on the stern platform, hanging onto the towing post and whipping down the bay through the darkness. Behind in the churning wake, flashes of small, round blue phosphorescences illuminate the darkness, as the propeller disturbs the tiny plankton and the comb jellies drifting in with the tide. Looking down into the water, it is as if we are traveling rapidly through time and space and the blue lights down in the sea belong to some other world. Ahead on the black horizon, channel markers flash red and green as boats head out to the bars where the mullet gather.

We were hunters, roving the tideflats, seeking our quarry. Jake shut off the motor and we drifted, listening to the sounds of the waves and waiting for the splash of mullet. Suddenly we were in a school, and torpedo-shaped fires sped past us.

We waited and listened in silence, hunters and hunted in a soundless world. Suddenly, with a hard snatch or two, the outboard roared into action. At Jake's command, John L. threw the sinker on one end of the net overboard. The tunnel boat sped ahead, spewing net off the stern.

The boat surged through the choppy waves, the corks bouncing off the platform as six hundred feet of webbing were whisked away by the forward force. Down went the lead line into the fiery wake, carrying the wall of webbing to the bottom. Corks bobbed along the surface.

The mullet were in a panic and fled, only to tangle and snare themselves in the wall of webbing. We made a full circle around the school and then sat there in the middle of it, beating on the sides of the boat to send the fish stampeding into the mesh.

When we hauled in the gill nets and shook free the illuminated blue blobs of jellyfish, we pulled out the sleek bluish-black mullet along with alewives, skipjacks, catfish, and small sharks and threw them all into the boat. And then when the net was hauled aboard, and the fish quit flopping and beating, there was quiet—an eerie quiet that comes just before the wind springs up, with its breath of chill, a wind that can turn the still waters into waves that rise up with energy and power. In a tunnel boat not designed to withstand rough seas, you must sneak out when the weather isn't looking and reap a harvest if you can find it, then hurry back to land. For the great protector of the fish is weather.

We had managed to catch more than enough to eat. Jake picked out a half-dozen mullet, still flopping and very much alive, to cook for breakfast. He mashed his big callused thumb and forefinger into the gills and ripped open the throat. "Seems cruel," he said, letting the dark red blood spill onto the deck already covered with scales and fish slime, "but mullet's a whole lot better if you get the blood out while he's still alive."

We headed for shore, slept for a few hours until the sun came up, and then started preparing breakfast. Jake was cleaning fish, the keen edge of his pocketknife sped through the tissues and bones, and in a moment he had a pan full of perfect fillets.

It is a good bet that the Indians were just as fond of the plump red mullet roe as we are today. This is a true Southern delicacy: fried along with the eggs, or mashed up and mixed with scrambled eggs and fried in a hot skillet, or cooked separately and served with grits and red-eye gravy—nothing short of a wonder.

"You eat gizzards?"

"Yes," I said, "and livers too." Jake nodded with satisfaction. That made me a proper Florida cracker. It was one of those little nuances of acceptance.

We sat around the campfire. As usual, John L. said little, but Jake was in a talkative mood. All the silence of the night before was gone.

"Back when I was a boy, we didn't throw none of the heads and gizzards away. We saved the white roe too. We used to make camp and cook up a batch of mullet head stew. Put onions, carrots, some milk in with it, and you had something plumb delicious. The oil in this head is what gave it the flavor." He held up a skewered gizzard on his fork. "I've always wondered why a mullet's got a gizzard. It's just like chicken."

"They use it the same way for grinding up mud and sand," explained Anne, who was sleepily propped up against a log, enjoying the warmth of the fire.

Jake winked at her. "I think it's 'cause a mullet is half-fish, and half-bird. Ain't no other fish got one; that's why he jumps all the time."

"Gizzard shad do." She yawned.

"Well, they do, that's true, but shad jump sometimes, especially when they hit a net, so it must be so!" Jake said triumphantly.

When breakfast was finished, I gathered up the dishes and the mullet remains and carried them all down to the water's edge. We had to get back. The real world was calling, the article was due in three weeks, and this was the end of our trip. I tossed the backbones, heads, and viscera into the water and began scrubbing the pans with sand.

The moment the discarded backbones hit the water, a small blue crab scurried out from beneath its blanket of sand and began tearing at the flesh. Moments later there were longnose killifish everywhere, worrying the meat, shaking their bodies to and fro, ripping off particles. And finally came the mud snails, erupting from the sediments, sliding over the bottom, attracted by the taste of blood.

It was a ritual, one I always followed at home. Whenever I ate seafood, I carried the shrimp shells, the fishbones, or the broken stone crab claws out to the end of my dock and dropped them into the sea. The cycle had to be completed. We had had our share of the mullet and were returning the rest to the ocean whence everything came.

3. The Fish That Roared

"Beep-beep, beep-beep" seeped up through the dark waters surrounding my dock at Panacea. A soft, high-pitched, almost melodious note, it was a far different sound from the bubblings of oysters and barnacles on the wharf pilings and the periodic clickings of snapping shrimp down in the mud.

That night, the sea was alive with mad, whirling dervish little creatures that emerged from the black waters and danced under the dock lights. Needlefish, halfbeaks, tiny blue crabs: there seemed to be an incredible amount of life displaying itself, almost like actors in a theater of the absurd coming out to take an encore. In the drift grass, little brown flatworms were endlessly undulating their leafshaped bodies almost in rhythm to the sounds of the night sea. Now and then a mullet leaped into the air and landed with a splash, and as the tide dropped, the clickings and bubblings of the barnacles increased in a gentle crescendo. But the most eerie and melodious sound of all that emanated from the depths was the song of the lovesick toadfish.

I had to remain absolutely still lest they cease their serenade. A scientist had discovered while working with the Atlantic toadfish that if he so much as leaned on the rim of a ten-thousand-gallon tank, the mating calls stopped. And simply walking on the dock sent such vibrations down through the pilings that mullet were often startled and went speeding off through the darkness leaving a searing, fiery trail of phosphorescence behind.

I sat completely still, listening to the toadfish's song, watching schools of halfbeaks, elongated green fish with spearlike lower jaws that resemble a swordfish's bill, move across the light. From down in the mud, transparent wormlike sea cucumbers slowly and gently turned loops and squiggles in the water column like ghosts being swept along in the falling tide. Multitudes of newly-hatched larval fish, so small that one could barely isolate them with the naked eye, moved in to feast on the caviar that saturated the open water. Again and again the toadfish called out its mournful sweet whistle. I wondered whether the giant toadfishes in Surinam made calls like that.

In a few days we would be flying to South America to capture what I hoped might be the world's biggest toadfish. Our house was in chaos from suitcases' being packed, gear readied, equipment bought, piles of checklists on checklists of things needed for the expedition, from malaria pills to nets, pumps, and aquarium supplies. Anne was busy packing, and I took refuge on the dock to clear out my mind.

The toadfish's "boat whistles" are made only by nesting males calling the females early in the mating season. It is a true song, a particular pattern of notes generated by specialized muscles in the swim bladder. To attract the female, the love song must be of the correct duration, have just the right frequency and volume, and be intermittent.

Scientists have confirmed that the calls average about seven whistles a minute. When a female arrives, the calls increase. And when one male starts calling, the others join in, all trying to attract her. The sea becomes a chorus of high-pitched beeps, hoots, and grunts. Sitting on the dock listening to the males calling, I tried to make out how many there were down beneath those murky estuarine waters. The sound traveling through the water seemed to be omnidirectional. The love songs were intensifying, and I guessed that a female was passing by. A male calling at the rate of ten calls per minute will increase to twenty-five as a ripe female enters his little kingdom of oyster shells and rocks. She is won by the loudest and most persistent of her suitors and stays but a minute or so in his nest, laying eggs and moving on. A mature bull toadfish attracts several females in turn to his nest and fertilizes their eggs until he's nearly spent.

Male toadfishes make good mothers. Hiding under rocks and in their burrows, they brood the eggs, protecting them until they hatch. I learned this years ago when I was a boy, barely fourteen years old and had just moved to Florida. I was exploring the rubble of a fallen seawall at low tide and probed my finger into a dark hole that was filled with water among the rocks. Crab shells and debris were strewn about the entrance.

Common sense should have told me to stay away, but curiosity prevailed. I almost went into shock when something crunched down, hard. I yelled, snatched my hand out, and shook off a six-inch, smooth-skinned brown fish mottled with yellow. What an ugly beast it was, with its bulldog face and mean little eyes. Big fleshy pendants hung down beneath its chin; it was all mouth and no body, a grotesque giant tadpole with teeth.

It swam back into its lair, and when I turned over the rock, I saw that it was protecting hundreds of tiny, newly hatching babies. They don't spawn into the sea as other fish do, but sit on top of their eggs, fanning them with their fins, pumping water and aerating them with gills, ready to deliver a savage bite to any would-be predator. They stay until the young absorb their yolk sacs and swim off to take their chances in the sea, not as helpless half-formed larvae, but as fully-formed, mobile miniatures.

Masters of adaptation, toadfishes can survive in low-oxygen water and even in polluted water. They sit under a log, or a broken piece of culvert pipe, with their big hoary heads guarding the entrance to their burrows. Their jaws are studded with tiny, sharp teeth, waiting to clamp down on an unwary crab or shrimp. Then the toadfish lunges, virtually inhaling its prey, and gulps it down.

The only thing more formidable looking and pugnacious than a toadfish is a bigger toadfish. So when I happened upon a giant in Surinam, at the mouth of the Marowijne River, I was stunned.

We had joined a New York Zoological Society expedition to bring back a variety of freshwater tropical fish including piranha, electric eels, and freshwater stingrays, with a few lizards and frogs thrown in. The trip was financed and led by a longtime friend, Nixon Griffis, a trustee of the New York Zoological Society, which operates the Bronx Zoo and the New York Aquarium.

At the time, I was working on a book on sea turtles, and Anne and I took a side visit to the bleak coastal village of Matapica, where leatherback turtles nest.

On this visit to Surinam, we traveled for hours through meandering creeks bordered by towering mangroves in a precariously balanced, elongated canoe propelled by a rickety outboard motor. Our guide spoke no English. Matapica Creek was located behind a vast expanse of barrier beach where the rolling breakers of the Caribbean pound incessantly on the shore. The nearby village consisted of a few huts, a small dock, and a number of Javanese fishermen who spent their time drying shrimp and catching fish to sell in the marketplace of Paramaribo. It was located in the middle of wretched, drained polder lands, swarming with mosquitoes.

We set up camp in one of the huts, and when darkness came, we loaded our gear into the canoe and started down the creek to the opposite shore where the leatherbacks were known to nest. Scrambling ashore, we agreed to meet our guide at two o'clock in the morning and started down the log-strewn beach. It was the most desolate, remote, godforsaken beach we had ever seen, but it was perfect for turtles. Hordes of giant ghost crabs, far larger than any we had seen in the Gulf of Mexico, clattered away in all directions. Everywhere there were trails of nesting turtles emerging from the water and later returning to the surf.

All night long we stumbled over giant leatherbacks and huge greens. Anne's strobelights flashed over and over again as she recorded the turtles' nesting habits. Finally, after we had taken endless photographs from every possible angle, whenever yet another of these magnificent creatures appeared, it seemed to us just one more turtle. We were tired, it was late, and we headed back to the landing at the mouth of the creek.

We were exhausted from the ten-mile trek, scratched and bruised from tripping over logs and branches in the dark. Our boatman was a welcome sight. We piled into his unstable canoe, and we pushed off from the dock.

Suddenly, the night turned into a disaster. Somehow the weight in the boat shifted abruptly—perhaps the stern was caught by the swift current—and the canoe flipped. All of us spilled out into the sea, camera, film, lights, and all. But the gear was the least of our worries. The current was swift, and the next thing I knew we were being swept out into the center channel that fed out to the sea. Turtle beaches swarm with sharks. The thought of enormous hungry bullhead sharks propelled me through the water, and I scrambled up the bank, dragging myself through the slippery mud into the mangroves. Anne had been swung closer to the bank and managed to get out with the boatman. But the outboard motor was flooded, and the salt water ruined the camera. It was a serious setback for us as the camera was an important part of our work and was not insured.

It took the rest of the night to paddle up the creek back to our shack. We spent most of the next day chilled, trying to sleep while trying to hide from clouds of bloodsucking mosquitoes while waiting for the boatman to finish overhauling the outboard motor so we could return home.

Anne managed to fall asleep, but I could only catnap and finally got up and wandered around the rickety walkways that traversed the marshes. I watched big, red-clawed fiddler crabs sit at the entrance of their burrows waving their claws, and schools of semiterrestrial, air-breathing mudskipper fish scurry over the slimy mud.

The Javanese fishermen were smoking their catches, and I headed toward the pungent aroma. We were low on groceries and hadn't come prepared to spend an extra day, so I decided to try to buy some fish.

Two men were fishing with hooks and lines at the edge of the wharf. They had a thin chain hanging down in the water, and something was jerking on it. When I approached, they pulled it up, and there was the largest, ugliest toadfish I had ever seen. It appeared to be at least three feet long, possibly longer. It was all mouth, and when it was finally out of the water, I stared aghast at its many pointed yellowish-white teeth that made it look even uglier.

Always on the lookout for creatures that would make a novel exhibit for the New York Aquarium, I hurried over. "What's that?" I cried, pointing my finger. Usually, I try to be reserved, bide my time, and gradually make the acquaintance of villagers, but this creature was too shocking for nonchalance.

One young man spoke a few words of English. "Dat's lumpoe..." he said and laughed. "Ugly fish... mean, bite you."

The fish grunted and thrashed, but apparently most of the fight was out of it as it had been on the line for quite some time.

"In America," I said eagerly while jabbing my finger down at it, "that fish is only this big." I spread my hands eight inches apart, and then moved them another four inches as I said "the biggest [in America]."

The bushy-haired Javanese fisherman laughed again and shook his head. "Lumpoe here... this little." He pointed to the creek, "catch beeg lumpoe sometimes," he said, spreading his hands far apart and then made a barrel hug to show how big around they were.

"Lumpoe," what a good name; it didn't need much to translate, a lumpish, recalcitrant, mean ugly fish. The name was as good as "toad-fish."

"Lumpoe good to eat," the young man went on. "Cook with tomatoes, onions, rice, and spices, very nice." He hoisted it out of the water and plopped it down on the dock, where it thrashed around and grunted. Then the fisherman picked up a sizable rock and slammed it down on the fish's head. Its mouth sprung open as it reeled around to bite, but again and again the fisherman's blows rained down on it until the giant toadfish was still. I walked off, not wishing to watch the slaughter.

But if one were going to eat a toadfish, it was the only way. Normally, when you clean a fish, killing it isn't a problem. You simply let it lie there out of water for a few minutes until it expires. But with a toadfish, you could wait all day and it still wouldn't die, so it had to be bludgeoned. All along the west coast of Florida, where people fish from piers, docks, and bridges, it's commonplace to see discarded toadfish lying at their feet, burning up in the sun, dying for no particular purpose. Even after hours out of water with their skin dried, I've seen them stay alive.

But in Surinam the entire fish is eaten. The head is severed to make lumpoe stew.

Some months later I was in New York walking around the New York Aquarium with Nixon Griffis, and my excitement over the fish was as great as ever.

"You're quite sure it was a toadfish you saw, not a grouper or a warsaw?"

We walked past the two white beluga whales that were pressed up against the glass walls, their melodious sounds broadcast through a hydrophone.

"Positive," I insisted, "and it was huge." I spread my arms far apart, saying, "It was at least three feet long and had a mouth that looked big enough to swallow a basketball. They called it a 'lumpoe' and told me they sometimes catch them this big," I said, as I spread my arms as far apart as they would reach.

Nixon was fascinated by the possibility. "If it's true, a giant toadfish would make a fantastic exhibit," he said as we paused in front of a large tank where brightly colored marine tropical fish swam back and forth amid the bleached white coral. "People get awfully tired of seeing the same pretty fish year in and year out. Something really ugly might boost attendance."

Nixon Griffis is one of the few people I know who doesn't let money get in the way of their interest and pleasure in life's mysteries and marvels. When he was young, he owned and operated bookstores in the United States and abroad, but his real interest always lay with the sea. Sponsoring archaeological research, he dove for Bronze Age wrecks in the Mediterranean, in between his business obligations. When his father died, he took over the family foundation and sponsored a series of expeditions for the New York Zoological Society. Into the New York Aquarium came giant spider crabs from Japan, the largest crustaceans on earth. He helped bring back rare crocodiles from South America for the Bronx Zoo, as well as collections of hammerheaded bats and other bizarre creatures. His green scorpionfish from New Guinea was a smash.

"You know, we're going to Peru to collect freshwater frogs from Lake Titicaca and then on to Bolivia for clingfish. I don't see why we couldn't stop in Surinam for a few days. You could fly them back to New York. Get me some literature on these Surinam toadfishes, Jack, and we'll see whether we can do a trip, but you'll have to hurry," he said.

At last I located a toadfish specialist, Dr. Carter Gilbert at the Florida State Museum in Gainesville. I met him in his laboratory, where jars of pickled fish were stacked on shelves from ceiling to floor. "Can you tell me something about the giant South American toadfishes?" I inquired, spreading my arms apart again. "You know, the ones that get this big."

He looked at me as if I were insane and shook his head. "You must mean catfish, don't you?"

"No, I mean a toadfish; it looks like our *Opsanus beta*, but much, much bigger. It must weigh fifty or seventy-five pounds." And then I related the story of the fish that was pulled from the Matapica Creek.

Dr. Gilbert listened incredulously and shook his head. He showed me the scientific literature from ichthyologists who had made collections in Surinam, even in Matapica Creek. "The biggest *Bactrachoides surinamensis* reported weighed only seven pounds and was just over two feet long," he said, and then added kindly, "You know it really is difficult to tell how big a toadfish is unless you measure it. When you pull one out of the water, all you see is head, nothing more; the body tapers off to nothing. If the body really matched the head it would be enormous, a monster to be reckoned with."

So here we were on our dock in Panacea, getting ready to depart for Surinam in a day or two, as I wondered whether I had really mucked it up. Maybe I had created the ultimate fish story. But it was too late to cancel the trip: Nixon had already departed for South America, and we were supposed to meet in Surinam. As I listened to the quiet "beep-beep, beeeeep" of the lovesick toadfishes underneath the water, I wondered whether I had invented the whole thing. If only Anne had been awake that day at Matapica Creek to see what I thought I saw. But then

I remembered that the Javanese fisherman had had to lift the giant toad-fish up with both hands to get it on the dock.

A few days later we arrived in Surinam and joined Nixon at the Torarica Hotel. They had clearly remembered us from the previous expedition. Little printed signs were placed on the bed tables where they couldn't be missed: IT IS STRICTLY FORBIDDEN TO BRING LIVE ANIMALS AND PLANTS INTO THE ROOM, THE MANAGEMENT.

They did have a point. We had had electric eels in the bathtub and sacks full of boa constrictors that had terrorized the maids. Perhaps it was the armored catfish we stored in the garden lily pond or the Surinam toads that hopped across the swimming pool near the bar that made us so agreeably remembered by the management. Anyway, this time we promised not to bring anything back to the hotel, and they reluctantly handed over the room keys.

For keeping fish, we encamped at the Surinam Department of Fisheries in a fenced-in compound next to the shrimp boat docks where the Minister of Fisheries gave us building and tank space in an old shed. We had aquariums and tanks, and it was perfect for our purposes.

The first problem that presented itself was the river, more of a liquid, muddy soup than water. The banks were great boggy borderings of mud that wouldn't support a large spider. The riverbank offered as little as an inch of visibility. We pumped the water into our tanks and started the aerators and subgravel filters so we could see whatever we caught, but all of our equipment was little match for the chocolate torrent that poured down the river on its voyage to the sea.

We put out the word, and fishermen began bringing in toadfishes, but all were small. We went net-fishing near the docks, catching strange catfishes, but no matter what we brought in, when we put them into the tank, they disappeared from sight. We soon had no idea how many fish we had in the two-hundred-gallon tank or whether they were dead or alive. The filters clogged, and the aerators stirred the silt even more.

Finally, we discovered the secret of cleaning up water. The river water was pumped into big settling vats and allowed to sit overnight. By the following morning most of the heavy material had settled to the bottom; if the top was siphoned off, we got more or less clear water. Soon we could see our armored catfishes swimming about and our toadfishes nestled down among the gravel and sand on the bottom, fanning out depressions for themselves. Every now and then some confused catfish, possibly blinded by the dazzling light, strayed too close, and he received a nasty chomp from one of the bad-tempered toadfishes. Eventually, we had to set up new tanks to isolate them from each other. Then we found that the toads also fought each other, when jammed together in a tank. We began to wonder how well the Surinam fishes would survive in the sparkling clear waters of the display tanks at the New York Aquarium.

Three days passed and we had amassed a considerable collection of fish, but nowhere had we been able to find a truly giant toadfish.

Our expedition was becoming a joke. The hotel maids were giggling and calling us "lumpoe." I was beginning to wonder whether the giant toadfish I had seen a year ago was a mirage or maybe that gigantic, flat, ugly head with its little tapered body made it look so terrible that it grew and grew in my imagination as Dr. Carter Gilbert suggested. By the time I had described it to Nixon at the New York Aquarium, it had grown to be a monster, at least in my mind.

Soon, sympathetic people began to say, "You get Boudji; he can catch beeg lumpoe.... Boudji can catch anything."

Thank God for the Boudjis of the world. There's always one in a village, the man who lives by the sea. There's a Boudji along practically every cove, town, island, or whatever if you look long enough. I knew one in Panacea, uncompromising, unwilling to work at construction or any other kind of work except following the fish.

We found Boudji mending his net down at the fisheries dock one morning. He wasn't a very impressive figure, a squat, brown-skinned Hindustani barely five feet tall with a bald head and a short moustache. "Ever since little boy, I fish river," he boasted. "We catch beeg lumpoes," he said, spreading his arms far apart, "good to eat; you cook with peppers, tomatoes, onions. You pay me fifty dollars a day, buy all de gas and food, and we catch... No problem. We go tonight in de river." He pointed up toward the industrial docks where we'd been fishing.

"But we've had no luck there," I protested. "Can you take us to Matapica?"

Boudji shook his head emphatically. "No good there, too much mosquitoes, too much mud. No one there now."

Anne and I didn't care to argue, remembering our last torturous foray. Besides, as Nixon pointed out, it would be a three-day roundtrip, and we were fast running out of time. He had to meet the rest of the New York Zoological Society's expedition in Bolivia.

That night we loaded Boudji's long seagoing canoe with styrofoam boxes, an oxygen cylinder, and other paraphernalia for keeping fish alive, his three-hundred-yard trammel net, and ourselves. Boudji snatched the starter cord on his decrepit forty-horsepower Johnson motor. Again and again he pulled it and nothing happened. I was beginning to worry that our last desperate night's fishing was going to end in a fiasco. But at last it sputtered, ran a few feet, and cut off. With endless patience, he cranked up the ten-year-old motor. It was worn out, rebuilt, and rebuilt again until the metal had worn thin, but soon we were moving down the river.

After several hours and repeated strikes with the gill net, we still hadn't caught a giant toadfish. The night was beautiful, with a half-full moon shining on huge cumulus clouds. They floated above our heads on a starry sky, like white castles. The lights of a freighter anchored off in the river channel glittered on the black water.

Once again Boudji and his teenage son, Franz, struck the net, let it fish for thirty minutes, and began hauling it in. Almost half of the three hundred yards of webbing had been hauled into the dugout canoe when an eerie, penetrating, almost strangling sound came up from the depths of the vast muddy Suriname River.

Hurriedly I switched on my flashlight and beamed it onto the small brown devilish-looking fish that writhed its flattened eellike body to and fro in the webbing, flashing its milky white belly and whipping its long set of whiskers back and forth. "Waaaaark... waaaaark... whaaaaark," came from the joints of the long, dangerous-looking sawtooth pectoral fins that sprang out from its sides. With great force this creature of the mud snapped its fins shut, then expanded them again.

"Good God," cried Nixon, "look at those tiny eyes. That's about one of the strangest fish we've seen yet in Surinam. Too bad it isn't bigger, but let's try to get it back alive anyway. What do you suppose it is?"

"Some kind of catfish, I would imagine," I said, grabbing the writhing, mucus-coated body and trying to unravel the webbing from its serrated flat spines. "Almost everything we've seen in this river has been some kind of catfish," I grumbled. It was almost impossible to free it. With each sinuous twist the fish became more tangled and my gloves were making the job even more difficult.

"Mister, you be careful," warned Boudji. "Dat trumpet fish... he hurt you bad!"

I was growing impatient—if this bizarre creature stayed out of water too long, it would die. Had this been my own net, I would have cut the webbing away to free it. But the old, threadbare, patched, and repatched net was Boudji's most valued possession. He told us proudly that he had had it for fifteen years, and in those wild jungles of Surinam where people exist on a sparse economy, a net means subsistence.

The entangled trumpet was screeching even louder. Finally, I yanked off my gloves, worked the fins free, and just as I started to drop the fish into the waiting box, the saw-toothed arsenal of spines on the fins slammed closed like a guillotine, pinning my fingers against its bony side. Blood spurted out as the searing poisons shot through my hand. The fish writhed to and fro, cutting deeper.

I yelled with pain as Boudji struggled to pry it off me. And when at last it was free and whipping its snakelike body around the collecting container, he turned to me angrily and said, "I tell you she hurt... now maybe you believe!"

"I believe," I repeated, stunned.

"Are you all right?" Anne asked with concern, as Nixon shined the light on my wounded hand.

I cursed my stupidity and nodded, then sat miserably in the dugout sucking the fingers that burned with pain, in too much agony to slap the mosquitoes that hummed in my ears and sucked my blood. Boudji and Franz continued hauling in the nets, snapping off the venomous spines of the brilliant gold catfish before tossing them into baskets. In the morning, the Hindustani fishermen would sell them in the Paramaribo marketplace.

Nixon's flashlight illuminated the wondrous gold aura of the catfish, making them look like the gleaming treasures of the Pharaohs. "Fool's gold!" he muttered. "It's a damn shame."

When we had first arrived and started fishing the wide, deep, muddy rivers that drained out of the jungles into the Caribbean, we were enthralled with these common golden catfish. "What a fantastic display they'll make at the Aquarium," Nick declared. "People love the color of gold. I can just see them in a black-walled tank with a dim yellow light to bring out their color. They'll be fantastic." Not only were they bright yellowish gold, but when the males came up fighting in the nets, they often spat out marble-size greenish eggs and tiny spiny babies.

With great enthusiasm we had worked through the night, changing the water of the gold catfish, selecting the best specimens that were free from net bums. But by morning, to our woeful disappointment, they had settled down and faded to what we learned was their normal, nondescript gray color—all too typical of the common sea catfishes found in the Gulf of Mexico and the south Atlantic coast of the United States. We felt like Cinderella when her gold coach turned back into a pumpkin.

Now almost nothing surprised us about these bizarre Surinam fishes. This was the land of the piranha, the electric eel, and the freshwater stingray. Here in the muddy waters where virtually no light penetrated, fish evolved armored bodies, wickedly sharp teeth, and venomous spines. To escape their attackers, they could change color or make loud raucous noises. The diversity of South American catfish was mind-boggling. In North American rivers and lakes we have ten or twelve species that all look more or less alike. But here there were hundreds of species, some with heavy-plated armored bodies that looked more like armadillos than fish. Others were soft and milky white with black tiger stripes, and some had taken the form of eels. Still others had evolved strangely flat heads and long whiskers that bent back along their sides. All of them had a nasty arsenal of spines.

As Boudji and Franz hauled in the last section of net, I heard him cry happily, "Aaah, here's beeg lumpoe!"

Instantly I forgot the burning fire in my fingers. I hurried forward and helped pull the Surinam toadfish, *Bactrachoides surinamensis*, into the canoe. It landed with a flop and began thrashing around, making menacing grunts.

Its shocking jaws sprang apart, displaying the whitish mouth that seemed to go all the way down its narrow, tadpolelike body. The lumpoe's bone-crushing jaws slammed shut and sprang open again. Quickly I closed my gloved hands around its soft, flabby body, taking great care to avoid the tiny, thorny, poisonous spines on its gill coverings. Before it could turn and bite, I catapulted it into the styrofoam box. It smelled ghastly.

The lumpoe backed into the comer of the styrofoam box and sat there with its mean little eyes glowing up at me. As its jaws opened and closed, the fleshy brown pendants that hung down from its broad flabby chin swayed like seaweed.

"Dis one big enough?" Franz demanded. The boy was getting tired of fishing with us night after night and being away from his friends.

Soon the clutter of docks and wharves disappeared behind us, replaced by mangrove bushes that grew thickly along the muddy shoreline.

"No, it's not," I replied. "We need one at least three feet long. This one can't be much larger than fourteen inches."

Franz shook his head. "You fish here all year, maybe not catch one dat beeg!"

Nixon chuckled, "Well, Jack, it looks like your giant toadfish may have turned out to be the ultimate fish story."

"Not to worry," Boudji put in reassuringly, when he saw my disappointment. He snatched the starter cord on his motor. "We catch… it take two, maybe three more days… but we catch." The motor spluttered, ran a few feet, and then cut off again.

Nixon puffed his cigarette, making the orange tip glow brightly in the darkness. "Boudji, this is our last night. Tomorrow we have to start packing the fish to go back to New York. We don't have two or three more days. But we'll pay you a big bonus if you catch one tonight."

Anne and I looked at each other in the darkness; Nixon's cancellation was a couple of days early. He had already written off the trip, and we couldn't blame him. Even though he was a close friend, it was still an embarrassment, one that would be hard to live down.

The squat Hindustani scratched his bald head. "My cousin tell me dat he see beeg lumpoe at de old sugar plantation. Very far down de river, but we go tonight."

When we finally got the motor running, we sped on down the main river channel around the broad twisting bends that wound down to the sea. Soon the clutter of docks and wharves and houses on the outskirts of Paramaribo disappeared behind us, replaced by mangrove bushes that grew thickly along the muddy shoreline with thick tangles of prop roots.

At last, much later, we reached the abandoned sugar plantation. It was three o'clock in the morning, and the rubble of the broken concrete sluice gates and crumbling buildings was silhouetted by the moonlight at the river's edge. Worm-eaten pilings rose ghostlike from the sluggish, dark Suriname River. Mud covered everything. The cabins of two sunken cruisers emerged from the thickly silted waters, and the whole place had a feeling of decay, of jungle rot. Boudji cut off the motor well before we approached the decaying boathouse. When the water shallowed, he and Franz jumped overboard for the fifth time that night, dragging the dugout toward the wreckage. When the keel dragged over the sandbar, I started to get out and push, but, as before, the squat Hindustani fisherman shook his head. "No, no, Mr. Jack, you stay in de boat. Much sharp shell, glass… cut your feet."

I didn't need much convincing. There was something dark and ominous about this part of the river, something I hadn't felt before. The empty shadows of the plantation ruins stood cold and unfriendly. As the two men pushed and pulled the dugout along, the ground periodically gave way beneath their feet. Once Franz had to pull himself out of the ooze. At another point the bottom dropped off into a deep hole, and the motor wouldn't crank, so they had to swim along the side while we paddled through the opaque muddy waters.

My mind flashed back to the stories we'd heard of the voracious bull sharks that prowled the rivers at night. And then there was the *lau-lau*, the colossal catfish reputed to snatch little children from the riverbank. Two days ago I would have thought that story fiction, but now it seemed all too real.

Right after we arrived in Surinam, we had made forays into the bustling marketplace in Paramaribo to see whether anyone had brought in a giant toadfish. We moved with the morning crowd, past the racks of drying sharks and shrimp, smelling the pungent odors of smoked mangrove snapper, snook, and mullet, which blended with the overripe fruits and vegetables. Through the crowds came a flatbed truck, blaring its horn for everyone to make way, sagging on its axles, straining under some tremendous weight. It carried a single monstrous catfish that easily measured twelve feet and weighed nearly a thousand pounds. It was still alive, slowly opening and closing its gills while its eyes glazed over. Now, as we moved along the fluid muck of the Suriname River, I half expected to see the Loch Ness monster come slithering out.

Suddenly there was a swirling sound in the shallows, and I automatically switched on my flashlight, catching the gleam of dozens of raised, green eyes of little fish scurrying on top of the water. They looked like scaly brown frogs.

"*Anableps*," said Nixon, "they're air-breathers. You see them all over South America. We've already got some at the Aquarium."

"Turn off light!" Boudji whispered. "You scare fish." Then he whispered, "OK, be very quiet, make no bump or noise."

As we sat there hearing only the waves gently lapping against the mangrove roots and the whine of the mosquitoes in our ears, it occurred to me that in all the days we had spent lumpoe hunting we hadn't heard a single sound out of these Surinam toadfish. Not in the wild, and not in the aquarium. Perhaps *Bactrachoides surinamensis* didn't sing the way our North American species did, or perhaps we were there at the wrong season. I wanted to ask Boudji about it, but it was obviously the wrong time.

Steadily he dragged one end of the all-engulfing gill net toward the fallen ruin of the boat shed, while Franz continued pulling the canoe ahead until a wall of webbing stretched out and circled the wreckage. Soon the entire dock was fenced in so that no fish could escape.

For a long while we sat silently in the dugout, listening to Boudji and Franz talking softly in Taki-Taki, the local dialect. The moonlight's reflection gleamed golden on the river as Boudji crouched down and reached under the debris with his bare hand, groping around the wreckage, poking his hand down into dens and burrows. Only his head was sticking up, but periodically he would crouch down, hold his breath, and disappear into the muddy morass.

You couldn't find a more dangerous way to hunt toadfish. No other fisherman in Surinam would have taken the chance. We could just barely see the two fishermen in the moonlight, moving along ever so slowly, methodically prodding and reaching into the net. The night was deathly still; more mosquitoes whined in our ears. We slapped them and passed the mosquito repellent around again and again.

Something splashed in the net, and three corks pulled down. Probably another fair-size snook was gilled in the webbing; we had caught several that night. In the moonlight we could see that several corks holding up the wall of webbing were pulled down, snatched by other fish that had been driven away from the shelter of the fallen dock.

Suddenly we heard a loud, bloodcurdling shriek and water cascaded up in an explosion as Boudji jumped upward. Madly he flailed the water into foam, cursing in Taki-Taki, trying to shake something off.

"Something's grabbed Boudji." Nixon's beam caught the small man thrashing about, wrestling with something. Franz stood by, looking horrified. I saw the fear in Anne's face as I jumped overboard. But before I knew it I was lurching through the boggy mud, trying to make my way toward him, wondering what I could do to help without a weapon and in the dark. I was also wondering whether whatever it was might grab me next.

But I didn't have time to think. Boudji had broken free and rushed back, churning the water while shouting, "Stay in de boat… stay in de boat."

"What is it?" I demanded, running behind him, fast as I could go through semifluid muck. "What happened?"

We got to the dugout, and Anne's flashlight illuminated a large circular bite on his arm where a hundred small sharp teeth had perforated his brown skin; blood was trickling out of the holes. "Dat lumpoe, she a big one and got de eggs. When she got de eggs, she bite you bad, get mad," he said, while demonstrating by clamping his fingers abruptly on his other arm.

"Are you all right, Boudji?" Anne asked.

"OK, OK… we catch." Looking frightened, Franz hurried over to retrieve the other heavy pole and followed his father back toward the collapsed boat shed. With shouts of vengeance they attacked the inside of the net with a fury, trying to drive the fish out. Using their jabbing poles, Boudji and Franz slammed the water over and over, churning the peaceful Suriname River into foam.

Then, with an incredible amount of courage, Boudji went back to the exact spot where the lumpoe had sunk its teeth into his arm and submerged to grope in the mud again. We held our breath and the tension mounted as we saw him come up, gasp for air, and go back down again. Franz stood by, anxiously clutching his pole.

At last, Boudji surfaced, exhaled, and shouted, "She run out now; watch de net."

But the giant lumpoe was a long way from being caught. We shone our flashlights around the three-hundred-yard circle of bobbing cork line while the two fishermen walked around the inside, randomly thrashing the water, hoping to drive it into the curtain of webbing. We knew the odds were equally great that the big toadfish had run a few yards away and was sitting on the bottom, waiting for the net to lift when we began hauling it in. Then it would swim under the lead line to freedom.

When Boudji and his son climbed into the boat, Anne asked, "Do you think it got into the net?"

"Don't know, maybe yes, maybe no," Boudji replied grimacing from pain of the bite as he pulled in the first armload of webbing and piled it into the bottom of the canoe. More catfish, croakers, and snook came aboard.

"Look!" Nixon shouted, his flashlight illuminating something big and angry several hundred feet away in the net. Five corks that held the wall of webbing afloat were abruptly snatched under as something big collided with the net and fought to get out. There was an explosive splash; then the corks bobbed upward and pulled down again and returned to just below the surface. It could be nothing else but the lumpoe.

Boudji began pulling in the net all the faster. I was hauling back with all my might, trying to ignore my sore hand. "It should stay in that trammel net, shouldn't it? Almost nothing can get out of that," I said.

"Don't know," Boudji grunted. "Maybe yes, maybe she get out... we see." There was no way we could tell by looking at it whether the fish had been snared or had bitten a hole through and escaped into the soupy, protective mud of the river, leaving a tangled mess behind.

Boudji slid overboard and Franz followed, not looking very happy. Warily he danced over to the bunched-up net beside his father. Once again Boudji dove down into the black water beside the thing. A low growl arose from the mud, and then Boudji popped up. "OK, into de boat!" he shouted. With one mighty heave, he and his son hurled up the webbing, and something heavy plopped down into the bottom of the boat.

Prolonged bellows of pure rage shook the night, first one and then another. I shined the light down, and the beam caught the small green eyes sitting on top of an immense head. There seemed to be no limit to the giant white mouth that flew open, roared like an angry animal, and crunched down on whatever came within its reach.

Panic seized me. I clambered backward over Anne trying to get out of its way. I have dealt with every conceivable creature in the ocean and have never been completely frightened by anything nonhuman. But for a moment I was petrified. It was in the canoe with us, slamming, beating, stomping the bottom, and roaring. In karate, one disarms one's opponent with a bloodcurdling scream, and it works. "My God," cried Anne, "no fish should roar like that!"

The sixty-four-year-old trustee of the New York Zoological Society stared at it wide-eyed. "It's incredible; I'm not sure whether to bring it back to the New York Aquarium or the Bronx Zoo! What a monster. I've never heard a fish roar before!" he said, his voice filled with admiration and disbelief. Nixon was enjoying his prize at the same time he was retreating with us, giving it plenty of room as the creature went into a fresh rage. It thrashed around the bottom of the canoe, flailing the sides with its triangular tail.

I had to do something. I couldn't let our prize batter itself or get stuck by a discarded catfish. I slipped on the heavy welding gloves brought along just for this occasion, but I couldn't bring myself to handle it.

"Mister, you watch, that fish bite you bad," Franz cautioned from his now safe ground outside the boat.

I took a deep breath and mustered my courage. But when my gloved hands touched its body, another explosion rocked the boat. The monster whipped around, slammed its immense jaws shut with a loud snap, then went into another frenzied fighting tantrum. Again and again it bit at the struts on the bottom of the canoe, holding on like a bulldog, turning itself over and over. I regained control of my fear and started forward again.

"For heaven's sake, Jack," Nixon urged, "let the damn thing wear itself out."

"Yes, do," echoed Anne, who looked as if she were contemplating joining Boudji and Franz outside the boat.

Boudji came to the rescue. He leaned over the gunwale and motioned for me to give him room. "Here, I show you," he shouted. "This is the way to pick up lumpoe. First you make her go to sleep... like this."

Ever so gently, his bare fingers stroked the top of the immense slimy round head, in front of the thorny spines, right above its upturned eyes. Its huge white mouth remained open, showing all those tiny sharp teeth that had perforated his shoulder and arm, but it didn't snap. Like a true hypnotist, he stroked the head over and over, and he mumbled to it softly, "Make him go to sleep... so." In just a minute the monster became motionless.

"Get box ready," Boudji whispered. "I bring fish!"

His palms slid under the bloated, soft underbelly of the creature that had bitten him so badly, and ever so gently, he lifted it up. Suddenly the toadfish woke up and spun around. Boudji yelped as he tried to hold it, but its mucous body slid out of his hands and was headed overboard.

I saw that wide cavernous mouth spring open and thrust my already wounded but heavily gloved hand into its mouth. The bones felt as if they were being crushed in a vise as I fell to my knees and dropped hand and fish into the box. Fortunately, the teeth were too small to penetrate the leather, but God, did that toadfish stink! The sour stench was worse than the pain—it reeked of garbage and mud flats—and the lumpoe was in no hurry to let go. I kept my other hand pressed on its back to keep it from twisting around.

Finally, it released the pressure slightly, and I slid my bruised fingers out of the glove, leaving it clamped in the monster's mouth.

We slammed the lid on the box, and the toadfish began thrashing and croaking again. For a while it seemed as if the very sides were going to be torn apart. I sat on the lid until it settled down to a series of unhappy grunts, shaking my head in disbelief.

"I hope you're all right," said Anne, watching me wriggling my fingers. They were numb, but had no real damage.

Nixon shook his head in disbelief. "I know we need the fish, Jack... but it's not worth losing fingers."

"It's OK," I insisted. "Its jaws aren't that strong—otherwise Boudji wouldn't be here with us."

A few minutes later, when the box was quiet, we opened the lid and Nixon gazed down at the huge lumpoe with admiration. It completely filled the cooler, its tail circled around a corner. My glove lay floating where it had finally dropped it, and I fished it out cautiously.

There was the largest, ugliest toadfish I had ever seen.

When the net was on board, and our growing assortment of local fishes was stashed away, Boudji paddled over to the big decaying dock once again, and he and Franz slid overboard.

"What's he doing now?" Nixon asked sleepily. The adrenalin and excitement of the night had passed, it was four-thirty, and we were tired. The fishermen took a good fifteen minutes pulling and snatching at something on the bottom.

At last he and Franz came dragging out a six-foot-wide board and lifted it into the canoe. The black muddy underside was coated with hundreds of pink larval toadfishes, each less than a half-inch long, looking like tadpoles clinging to the muddy surface. Under our flashlight, pulses of movement ran through the colony as their orange tails wriggled forlornly back and forth.

For a moment a feeling of guilt had come over us all and put a pall on the expedition. "Well, I guess we'll call her 'Big Mama,'" declared Nixon. "Her babies will just have to go with her to New York."

"'Big Mama' is probably a male," Anne pointed out. "Remember the males guard the young."

"Male or female," I interrupted, "what are we going to do with a six-foot board? We don't have a saw to cut it down to fit into a box."

All during the trip back to the dock we took turns slowly bailing water over the nursery, watching the pinkish-orange fish waving their tails. Pulses of movement went through the colony as they wriggled back and forth, glued to the surface of the wood by their egg pouches.

Dawn was breaking by the time we arrived back at the docks of Paramaribo. The masts of the shrimp trawlers were silhouetted against the pale tropical sky. I opened the lid and regarded the puffy brown toadfish as he looked balefully up at us. "A little over three feet," I said. "I guess that's about as big as they come."

"Well, I'm not sure we could have handled one any bigger," Nixon said reassuringly. "She acts like she's ten feet long. Big Mama's a monster all right."

Aside from the show of bad temper that first night, our big lumpoe remained docile and gave no trouble. I was soon able to handle "her." Whether she was a he didn't seem to matter. By virtue of its maternal behavior, it was female to Nixon and me. Anne insisted on calling it "he," which was just the opposite of her usual complaint—that almost all animals encountered were automatically referred to as "he," as if the female sex did not exist.

The lumpoe seemed content, sitting on top of its babies, making only an occasional grunt. The day we were packing up to leave, Boudji came to help pack and collect his money. He reached over to touch Big Mama in the shipping box, and the lumpoe charged him like a freight train. Once again its jaws clamped down on his hand. He yelled and snatched back his bruised arm that still bore her teeth marks. "Oooohow!" he yelled, and jumped away.

"Big Mama doesn't like you," Nixon laughed.

"That's because I cotched her," Boudji said philosophically. He looked down at her happily. "Next year, you come back and we catch great beeg lumpoe that make this one look small. I can catch."

Three days later we unpacked fifteen large styrofoam coolers at the New York Aquarium. The flight out of Surinam had been delayed, and we had lost some specimens in the torpid tropical heat. When I sliced through the filament tape of the box marked "Big Mama,"I reeled backward at the rush of putrid air. She had fouled her water during the long transit and lay motionless in the big plastic bag of putrid brown river water. With great sadness I reached for her remains only to be startled by a warning growl.

Sadness turned to joy as we slid her into a tank of clean water. And there she sat, on top of her babies, glowering at the crowds of curious onlookers through her tank window, no doubt missing her muddy morass. Nixon and I sat on the brass railing, watching her triumphantly through the glass wall.

"You know," Nixon said as we walked around the tank months later, "I just heard that they have really big toadfishes off the coast of South Africa. That's where we should go. Let's see whether we can catch one this big," he said, smiling, while spreading his arms apart as far as they would reach.

4. A Green Turtle's Story

The large green sea turtle lay on her back, blinking in the harsh afternoon sunlight. Her body felt the rolling swells as our little shrimp boat chugged down the Panacea channel out into Apalachee Bay. Did she know she was going back to the sea after seven years of captivity, seven years of being imprisoned and displayed at the Cleveland Aquarium?

The last time Evergreen, as they called her, had felt the rise and fall of the waves and the crispness of the open air was when she was captured off the Miami coast and was only slightly larger than a dinner plate. In the intervening seven years she had quadrupled her length and turned flabby and white.

Patches of her brown plastron were peeling away because of a vitamin D deficiency, a lack of natural sunlight. That was the main reason the curator at the aquarium wanted to set her free. People were beginning to worry that the aquarium had diseased animals.

She wasn't diseased at all; it was just the years of captivity showing, the years spent swimming perpetually back and forth inside the darkly lit glass aquarium. She had also outgrown her tank, and none of the other public aquariums with larger facilities wanted her.

So we agreed to set her free for them. Would this endangered sea turtle survive after all those years of being hand-fed by her curators? Would her pasty white skin catch the eye of roving sharks that would tear her body to pieces? Seven years of swimming back and forth beneath the artificial lights of a forty-thousand-gallon tank while hundreds of thousands of curious onlookers peered at her through the glass walls did little to give the turtle muscle tone.

When we pried the boards off her coffinlike shipping crate, the very idea of turning this big flaccid piece of turtle meat back into the wild seemed hopeless. With grunts and groans, we heaved her three-hundred-pound bulk into our fourteen-foot holding tank, where Evergreen swam about uncertainly. She looked at this new tank, smaller and shallower than her own home at the aquarium, and banged into the walls. Her peeling shell rose above the water, bobbing like a cork.

Her panic finally ceased. The tank was different, but still she was being attended by humans, the same species she had known all her life. The turtle looked expectantly at us for food. All her life she had been fed fish, even though her diet in nature would have consisted of sea grasses and algae. Her daily aquarium diet was thawed sardines or chub mackerel from the hand of her keepers. Green turtles are normally carnivorous only during their first year of life after they hatch out of the egg and take to the open sea. Afterward, greens become grazers, with the specialized serrated rounded jaws designed to chomp away at seafloor vegetation, rather than to the crushing jaws of a ridley or loggerhead that eats crabs.

I was not about to feed her dead fish. Somehow, I would have to get her back to her natural diet of sea grass, but I had a time and space problem. Our tank was not designed to hold such a big animal. She was already stirring up the gravel and churning the tank into a nightmare of siltation that was disturbing the other creatures. Very soon she would have to go back to the sea or we'd have to turn our facilities upside-down to keep her.

We didn't want to detain this imprisoned green turtle a minute more than necessary. However, we decided that only after she started eating her natural food, turtle grass, would we set her free.

It was called "turtle grass" because green sea turtles in the lower Caribbean feasted on it.

It was a warm summer day, so Anne and I decided to make grass gathering a family affair. We loaded our two children, Sky and Cypress, into the speedboat and headed across to Dog Island off Carrabelle, where an abundance of fresh drift grass often washed up onto the beach. It was also a good place to find small sea worms that we used to feed baby electric rays.

Since we had had children we had come to appreciate the beach as never before. There were no incessant wants, needs, complaints, and fighting at the shore. The beach was a perpetual warm weather baby-sitter.

With children, I also realized why the taxonomy and biology of the near-microscopic creatures that live between sand grains have been so extensively studied at the Marine Biological Laboratory at Woods Hole, Massachusetts. For there, on one of the few sandy beaches amid all the rocky, gravel ones, the scientists also came with their families to sit and watch the water. But being men and women of science, they had to do more than watch the waves. So they studied and looked deeper at sand grains through microscopes and gazed down at the world of tiny amphipods, cephalocarideans, nematodes, and polychaete worms that no one knew were there. They described new species after new species, and the way they moved vertically with the tidal rise. They looked through microscopes whose lenses were made of heat-fused sand grains, melted at thousands of degrees centigrade, ground and polished into glass.

Micron-size monsters move through the spaces of boulder-size sand grains, predators and prey, diatom plants and animals. Meanwhile the scientists' children played in the sea and the waves washed in and reclaimed their sand castles. We watched our two little boys building a sand castle, piling up sand, and scooping out an elaborate bunker. Their barrow pit was filling with groundwater, seeping out of the sand grains, and a number of disturbed tiny white amphipods darted to and fro in the newly formed pool.

Cypress, our three-year-old, was after the mole crabs they unearthed, the little gray torpedo-shaped crustaceans that dart down into the sand as fast as a fish can swim through water. Giving up on catching them, he went back to pushing his toy car around in the sand, making trails like a horseshoe crab.

Sky Rudloe, who was six, stubbornly continued fighting the inevitable collapse of his sand castle with the resolve of the U.S. Army Corps of Engineers; and with about the same futility as many of their beach-renourishment projects, the sea took it back.

I sat there relaxing, watching the hypnotic waves blanking out my mind. Over and over again the waves broke, washed over the sand, and drained off into the interstices between sand grains. For a brief time there was dryness and the sands changed hue and became darker, dulled, only to be doused again and gleamed with renewed golden sheen from the sun. It was a moment of magic.

Just below my feet were countless thousands of living coquina clams amid the surf digging their way into the sands. On the east coast of Florida, they are so dense that yellow and white coquina sands from their fragmented shells have built the beaches, and compacted coquina rocks have been used to build houses. Here I had only to scoop away an inch of surface sand to expose their dazzling, lustrous array of colors, as pretty as gemstones.

Down the beach my wife was sitting in the surf in her bathing suit, working. Tediously she picked little pink worms out of the sand and put them in her bucket to feed her newborn electric rays. The rays were used in medical research, and we were involved in developing methods of culturing them. Food was a critical part of the problem of rearing rays in captivity. I thought about helping her, but I had other things on my mind, and there was plenty of time on the beach anyway.

My eyes went out to the dozen-odd shrimp boats anchored down, silhouetted against the horizon. Their exhausted crews were sound asleep, rocked by the waves, building their strength for another exhausting night of hunting shrimp, culling, icing, and working the rigging, trying to make a boat payment. Doubtlessly some of them would catch loggerheads and perhaps ridley sea turtles, and possibly some of those turtles would be drowned.

I thought of Evergreen in our tanks. What chance would she have if she swam into the fleet of shrimp boats? Although many of the captains and crews would send her on her way, if she didn't drown, and would let me know what the tag number was, others would happily eat her. Feelings about turtles were tense in the fleet nowadays, because the federal government and the conservation lobby were going to require that shrimpers pull special gear that would allegedly push the turtles out of the net along with the trash, and supposedly still retain most of the shrimp.

It sounded good, but most captains swore they wouldn't pull the cumbersome turtle-excluder device, that it wouldn't work, that it would clog up with sponges and crab traps, and jeopardize their already tenuous livelihood. The National Marine Fisheries Service, who developed and tested the gear, claimed otherwise. But whether or not it worked, the law would soon go into effect, backed by enormous fines, jail, and confiscated vessels. The shrimpers hated the idea, not only because they said the new nets would catch fewer shrimp, but because they were cumbersome and dangerous in rough seas.

I had mixed feelings. I hated to see turtles drown, and I also knew what hard work it was for those men trying to scratch out a living from an already overtaxed, diminished fishery. Many were saying I had betrayed them with the new law, that I was responsible for it, and in a sense they were right. Over the years I had worked hard for sea turtle conservation.

We had a grant to receive Kemp's or Atlantic ridleys, the world's most endangered sea turtle, from commercial fishermen and to rehabilitate them in our tanks. If they were half-drowned in shrimp nets, or cold-shocked or injured, we did our best to keep them alive and feed them until they were strong enough to return to the wild.

The Kemp's ridley is the world's smallest sea turtle, weighing only a hundred pounds at maturity. It's endangered because it nests exclusively on a tiny stretch of wild shoreline at Rancho Nuevo in Tamaulipas, Mexico, about one hundred ten miles south of Brownsville, Texas, and only in broad daylight.

Environmentalists are forcing the use of turtle excluders on the shrimping industry because of the ridley's catastrophic population decline. In 1947 these round-shelled, olive-green turtles came ashore in great seething masses known as *arribadas* with forty thousand ridleys emerging at a single time. Over the years their populations have drastically declined, to five thousand in 1960, to only five hundred nesting females in the mid-1980s.

No one really knows the cause of the decline; egg harvesting by Mexicans, drowning in shrimp nets, and possible disease have been blamed. But the required use of turtle excluders is a desperate attempt to save what is left.

Before the devices were required throughout the Gulf of Mexico and the South Atlantic, I felt that a lot more should be learned about the whereabouts and seasonal occurrence of the ridley. In the past twenty years we had tagged and released over a hundred in the eastern Gulf, and I had never seen a mature specimen. They were all half-grown juveniles, seldom exceeding fifty pounds. Yet in the nearly landlocked Gulf of Mexico the distance between the western and eastern boundaries is not great, considering the other distances they traveled. Dozens of half-grown ridleys have turned up coldshocked in northern waters off Long Island and Boston Harbor, and they are among the most common of waif and stray turtles off Nova Scotia.

Over the years ridleys have also washed up on the shores of Europe. One that was raised at the National Marine Fisheries Service Laboratory in Galveston was released in Homosassa, Florida, and 502 days later turned up on the coast of France.

Although we had caught them far up creeks and in back bays and marshes, a few specimens have been taken seventy miles offshore at the edge of the Gulf Stream off St. Augustine. Perhaps the small ridleys that the shrimpers brought us had ridden the Gulf Loop current up from Rancho Nuevo, Mexico, as hatchlings, and would follow the Gulf Stream when they left. Some might become lost and end up in New York; most followed the great gyre around the Atlantic, eventually to return home by some unknown route to lay their eggs. The presence of small ridleys in the Azores off the coast of Portugal and the absence of big ridleys in the eastern Gulf would fit the theory.

I felt it a dreadful shame that conservationists and shrimpers were pitted against each other when they should be working together. Archie Carr once termed the Atlantic or Kemp's ridley "the most mysterious animal in North America." If they became less mysterious, blanket laws requiring shrimpers to use turtle-excluder devices in all waters at all times might not be necessary.

What bothered me most was the total absence of ridley bones in ancient Indian middens. Zooarchaeologists sifting through coastal shell middens have uncovered plenty of loggerhead and green sea turtle remains along with manatee bones, fish, and other coastal fare, but never a single ridley, according to Dr. Elizabeth Wing of the Florida State Museum. Certainly ridleys are good to eat. The old turtle fishermen in Cedar Keys said they were almost as good as greens, and much better and more tender than loggerheads.

If the Mexican shores swarmed with nesting ridleys in 1940, what would the Gulf and South Atlantic waters have been like a thousand or two thousand years ago when the Indians built the middens? It's almost as if the ridley popped out of nowhere, created by spontaneous generation; or perhaps the Indians regarded them as taboo.

I tried to push away all these problems by going for a walk down the beach to see what creatures nature had tossed up. Dog Island in the northern Gulf was a good place to find shells, almost as rich as Sanibel Island much farther south, which is famous among shell collectors. Today there were lots of cockleshells, with linear markings, distinctive yellow and brown colors, mixed with beachworn whelks, quahogs riddled with worms, and boring barnacle and boring sponge holes, all retaining some vestiges of their individuality. All rolled in the surf, soon to be lost to a sandy oblivion. But the renewable life-force would bring new shells to the beach.

South of Tampa, the Gulf beaches are made up almost entirely of carbonate sands from untold billions of eroding shells. South Florida has a greater abundance of mollusks, coral, and calcareous algae growing in the warmer tropical temperatures. The north Florida Panhandle beaches, where we live and work, are almost all quartz sands eroded from mountains hundreds of miles away in Georgia, carried by rivers all the way down to the Gulf Coast. Geologists prospecting for oil say the sand on the west Florida shelf is twelve thousand feet deep in places, yet in others it lies only a few inches deep on top of limestone rocks. Far down beneath the sand is another layer of carbonate limestone that is more than 100 million years old.

Lying on top of the sand that day and mixed in the abundant seashells, pieces of pink- and rose-colored sea pork glistened in the sun along with clumps of calcareous bryozoans and yellowfinger sponges. But the remains of white rubbery cannonball jellyfish were everywhere. Sometimes shoals of these firm rubbery balls would be carried to the beach by the winds and currents and caught on a falling tide. Then the sun would scorch down, leaving their gelatinous umbrellas dehydrating and pulsing in the shallows until life passed away. Their whitened carcasses became part of the flotsam, to wash back and forth with the surf until the sand and sea made them disappear. They were recycled back into the great oceanic soup of plankton that in turn nourished those intertidal creatures down in the sand grains beneath my feet.

I looked at these rotting jellyfish with apprehension because in the following month, I had to make another electric ray trip. Until methods of culturing them were perfected, we collected wild ones from the ocean. If they were too thick, we wouldn't be able to drag our nets. Last time we deck-loaded with jellyfish, they stung all the rays to death, and I got an eyeful of nematocysts and spent a miserable night. The jellyfish got so thick we had to cut the trip short.

Shrimpers hate all jellyfish, but especially the big cannonballs. When they see their round white bodies sweeping out of the island passes into the Gulf where they're dragging for white shrimp, most of them pick up their nets and leave. Each jellyfish weighs anywhere from three to six pounds, and five hundred of them will burst a net and break a block and possibly kill someone.

As I walked along, I saw there were other jellyfish mixed with the cannonballs: gas-filled, beach-worn floats of the Portuguese man-of-war, along with boards covered with gooseneck barnacles, and clumps of oceanic sargassum weed. These were signs of Gulf Stream waters coming close to shore. Several weeks of strong south winds and dry weather had brought the great oceanic gyre closer to the beach.

The inshore circulation over the west Florida shelf comes largely from strong tidal currents, winds, storms, and cold fronts, but fifty to a hundred miles off shore is the warm blue water of the great oceanic current. Giant whirlpools of Loop current waters sometimes break off and move along the coast, dispersing tropical red sea anemones and butterfly fishes to the jetties of Panama City and bringing floating purple oceanic snails to the beaches of Port Aransas, Texas. Sometimes upwellings throw deep-water octopuses and luminous lantern fishes onshore, creating a beachcomber's adventure.

Gazing out over the horizon, I pondered the ocean highway that connected the Gulf of Mexico to the Atlantic Ocean, Europe and Africa to South and North America.

Passing through the straits of Yucatán, the Gulf Stream enters the Gulf of Mexico, where it is called the "Gulf Loop current." There is a river of warm tropical water several hundred miles across, two thousand feet deep, slowly churning around in a great gyre. It pushes up into the Gulf, bringing a constant flow of tropical clear water to this almost landlocked ocean, coming closest to shore along the west Florida coast.

As the current churns, it sometimes entrains fifty-mile-wide eddies of Mississippi River water. Satellite photographs have shown it carrying the muddy brackish water south at a rate of three-and-a-half miles per hour through the Straits of Florida, transporting river water around the tip of the peninsula as far as north Georgia before it mixes and loses its identity. By entraining a great pulse of brown shrimp larvae from the Louisiana delta, it may give North Carolina a bumper shrimp season, or possibly put our ridleys into Long Island Sound. Only when it leaves the Gulf, rounding Key West to head north to North Carolina, is this planetary-scale eddy called the Gulf Stream. It clips along at fifty miles a day before it turns east, moving away from North America out into the open ocean toward Europe and Africa. Once freed of the continental shelf, it no longer touches bottom and its flow resembles a garden hose madly thrashing around in a swimming pool. After reaching Europe, it flows in a broad sluggish stream called the "Canaries Current," past Portugal to the North Africa coast.

Then coming back across the Atlantic from Africa, another branch of the Gulf Stream is called the "Equatorial Current." The water literally piles up against the American continent and generates a swift current that races up the coast of South America and into the Gulf of Mexico, as the "Yucatán Current," and finally the "Gulf Loop."

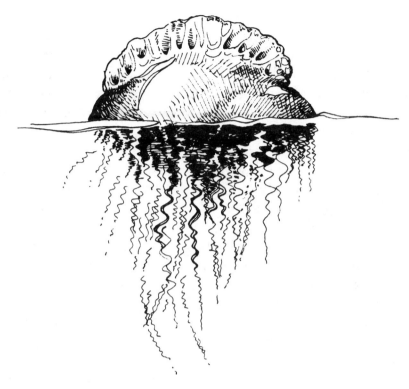

Gas-filled, beach-worn floats of the Portuguese man-of-war were strewn along the beaches, signs of the Gulf Stream waters coming close to shore.

All these names are attempts by mankind to grasp the great cosmic flow of movement and energy. And it's as futile as trying to explain the Tao, or convey the great eternity and vastness of it all. Oceanographers have bounced around the ocean taking hydrocasts, temperatures, and salinities, and measuring a segment here and a segment there. But with satellite photography, which shows the flow in one picture, the names become practically meaningless.

As I walked along, I looked through the great piles of turtle and Cuban shoal grasses that were washed ashore, hoping to find some rare waif or stray from the Gulf Stream. Sometimes tuna fishermen saw rafts of floating sea grasses hundreds of miles out in the Gulf when the north winds pushed them out to the edge of the great gyre.

For the past week a strong south wind had been blowing, pushing windrows of sea grass and sargassum up onto the white sandy beach.

This happens every summer. The grasses grow until they become so tall and ungainly that wave action rips them up from the seafloor and currents send them drifting around the ocean. Then the leaves pile up on the beaches, eventually dry out, and rot. It reminded me of the reason we came here: to feed Evergreen and to feed our lugworm farm.

Anne was still digging up the tiny pink worms in the surf zone. They were there because of the abundance of sea grass and other detritus that washed up and rotted. She was getting sunburned. "Who ever thought I'd get a Ph.D. so I could sit here and dig worms for a living?" she groaned, stretching her back and legs. "Why don't electric rays eat frozen fishsticks like crabs do?"

"Beats me," I said, looking in her bucket at the tangled pink vermiforms. "Why do people work all year in offices and factories to save up enough money so they can come to the beach with their kids just like we're doing for a living?"

"It's because the Great Turtle Mother so wills it. She also wills that we get this grass together and get back across the sound before it gets dark."

Our children wanted no part of gathering up armloads of drift grass and stuffing it into meshed bags, and I couldn't blame them.

The grass was full of beach hoppers, or sand fleas, little bouncing amphipods that pelted our faces and got all over our necks and arms. They bite, even though they are not supposed to.

We often had grass-gathering parties, because we needed stacks of it to feed lugworms, which we used for electric ray food. We piled up the grass and allowed it to decay in the sun and then put it through a meat grinder until it turned into sea mulch. We farmed black, oversize earthwormlike creatures that feasted and grew rapidly on the mushy black soup.

We went into farming worms because, even with buying long pink bait worms from Maine and adult lugworms from a bait supplier in Tampa, it was still a constant struggle to keep the rays fed. Then we got help from an unexpected source.

We found thousands of three-inch-long slender marine earthworms growing in our composted heaps of turtle grass. Minutes after our discovery, the baby rays were inspecting them and deigned to eat a few. So we had a new animal to get to know.

One doesn't think of earthworms as living in the sea. But there are hundreds of very similar species out there. Most of them are microscopic, living down among the sand grains. Only a few species are visible. But these were large, a good three inches long, almost large enough to bait on a hook if they hadn't been so skinny.

It took a while to get them positively identified, since there are very few marine earthworm specialists, but finally we learned they were *Pontodrilus bermudensis.*

They play the same part in breaking down the vegetable matter piled up on the shore that earthworms do everywhere on land. They transform dead sea grass into a sort of marine humus, food for fiddler crabs, amphipods, and other small creatures to feed upon and in turn provide food for the rest of the estuary. The importance of these little-known worms in the food chain may be greater than anyone suspects.

Pontodrilus, we discovered, when we typed its name into a computer, is widely distributed around Central and South America, Mexico, and Bermuda, hence its name. It is found throughout Florida and was first described from specimens found on the south Gulf Coast in Naples, Florida, in 1941.

There were billions of them out there. We had only to go to a sheltered beach where the grass piled up and rotted, dig down a foot in the sand at the high-tide line, and there they were in multitudes. We also learned from studies at the University of Georgia that, wonder of wonders, they have luminous spit that glows in the dark. The god of earthworms no doubt knows why, but nobody else does.

As we scooped the grass into the bags, we wondered whether the blades were plastered with the microscopic cocoons of these marine earthworms. Perhaps these sedentary worms were also children of the Gulf Stream. When the grass washed ashore, they crawled out of the sand, laid their eggs on it, and on the next storm swept it back out to sea. We speculated that these humble worms might be distant ocean travelers, like the great green sea turtles.

When we had a boatload of grass, and a bucket of worms, and the kids had enough of the beach, we pushed the boat off to take the soon-to-be-free green turtle her supper.

Later that night we dumped handfuls of grass into the tank with her. Evergreen was certainly hungry, especially since her curators had fed her three times a day as part of the show. But would she eat grass as wild greens do?

The great patchwork quilt of a turtle looked upon the strange greenery with intense curiosity. Then to our delight, her jaws opened and crunched down on the grass, swallowed it, and crunched again. She seemed to go crazy with delight. The grass acted as a tonic, her lethargy was gone, and her interest in life returned. A wildness seemed to come upon her by the time the last sprig was devoured, for she moved about the tank not as a shelled lump with flippers, but with a new awareness. Perhaps it was my imagination or even wishful thinking, but she seemed to avoid the part of the circular tank where we stood watching. We could let her go.

Several days later, a number of Anne's students from the university helped us haul her out of the tank with much splashing, load her onto the truck, and carry her down to our boat.

All during the voyage to Dog Island, and past it, we had kept Evergreen lying on her back in precisely the same manner that she had been shipped to us from Cleveland. If you turn a full-grown sea turtle onto its belly on land, all of the weight of shell and body comes to rest on its heart and lungs, and it can suffocate.

"What do you really think her chances of survival are?" one of the students asked, as we passed the last channel marker.

"She's already beaten the odds," I replied. "She's survived. Less than 1 percent of all hatchling sea turtles make it to maturity."

Of course, no one understood the odds, or could tell how many little sea turtles really survive. Often the newborn turtles are devoured by large ghost crabs and seabirds as they scurry off the beach. They are gobbled up by bluefish, mangrove snappers, jacks, and sharks as they dive into the waves. Divers off the east coast of Florida have swum behind fleeing turtles on bright moonlit nights in calm seas and watched schools of gray snappers rise up from the bottom and grab turtle after turtle. But would that have happened if the clutch of eggs hatched on a dark night, during a storm with offshore winds when the predators were scattered? Survival is a matter of luck, coupled with instinct and all the inherent tools of survival that nature provides.

I sat beside the turtle, pouring seawater over her plastron to make the trip out as comfortable as possible. Even the weather seemed to cooperate, as a cool breeze played across us while the boat was gently rocked by the rolling swells. In the distance I could hear a sea bell buoy clanging mournfully.

For a moment I wondered whether I should turn the boat around and go back into the sheltered bay. Had I made the wrong decision to release her here, where we had pulled up some enormous tiger sharks in the past?

The big turtle's head arched backward and her tagged flippers waved almost gaily, while her yellowish-white belly shell swelled with air on every in-drawn breath. I had the feeling that she knew she was going home. Whether it was home to death or to the freedom of the open seas almost didn't matter. She was a child of the ocean, and it was right that she should return.

We were bringing her close to an area where a fully mature male green turtle, weighing over three hundred pounds, was caught six miles off Apalachicola in ninety feet of water one summer on a shrimp boat. What a ferocious beast it was, growling and hissing at anyone who came near, snapping like an angry dog. Shrimpers in the northern Gulf had never seen such a turtle before; they were used to relatively passive loggerheads, not the fighting muscle of this outraged herbivore.

Most of the greens that appear along the west Florida shelf are the size of a dinner plate and weigh about ten pounds, although they seem to increase in size the farther south one goes. Full-size green turtles graze in the grass beds and underwater meadows off the coast near Cape Sable and the Florida Everglades, but do not nest there. Only on the southeast coast, around Palm Beach and Fort Lauderdale, do a handful of greens lay eggs.

But I wanted Evergreen to have the best possible chance at finding her natural migration route, so we proceeded farther out to sea as our little shrimp boat bobbed and rolled with the increasing waves. There was now a strong south wind blowing, and the tide was rising.

The water was a transparent, oceanic blue, not its usual greenish estuarine color. The dry summer, onshore winds, and proximity of the Gulf Loop current to shore brought oceanic influences.

Before us were great golden rafts of sargassum, gulfweed that had been transported hundreds of miles up from the Gulf of Mexico and the Caribbean, floating on the surface. It formed a weed line that piled up at the edge of the Stream, and there blue and lavender Portuguese man-of-war jellyfish bobbled along the surface, and more silver flyingfish skipped over the waves as if running through air on their tails. Mixed into the vegetation were debris, wooden planks, styrofoam, sea beans, rafts of animal and plant life.

Sargassum is as characteristic of the Gulf Stream as the bright purplish-blue water itself. Ships traveling across the Loop current in the Gulf of Mexico between Florida and Texas have reported running through tremendous floating patches. The golden weed stays afloat with little round air-filled flotation berries. Clumps and pieces move with the wind, swept by the currents, and bunch together at the edge of the Stream to form a weed line.

With the tremendous diversity of life that lives in clusters of hides beneath them, the sargassum community is one of the most productive habitats on earth. Eventually it sinks down into the depths, fertilizing the sea and providing needed nutrients to the empty abyssal depths.

Although there is only a little bit of evidence to substantiate it, biologists suspect that these dense floating rafts of vegetation in the Sargasso Sea provide a haven for little sea turtles. When newborn loggerheads break through their eggshells to scramble up into the night, they are almost the same color as sargassum. They join the world of camouflage, where all the creatures that live in the weed are subtle browns, reds, greens, and blotched color combinations.

Occasionally, when those magnificent golden and green and blue shimmering dolphins that lurk beneath the weed line to swallow flying-fish whole are landed, fishermen find small green and loggerhead sea turtles in their stomachs.

"Slow her down," I called out to Doug Gleeson, our chief collector. "We can't miss an opportunity like this. No telling what we'll find in this weed."

We jabbed our dip nets into the floating rafts of sargassum weed, scooped it up, and shook it out on deck. Sargassum crabs, looking like miniature blue crabs, but colored mottled brown and red, fell out, scattered, and had to be chased down. Filefish, and strange-looking frogfish that live nowhere else but in this matrix of stems, leaves, and little round air-filled balls, flopped about.

It took only a minute to accumulate bushels of gulfweed on deck. Always there were tiny pipefish, writhing like snakes, and hordes of brown little shrimp, and sandpapery-skinned filefish. Once a large transparent, glass-clear larval mantis shrimp that bent and flexed its needled body dropped out, and as I picked it up, its sharp rostrum stabbed into my finger. This was nothing new for mantis shrimp, no matter where or what size they are.

Growing on the weed itself were encrusting colonial animals, bryozoans and tiny sea anemones. It was a world unto itself, with fernlike hydroids that could sting as badly as their jellyfish relatives branching up festively from the stems and leaves. And feeding on them, absorbing their stinging cells into their bodies and passing them on in defense, were golden and brown nudibranchs, tiny snails without shells. Beautifully marked with neon blue speckles, they twisted back and forth in our buckets, waving leafy flaps from their weedy perches.

Surely all these invertebrates and slow-moving fish would make good forage for little sea turtles, but no matter how much we dipped, looked, and checked, we saw none. Not loggerheads, not ridleys, not any. Nowhere along the weed fine was there a sign of a little brown or black head popping up above the waves, even for a moment. If little turtles lived in the weed, it was only part of their unfathomable habitat.

Mixed in with the floating plants, logs, and sticks covered with gooseneck barnacles, were windrows of plastic, styrofoam, and tar balls. It isn't surprising that often when sea turtles wash up on the beaches dead, autopsies reveal all kinds of man-made garbage in their guts. The big turtles prey on jellyfish that bob along the surface; they often consume lethal plastic bags and styrofoam by mistake.

My real worry for Evergreen was not her eating styrofoam, but being caught by shrimp trawlers in open water.

This time of year the white shrimp run, and hundreds of boats gather to swoop up the rich harvest of green-tailed shrimp that flow in rivers over the shoals and gullies outside the barrier islands.

But as we rounded the pass, there was a curious lack of boats. I expected to see them dragging all up and down the beaches, but only one or two boats were working. And then we saw why. Far ahead of us was a polka-dotted ocean. There were not thousands, but millions of cannonball jellyfish, more than I had ever seen, white balls, rising up and down with the waves, so close that they were touching. There seemed to be more jelly than water; the ocean was freckled and pigmented with them.

We moved into their midst, slowed the boat, and gazed out in wonder and awe. Evergreen responded to the change of pitch and began flapping her pale white flippers, but no one paid her any attention.

Everyone stood up on the culling platform to get a better view. As far as the eye could see there were jellyfish, moving in vast armies. "I've read about occurrences like this," Anne remarked, "where two million an hour were reported moving through the Aransas ship channel, but to see it is truly awesome."

"How come there are so many?" one of her students asked.

*Green turtles begin their lives eating crustaceans and fish; after a
year or so they become herbivores, feeding on sea grass and algae.
But they never lose their taste for jellyfish.*

"Don't know. Conditions just got right this year: it was a warm winter; there wasn't much rain, so there was high salinity; and there must
be plenty of food for them. It's hard to say."

Cannonballs, *Stomolophus meleagris*, are beautiful embodiments of
water. Some had bright purple imbricated margins ringing their
umbrellas and others were all white. They are one of the densest, most
rubbery of all jellyfish. Every year they will suddenly appear as tiny
balls in the spring, grow rapidly, and become a plague to shrimpers in
the late summer and early fall. But they are anything but inert blobs of
jelly.

They are masters of their own fate. Even as they are swept along in
the tidal currents and winds, they remain within five miles of the beach
and avoid being swept out to sea. Most of the time they move crosswise

to the currents. Pulsing steadily with strong muscular action, they can travel miles in a single day. Neither randomly scattered nor in tight formation, they stay evenly spaced out. Normally you never see cannonballs colliding; it is as if they maintain their own individual spaces. But they were so thick that day that they seemed to have no choice. Cannonballs were colliding with each other. We could look down into the water and see them from the surface down to the bottom.

Little is known about their movements, but they grow rapidly in the brackish water, perhaps doubling their mass each week until they reach the size of grapefruit. Biologists have found their guts gorged with plankton, never large minnows or shrimp as some jellyfish prefer, but thousands of tiny copepods, clam, and oyster larvae. One jellyfish could eat a ton of future oysters.

"But who eats them?" asked one of our students, looking at the quivering cannonballs I had just scooped up in the dip net and dropped out on deck.

I held up one that had nicks taken out of its flesh. "Probably spadefish or tripletails did this," I said, pointing to the watery indentations, "or maybe it was blue crabs that also eat them. But sea turtles are their main predators."

All species of sea turtles eat jellyfish. Green turtles begin their lives eating crustaceans and fish. After a year or so, they suddenly switch and become herbivores, feeding on sea grass and algae. But they never lose their taste for jellyfish. There seems to be some highly nutritious element in the small amount of protein and mineral salts contained in the watery tissues, because the ocean sunfish (*Mola mola*) and the leatherback sea turtle attain massive size eating nothing but jellyfish.

Orientals once attributed magical efficacy to the dab of protein and mineral salts contained within medusae. Each year about 65 million pounds of jellyfish are landed by fishermen. The Chinese eat about seven different species, including cannonballs. They're not only considered an epicurean delight, salted and dried until they look like gelatinous white pancakes; they are also used in the Orient for medical purposes, for the treatment of high blood pressure and bronchitis.

"They're so popular," I went on, "that they're making imitation jellyfish out of chicken eggs and manipulating the biochemistry so that they taste like jellyfish."

I held up one of the rubbery balls. "You're looking at a future resource. Properly dried, they bring ten dollars a pound in China. Someday you'll see them all decked out in the fish markets, along with shrimp and mackerel."

We ran another half hour through a sea of cannonballs before turning our attention back to Evergreen.

The time had come to set this great turtle free, to end her years of captivity, and set her loose right in the middle of all those millions of cannonballs. With heaves and groans, one person on each flipper and two on each side of her shell, we hoisted her up to the culling platform, her pale white belly shell up toward the sky.

Each of her foreflippers bore a metal tag that we had double-checked to see that it was securely fastened. Then the students helped me turn her over, and she lurched forward, heaving her great girth toward the open blue. She expelled air from her lungs with a grateful hiss, plunged overboard with a thunderous splash, and sank like a stone. But it was only a moment before she was back at the surface, swimming about, looking confused.

I wondered what she was thinking, seeing and feeling the openness of the sea and blue horizon after all these years. What was it like for her to feel the roll of the ocean, after the stillness of the tank? Whatever her fate, she would no longer have to move back and forth in an aquarium cage. Before her was the boundless ocean.

We watched Evergreen circle the boat, her shell all too white and visible in the transparent offshore water. But after the initial shock of being dumped overboard, something seemed to take over, some other force. She moved about, getting her bearings, making a narrow circle around us, then a wider one. With the waves lapping on her shell, she swam round and round. Again I believed this was an indication of magnetic orientation, for that is exactly what honeybees and homing pigeons do when they're released away from their home grounds; they circle until they seem to pick up on a magnetic gradient and then depart.

As she swam farther away and deeper under the water, the whiteness of her shell became dimmer and dimmer until she rose to the surface again for another look. Her head popped up, and she caught sight of us. Instantly, she ducked under and swam off. With our diesel engine rumbling, we moved behind her, and when she saw that we were following, she took off as if there were a thousand sharks after her. Perhaps she was afraid that we were going to change our minds. Perhaps she was just now beginning to adjust to the idea that this new freedom was real and was not just a long-suppressed dream.

We followed behind slowly and caught sight of her one last time. We could see her pale patchy shell beneath the waves; she seemed to be following a vector, headed due south. Perhaps she was feeling the pull of the earth's magnetic field, or the force of the Great Turtle Mother, the legendary rock in the shape of a turtle that sits on top of the mystical turtle mountain in Tortuguero, Costa Rica. Turtle Mother, it is said, directs the movements of all turtles and protects them everywhere.

We watched the last pale underwater glimmer disappear from view. We hoped that someday she might crawl up on a beach somewhere, lay eggs, and continue her kind, but whether she lives or has died, she is free.

5. Night of the Electric Ray

A blinding flash of lightning banished the night. It revealed a flock of ghostly sea gulls riding on the surface of the rolling Gulf like ducks on a pond, waiting hungrily for the nets to come up. In that momentary eerie blue light, we could see the distant wooded shoreline of St. Vincent Island, the breakers pounding on sand and fallen trees. There was West Pass, the gap between the islands where the muddy waters of oyster-rich Apalachicola Bay emptied out into the Gulf of Mexico.

Edward Keith, captain of the sixty-eight-foot shrimp trawler *Dena Dini*, came out of the wheelhouse to haul back the two forty-five-foot trawls. He grimaced at the electrical storm. "I been listening to the other boats on the radio. They're catching hell out there; most of them's coming in. What do you want to do, head in or keep on electric raying? It's your charter."

Again the lightning flashed in the distance. "I don't know. What would you do if you were in shrimp?"

"I'd keep right on dragging. That storm may come this way, or it may blow over and go the other way. You don't never know out here."

I looked at Anne to get her opinion, and she reluctantly nodded assent. We both knew that we were taking a risk with the *Dena Dini*. She was thirty-five years old; many of her timbers were rotten and in need of replacing. Her pumps ran constantly, circulating the Gulf of Mexico through the worm-eaten boards. As long as the engine kept running to provide power to the pumps she would remain afloat, but because she sometimes ran hot and boiled like a caldron, that wasn't much assurance. Still, she was all the budget could afford.

Edward Keith had worked with me since he was a boy, for nearly fifteen years. Although most other shrimpers couldn't care less about anything in the catch except shrimp, Edward was one of our major suppliers, always saving horseshoe crabs, bringing back live octopuses, and faithfully packing up electric rays in plastic bags inflated with oxygen. It was with his help that we had located the mysterious "ray bars" where the electric ray, *Narcine brasiliensis*, gathered off the Apalachicola drainage.

Again the heavens blazed with light, and I thought how strange it was to be out here in an electrical storm at three o'clock in the morning dragging for a curious slimy fish that possessed the same powers that flashed in the skies above. By what curious design of nature did they make it happen? All they did was tense up their muscles and let it flow. How did they produce the shock? The neurochemistry of the reaction was of intense interest to medical laboratories.

The same power that rays use to capture food and defend themselves from sharks may soon help medical science learn how Alzheimer's and other brain-degenerating diseases work. All of the nerve endings in their specialized electric organs use a chemical called acetylcholine to trigger the actual discharge of the nerve. The same substance is used in many nerves in the human body, especially those that stimulate muscle cells, and in parts of the autonomic nervous system.

Defects in the acetylcholine system are involved in human diseases such as myasthenia gravis and the devastating Alzheimer's disease. However, in the body of the human and most other vertebrates, the acetylcholine nerve cells are mixed in with a wide variety of chemically different nerve endings, making their isolation and study extremely difficult.

Biomedical researchers, seeking a better understanding of this chemical and cures for these diseases, have known for years that electric rays have unmixed acetylcholine nerve endings that occur in huge concentrations in the electric organs, and biochemists and physiologists have eagerly sought them for their work. Previously the supply of specimens was erratic. An occasional fisherman would bring one in, but getting them on a routine basis was difficult. So secretive were the electric ray's habits that many lifelong residents of the Florida Panhandle who fished in the surf, and went floundering at night with a gasoline lantern and a gig, never saw one. Now and then someone steps on one and dances, however.

We returned to Apalachicola on the *Dena Dini*, dragging our nets in the same spot twice a month, during calm weather, stormy seas, on full and new moons, and even during lightning storms to bring them back to send to the Massachusetts General Hospital. We had a grant to study their movements and migrations, as well as to supply electric rays to their laboratories for study. If the biomedical community were ever going to use electric rays for routine laboratory assays, first something about their natural history and behavior had to be learned so they could be collected and reared reliably.

The sixty-eight-foot trawler shook and reverberated with a noisy rattling as the salt-eaten winches turned on their pitted bearings. The spools fattened with rusty cable until the otter doors were hoisted out of the sea and dangled wetly from the corroded outriggers.

As the first of the two forty-five-foot nets were hoisted up by the creaking machinery, Anne and I slipped on our rubber gloves and got ready. It was the most stressful part of the trawling operation, when all those sea creatures surfaced in one large seething ball of life. Edward hurried forward, moving warily, ready to jump back if the boat started rocking and the bag with all its protruding catfish spines started swinging. Hastily he grabbed the release ropes and snatched back and forth until the net bottom opened.

An avalanche of squirming creatures emptied out onto the bare wooden decks. Time was of the essence; our eyes roved around the confusion of life, searching for the round mottled bodies of electric rays. The glowing orange eyes of shrimp were everywhere. Thousands of croakers beat their tails and splattered mud and water in our faces. Blue crabs and portunid crabs scattered about the deck, and an octopus writhed. "There's one," Edward called out, pointing to a round form of an electric ray that had landed on its back, showing its white underbelly. Its whiteness was no different from the whiteness of the diamond-shaped underbellies of skates and stingrays that also abounded in the pile. "And there's another, and another." Over the months we had become good at recognizing the forms, but it wasn't easy.

We waded in, sliding our booted feet through the mass of creatures, mindful of the venomous spines of catfish, squinting to protect our eyes from the flyingfish scales. Hurriedly, we snatched out electric rays by their thick tails and passed them across the deck like a bucket brigade to a large vat of seawater with aerators bubbling. Back in the water they were on the road to recovery, but the longer they stayed on deck, the more damaged they became.

Normally one waits for the fish on deck to exhaust themselves before culling shrimp out of the pile, but not on an electric ray trip. Our cull sticks churned over the pile of life, exposing buried rays from beneath the pack of dying sharks, flounder, anchovies, squid, and eels. It was like pulling victims out of an earthquake.

"Oh hell, here's a pregnant female stuck with catfish," Anne said disgustedly, after exposing a ray and picking it up. It had two small catfish with sharp venomous spines jammed deeply in the ray. She snatched them out and handed the damaged ray to me, and I put it in the tank. It sat there in the tank's screened baffle respiring heavily and then started swimming, blood trickling from its wounds.

"She'll be OK; we've had worse than that recover from catfish," I said.

Before the second of the two nets was dumped on deck, we had pulled most of the obvious rays out. There would be others that were down on the bottom of the pile, smaller ones or ones that had managed to escape our eye, and some of them might die. The babies, rays measuring three inches or less, were the most susceptible.

Edward retied the nets, threw them back into the sea, and steamed back to the ray bar. Black smoke belched out of the stack, and the *Dena Dini* surged ahead over the choppy waters, returning to the same spot we just dragged. When he and his deckhand, Frenchie, dropped the trawls and finished feeding out the cable, I hurried into the pilothouse and copied down the familiar loran coordinates on the data sheet.

Who would have dreamed that these rare fish occurred in such sharply localized areas—two pieces of sea bottom where the Apalachicola River flowed around the barrier islands into the Gulf of Mexico and a few sections of beach in the surf. When we first began the project, there was only the great rolling Gulf of Mexico with its interminable blue waters, bays, estuaries, and barrier islands. Electric rays were only brought up as part of shrimpers' incidental catches. Sometimes they caught them, and often they didn't.

But going from boat to boat, talking to shrimpers on the VHF radio and working with Edward, we had narrowed it down to a small number of bars off barrier islands. Edward saved all the rays he caught when he was shrimping, faithfully packing them up in plastic bags and oxygen, bringing them in alive, and keeping locality data. And finally a picture began to emerge. Every two weeks we went back to the ray bars. It didn't seem to matter whether it was full or new moon, whether the seas were rough or calm, drizzling rain or fog, we caught them. The rays stayed there until winter came, when the arctic fronts came plunging down, chilling the Gulf. Then the rays picked up and moved well offshore into sixty- to eighty-foot depths.

The ray bars were relatively shallow, in depths of twenty to thirty feet. Topographically, the bars off St. George and St. Vincent islands and Cape San Blas are nearly unique in the Gulf of Mexico because they run perpendicular to the shoreline. They are filled with muddy gulleys and rises. But the rays only aggregate on specific parts of the bars. Edward soon discovered that if we dragged outside the area, by even a few hundred yards, we caught few or no rays whatsoever. But if he returned to the top of the same spot, which wasn't hard to do because of electronic positioning, we could average about eighty per twenty-four-hour trip. If we counted the newborns and the juveniles that could fit in your palm (a palm covered with a rubber glove, because the little ones can jolt almost as much as the adults), we caught twice that number.

Whether it was the outpouring of the muddy Apalachicola River, sweeping nutrients from the vast river swamp and drainage systems of Alabama and Georgia into the Gulf, or the peculiar crosscurrents driven by winds and tides sweeping across the sandbars that caused them to gather, we couldn't say. Perhaps they were drawn to the magnetic anomaly off St. George Island, a great iron deposit buried hundreds of feet beneath the sediments that had a magnetic field many times stronger than the earth's. Throughout their range from Brazil to North Carolina, they were often found around similar bars in the path of great rivers sweeping out to sea.

Perhaps the electric rays gathered there to mine grains of magnetite and other heavy mineral sands that were eroded from mountains and rocks hundreds of miles away and carried by the river to the sea. For some unknown reason, we found that all electric rays out there, from the time they were born, accumulated black sand grains in the labyrinths of their inner ears. They seemed to work the grains down into the chambers next to the brain through two tiny ducts on the top of the head.

Dr. Robert Johnson, the researcher who was receiving the rays at Massachusetts General Hospital, was the first to make that discovery with *Narcine*, although as far back as the 1840s naturalists knew that closely related *Torpedo* rays in the Mediterranean had black volcanic particles in their heads.

Robert found them while dissecting the brains. One afternoon in a laboratory at the nearby university marine station, he slit open the skull cavity to show us. Deep in the skull amid the connective tissue of body fluids were grains of black sand.

When I placed the dissected fish under the dissecting scope and turned the focusing knob, the blurry world came into clarity, and the grains were blown up until they looked like cobbles on a New England beach. They glittered up at me, with lustrous shiny blacks, some clear, others reddish and brown. Their shapes varied, but there was an abundance of transparent elongate grains that geologists later identified as zircons. All the rocks in their heads were heavy minerals such as sphene, ilmenite, garnet, and magnetite. They accumulated in a curved black band, sandwiched between clear or white grains contained in a membrane filled with electrolytic jellylike fluid. The entire thing could be pulled out with a forceps in a little bag.

It was not uncommon to find concentrations of such heavy minerals in the sand around the barrier beaches and offshore bars where rays congregate. But for some totally unknown reason, the electric rays carry these heavy minerals in their heads at concentrations many times higher than that of the seafloor.

Exactly why electric rays would collect such things deep in their body tissues was a complete mystery. Some scientists thought they got there accidentally, that they just spilled in through their endolymphatic ducts while the rays were feeding. Every time a ray gulps down a worm, it blasts a plume of sand through the large round spiracles on its back, right beside the duct opening. The theory was that the heavier grains settled and somehow worked their way down into the inner ears, through the tiny ducts on the top of the head.

One day I put a juvenile electric ray under a dissecting scope in a small bowl of water to see whether I could learn something about how it worked. It wasn't easy making it sit still, but at last I got it into focus. Its body was covered with tiny holes, the ampullae of Lorenzini, the jelly-filled sensory pits that enable all sharks and rays to detect electrical fields and depth. But no sand grains could enter there.

Then suddenly I saw two large white openings behind the eyes about the diameter of a large sand grain. When I brought them into focus, I almost jumped out of my chair. Something reached up out of the hole, like a jack in the box, a tendril of some sort, and drew back in. Scarcely believing my eyes, I took another look, and saw only empty, elliptical pits. Then it did it again; the thing popped out again.

Hastily I sprinkled some sand from the bottom of the dish on it, and the organ, which I had decided was functioning more as a flap valve, seemed to push them away or acted as a plug. Certainly the grains didn't fall passively into the rays' head, as some scientists believed.

The muscular action of the skin shook off most of the grains, but then something else was happening. A single black grain suddenly rolled uphill, right into the endolymphatic pore. The ray's body sloped downward, but this one appeared to defy gravity, as if it were being pulled by a magnet.

It landed in the pore like a golf ball making a hole in one. The organ appeared to be working it around and around, pulling it down into the pore. It was halfway down, almost out of sight, when the ray spit it out.

About a third of the grains were magnetic, we learned, and wondered whether the selecting organ could pick up on the tiny magnetic fields. Whenever we found dead rays on the *Dena Dini*, we saved them for later dissection. The grains would be identified with X-ray diffraction studies by the Florida State University's geology department.

As we madly culled the catch on the back deck of the trawler, I stared at the rays, willing them to speak and explain their story. None did. We kept working. The storm seemed to be coming our way.

West Pass was a boneyard of sunken trawlers, boats with their masts sticking up above the water, with their bottoms shattered and oysters growing on their muddy hulls. The current is so strong there at times that a small boat under tow can catch the sea wrong and turn over. If it weren't for the fact that it was one of the best shrimping areas in the northern Gulf Coast, no one would drag there. And it is especially dangerous in rough stormy weather.

We tried not to think about that as lightning blazed all around us. There we were, the highest thing around on the flat ocean with our steel masts pointing upward to heaven—a ready lightning rod. Nothing is more scary than a direct hit, when blue fire goes sparking all over the boat, the air tingles, your hair stands on end, and the shipboard electronics smolders and explodes.

But what really worried me were the gusts of winds and the building seas. Usually on calm nights when we tagged rays, and stood on the wide-open back deck beneath the overhead lights pulling rays out of the tank and tagging them, we could put the *Dena Dini*'s poor structural condition out of our minds. But tonight we worked in haste.

After the rays were all put into water, it was time to measure them and record the data for that catch. I grabbed a ray at random and pushed it down on the measuring board, trying to hold it still to record its length while it squirmed around. "It's a male," I called out over the wind, noting the two elongated reproductive organs that hung down from the rear of the body disc. "It's 30.5 centimeters [12 inches] and has leeches." The leeches were little worms that fastened their sucker mouths onto the rays' underbellies. Later they would be killed in our laboratories with toxic fish dips and antibiotic treatments.

Grimly Anne recorded the information on her data sheet and handed me tag number 603. It bore the name of our Panacea Institute of Marine Science, address, and a plea for locality data printed on the long bright orange shaft. The plea was to shrimpers, the only ones likely to catch electric rays, who occasionally sent the tags in. More often, when I got rumor of a tagged ray's being found, I had to chase the lucky tag holder down and present him with ten dollars.

Pressing the smooth-skinned, slimy electric ray against the measuring board, I perforated its hide with a large fat needle and grimaced as I rammed it deep into the muscle. That created an opening and passageway for the barbed head of the plastic tag, which I inserted deep into the wound. Once in there it stayed. It was a traditional fish tag, used on tuna, salmon, sharks, and many others. And although it looked as if it were traumatic, it didn't appear to damage the fish. The wound soon healed, and the fish behaved as if the tag didn't exist.

But the electric rays responded by doing their best to shock me while trying to twist out of my grasp. I could almost see the surge of electricity flowing out of the two kidney-shaped electric organs on the front part of its body, one on each side.

Wearing rubber gloves I usually felt nothing, but sometimes after working all night and walking around the decks of the *Dena Dini* in a sleepless daze, I got careless and received an unpleasant shock. It always happened when I reached down into the vat to catch a ray, instead of using the dip net, and then tagged it with water swilling around the inside of my glove. A rattling good shock went right through my bones, into my joints. Making me yelp and jump back, such a shock always served to wake me up. And as many times as I had been shocked, it was something that I could never get used to. As Anne had said, it was an effective weapon.

But our procedure was useless, completely useless against the inexorably dragging nets, those immense funnels that scooped up everything on the bottom. We shared the responsibility of all who love to eat shrimp for this carnage.

All the little shrimp, crabs, squid, and hammerhead sharks must relish bad weather, the "hangs" and rock piles and crab traps that make shrimping impossible in certain places. The great masses of jellyfish swarming into the area occasionally become protectors of all that swim and crawl, along with the "gumbo," the drift algae that suddenly explode into vast numbers when conditions are right. The algae weigh down the nets until they are impossible to lift.

But when the shrimp were running and the conditions were right, the vacuum fleet, as Edward called them, moved in. Hundreds of boats, all sizes, all shapes, every make of wood, steel, and fiberglass, moved in to scour the bottom.

There are winners and losers in shrimping. The flocks of sea gulls, jack crevalles, porpoises, and sharks gulped down the dead and dying as fast as the leftovers were raked overboard. And down below, crabs feasted on the sudden flood of protein discharged into the system. All the time we were culling, Frenchie the deckhand was madly picking out white shrimp from the catch, spurred on by the rumbling of thunder in the distance and the fire that zigzagged across the night sky. The waves were growing, and with each rocking motion, the water slopped back and forth in the ray vat.

"We'd better release some of these rays," Anne said above the wind, watching them all pile up against the baffles and wash back. "They don't need to get battered up."

"We usually do that in the morning, when we can pick out the best ones to ship to Boston," I reminded her.

"Yes, but I don't want to ship any pregnant ones, and there are a few that have catfish wounds. Let's release twenty now," she said.

I selected a large female, one that almost topped two feet in length, and when I lifted her up, she weighed easily five pounds with her bulging belly. Virtually every ray above 11¾ inches in length was pregnant this time of year, in July. As gently as I could, conscious of her condition, I lowered her down to the water and let her drop.

Tagging rays was important. If *Narcine brasiliensis* really turned out to be a good medical model for studying Alzheimer's disease, there would one day be an increased demand on their stocks. While collecting fish, we were also gathering fisheries data to try to estimate a sustainable yield, how many could be collected without depleting the pop-

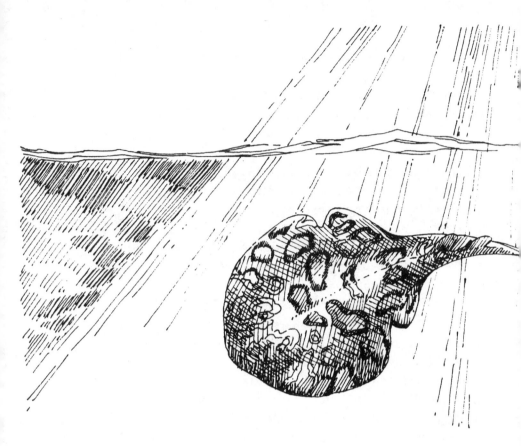

A six-foot shark materialized beside the ray like a menacing gray apparition.

ulation. On the basis of statistics applied to the two-thousand-odd rays we had accumulated, ranging from newborns to two-footers, it appeared that they grew to maturity in two to three years.

The more we tagged, and the more data we accumulated, the more questions about these remarkable fish arose. Where did they go when they were not on the ray bars? And how did they find those special spots on the seafloor? What drew them? Did they orient to magnetic fields—for the ray bars certainly seemed to coincide with magnetic anomalies—and did the crystals in their acoustolateralis systems play a part in their orientation?

We watched the first ray start to waddle its way down to the depths, almost outside our field of vision. Then suddenly, a six-foot shark mate-

rialized beside it like a menacing gray apparition, scrutinized it with the rapt attention of the hungry, and faded back into the shadowy murk.

We both laughed. "He knows better; he doesn't want any part of it," Anne chuckled, leaning over the side to get a better look. "Now that's what I call an example of learned behavior."

"Could be," I countered, "or it could be that the ray discharged its electric organs when it felt the pressure wave. Remember the porpoises."

Several trips before, we released a tagged ray and suddenly two porpoises came rocketing up from beneath the boat, their mouths wide open, displaying rows of sharp pointed teeth, ready to swallow it. They got within two feet of the ray, then broke off the attack in unison, veered sharply, and fled. The response seemed too quick, too simultaneous to be purely visual.

Only once during the entire tagging project did we ever find conclusive evidence that a shark will hit an electric ray. The ray had a fresh set of jagged tooth marks arched over its entire dorsal surface and part of its belly. The serrated wound looked as if it had been inflicted by a shark, but it only penetrated about half an inch down into the tissue. The ray was alive and in good shape, and we took it back to the lab and kept it for months in our aquarium.

That ray provided an astonishing piece of information about sharks. A shark is a creature that bites with the force of three thousand pounds per square inch in a fraction of a second, yet has the ability to change its mind in midbite. When it felt the electricity flowing through its body, probably causing excruciating pain to all its ultrasensitive sensory organs used to detect prey emitting weak electric fields, its jaws sprang apart.

As I was thinking, Frenchie started dumping the picked-over trash fish overboard. We had a heaping basket of white shrimp picked out and watched the discarded pinfish, croakers, skates, and rays sinking down into the depths and being scattered by the waves.

The sea gulls that had been hovering behind the boat, letting out impatient and scornful cries, berating the crew for their slowness, went wild.

Any fish small enough to get into their beaks was fair game. It didn't matter whether it were an anchovy, or a small catfish, or even a baby scorpionfish: they crammed it all down. But when we released baby electric rays, the gulls hovered above them, watching as the little ones moved deeper to safety. I often wondered whether the gulls could read the brown markings that looked like a warning inscription on their backs. Amazingly, when a dead one was thrown back, they didn't hesitate to swoop down and grab it.

What a sight our shrimp boat was, with its flocks of gulls overhead, screaming and screeching like an avian cloud, porpoises and sharks following along, becoming more excited with each shovelful of trash pushed through the scupper holes, spreading out fish juice, slime, and scale into the water with even more tantalizing smells. Every time a stingray or fish hits the water, they rose up from the depths to grab it. They were eating machines, and with each new shovelful of trash, the sea boiled with sharks. They were going in circles behind the boat, splashing, grabbing, and gobbling up all the little fish that drifted by. A discarded Texas skate, bearing the characteristic two handsome yellow and black symmetrical spots that looked like large fierce eyes, swam by on the surface, stunned but alive. Without hesitation another six-foot shark shot forward, engulfed it in one smooth wide-mouthed bite, and then was gone.

Perhaps the "eyes" looking up from the muddy seafloor might scare off a hungry predator, but not out there at the surface. The highly reflective eye structure of a shark identifies shapes and detects motion in the feeblest light. For more than 140 million years they have relied on a wide range of very specialized senses to survive.

With each new blinding show of lights from the skies, more sharks were revealed splashing and striking behind the boat. We wondered whether the electric discharges were stirring them up because they were far more active than usual, more sharks than we had seen on any previous trip. We watched the next ray attentively as it swam off, bearing its festive orange tag. It faded out of sight unobstructed, but suddenly we saw a shark explode out of the water tail first, stiffen, and shoot back down. "There went that ray," I said with surprise. "I don't think we should release any more." The electric organs could protect rays from sharks most of the time, but not when they were crazed by blood, fish juice, and the competition of their own growing numbers.

Edward stepped out of the wheelhouse and made his way back to the stern, when he saw our rapt attention focused on the churning wake. "See what I told you about West Pass," he said triumphantly. "You'd be out of your mind to try diving here."

When we had first started the project in March, I wanted to dive and explore the bottom. The water temperature had been 68 degrees Fahrenheit, and there were few sharks. But now it was 84 degrees, and the number of sharks kept increasing. One night we heard a boat talking on the radio; they made an oblique turn while hauling up their nets and had eighty six-footers in the nets.

"Edward," Anne said, "how about running a mile or two away from here next time we take up; maybe we can shake these sharks. We've got to release some rays; we're getting overcrowded."

"We may have other problems than releasing rays," he said shortly, "that's a bad storm coming."

The next flash turned everything blue, and all around us the approaching bank of black, ominous clouds hung down, with spirallike fingers—"witches' fingers," the shrimpers call them—full of venomous, lashing winds. Then it began to rain, a gusting deluge that poured down.

We left the rest of the catch on deck, and all hurried back to the wheelhouse.

Edward switched on the light of the engine room and went hand over hand down the ladder into the great noisy yellow Caterpillar engine room below. I didn't even like to look down there; there was always black oily water sloshing back and forth. It was a constant reminder of the wonderful garden of wood-boring isopods and shipworms contained in her hull and the rotten caulking on which our lives might depend. Edward checked the bilge level constantly, at least three dozen times during a trip, and saw that the pump was working. Shrimping had been bad for the last two years. The poor season, the low market price, and the fact that the whole industry is overexpanded and overcapitalized and in debt all led to the fact that they couldn't afford to haul it out at the shipyard and fix it right.

And when I heard him fire up the auxiliary gasoline pump, I recalled the scene of a few weeks ago when the *Dena Dini* had sunk at the dock and was being raised up from her dockside watery grave like Lazarus. Someone accidentally unplugged the extension cord that ran to yet another bilge pump when the crew went home for a couple of days, and she sank at the dock. Now the image of her muddy, oily hull rising up from the murk, water pouring off her decks, and four pumps running into the night, impinged on my mind. As the winds blustered, dishes rattled and crashed, and Frenchie hurried around battening everything down, I felt a twinge of fear. Could the *Dena Dini* really ride out a sea like this?

"Don't worry," Edward said, coming back into the wheelhouse, "we're not gonna sink. It's only the planking that's separated; the ribs are strong. She can take a sea like this; I've done it before. Long as the engine's running, the pump will keep her up."

That wasn't much comfort, I thought, as I listened to the wind howl vengefully across the Gulf, because on the trip before last, the engine ran hot, a great boiling caldron of rusty water boiled out of the reservoir tank that cooled the engine, and he had had to shut her off until it cooled. If it happened now, we'd sink.

We stood in the darkness of the pilothouse, holding on, watching the approaching storm on the radar. It was tremendous; it seemed to cover the entire field. Behind us were outlines of the two barrier islands. Ahead the sea buoy flashed red until it disappeared beneath the tumult of wind and water.

Then came a heavier deluge of rain, followed by fifty-mile-an-hour winds.

The bow rose up and crashed down. The pounding intensified. Then came a heavier deluge of rain, followed by fifty-mile-an-hour winds. Before we managed to shut all the windows, the screens puffed in and out like some respiring animal. Edward slipped the boat off automatic pilot and held it into the sea. "This is going to be a heap longer tow than you want," he announced. "We can't take the net up in this weather. If she blows sideways, that's all she wrote."

Making a run for the Pass to sheltered water was impossible now. We would just have to weather the storm because we were under tow. Enviously I watched two other trawlers fighting the seas back to the safety of Apalachicola Bay. They would be inside and anchored down in an hour while we and a few other boats that were caught by the storm stayed in the teeth of the wind. The whole cabin was shaking and reverberating, but the old boat moved steadily ahead, dragging the nets. "Look at that," said Edward with some amazement. "The wind is so strong we're not moving. I been watching the loran; there's hardly been any headway. We've made three microseconds in the past ten minutes."

Suddenly the auxiliary pump down below spluttered, faltered, and died. Edward cursed and told Frenchie to go down below and start it again. He thrust open the door and the winds burst in on us. It took all our strength to shove it behind him. After ten minutes, Frenchie returned. "Pumps died," he announced. "I tried to start it but I couldn't."

"Hold the wheel," Edward ordered his deckhand. "I'm going down and fix it."

Edward Keith was a master of putting junk and worn-out equipment together and making it get by for another time. However, sometimes his repairs worked and sometimes they didn't.

"This is a hell of a note," Anne muttered after Edward had slipped on his slicker and pushed out the door. "I'm not prepared to drown for these damn electric rays."

We stood in the pilothouse with only the dim red light of the loran and the green glow of the radar flickering on the soiled paneled walls. The empty pilot's chair, which Edward had custom built from an old car seat and a pole, looked vaguely gruesome with its stuffing hanging out as the vessel rocked to and fro.

"Don't worry; we're not going to drown," I said, trying to reassure her. But my voice lacked conviction. "This boat has been all the way to Key West and back in worse weather than this."

Edward came back. "I can't start it; the carburetor must have stopped up. But we're OK; the main pump is holding it down. She ain't gaining much."

His explanation was interrupted by a loud crunch that shuddered throughout the whole vessel. Edward and Frenchie looked a little more worried. "That was a 'crunch,' not a 'crack.' I'm waiting for that any minute," he said in an unsuccessful attempt to reassure.

Seeing our worried expressions, he added, "But don't worry, we ain't gonna sink. If she goes to taking on too much water, we'll just plow her up on the beach and walk home."

I tried to ignore the image of the *Dena Dini* aground on the barrier beach of St. Vincent Island with her bottom pounded out by the breakers, the vicious undertows and the sharks, and us trying to get off and swim to shore.

The safest thing to do was get into bed and hope to stay there and wait it out. I lay there wondering why I didn't have an office job somewhere. Finally, though, the storm diminished and passed on. As the seas quieted, it was as if nothing had ever happened.

Trying to get my mind off the near-disaster, I left Anne sleeping in the bunk and went out on deck, to check on the electric rays and see how they fared in the storm. They were fine; the baffled tank kept them from becoming too beaten up.

Then I glanced over the stern and had a sudden start. There were sharks swimming all around us, illuminated beneath the deck lights— only they weren't frightening any more; they were fascinating. Peaceful and beautiful in form and essence they swam among the luminescent plankton glowing like eerie spirits. They were much more in harmony with their watery environment than the porpoises that came speeding in, dropping back, and bobbing up to puff and blow and partake of the atmosphere as we do.

What magnificent creatures these elasmobranch fish were, totally in tune with their world. They were part of an arms race that had been going on almost since the beginning of life, hundreds of millions of years. A sleek body, razor-sharp teeth, and electrosensory devices enabled them to feed on their cousins the rays.

But rays in turn evolved defenses. The stingray had a poisonous tail. The spotted eagle ray had speed and grace and could leap high out of the water and sail through the air, landing with a spectacular explosion. The bat rays and butterfly rays glided over the sand bottom like magic carpets with a sweep of their wings to escape with firm muscle and vigor.

But the electric ray had traded away grace and muscle for power. Its body had become rounded, soft, and flabby to support the electric organs. Its swimming motion was awkward and slow, almost a waddle. It had to push itself along the bottom with its broad pectoral fins while it searched for worms. And when it swam, it sculled along with its sharklike tail in a slow sinuous motion and no shark bothered it. Yet locked away in that flabby fish's body were mysteries, secrets of energy and magnetics and the working of the central nervous system, and perhaps a cure for human diseases.

6. Tide of the Plumed Worm

The glare of my gasoline lantern cast shadows on the expansive sand flat off Alligator Point, accentuating the ribbed patterns left by the receding waves. I walked briskly, carrying buckets, my eyes roving the patch of illuminated ground before me for worm tubes. Sea cucumbers pulled their crowns of tentacles back into their burrows at the disturbance of my footsteps. Everywhere there were sand stars sliding over the bottom in the watery depressions, their tubed feet extended in flowing motion. Whelks and conchs with fleshy bodies rippling below their shells roamed the shallows as well.

But my eyes were searching only for worms: hundreds of worms, thousands of worms, enough to feed tanks full of starving electric rays; rays with rounded tubular mouths that telescoped out to slurp worms out of their burrows. They shocked their victims to death, paralyzed them, and yanked them out like limp pieces of spaghetti. And they were good at it, devouring fat muscular sipunculids or sausage worms that were devoid of segments and lived deep in sediments. If I found a dozen a year I was doing well, but the rays we often dissected on shrimp boats had their guts filled with such worms.

Dead worms simply wouldn't do. They had to be alive and healthy or the electric rays couldn't find them. Nothing else we put into the tank would tempt them, neither chopped shrimp, fish, clam, nor any other morsel—not even live minnows or amphipods. They ignored our offerings and grew thinner, weaker, and more emaciated. And when they finally died of starvation, because we couldn't get enough worms, their normally folded back mouths protruded, a final recrimination that we let them starve.

Wisps of fog were moving over the flat, driven by a gentle south wind. I needed a bone-chilling north wind that would have pushed the water off the tideflats, keeping them exposed for hours so I could cover more ground and dig more worms. But tonight the winds were variable,

able to turn any moment and push the water back in. In the fall of the year, when warm air blows across a cool sea, there can be sudden fog, and being caught in it out there on the flat can be an uncomfortable situation at best.

When we first got the contract to supply routine shipments of live, healthy electric rays I was confident we could handle it. After all, Gulf Specimen Company already sold worms to many zoology classes in the country to demonstrate the phylum Annelida. We knew where to get scaleworms, or dig lugworms out of the marsh, or dive for featherduster worms that lived in tubes in the limestone coral rocks.

But in retrospect, we sold a dozen here and a dozen there. Who would have dreamed that the rays would eat so many? Nights were spent on my "Living Dock," holding a light above the water dip-netting *Nereis pelagica*. The whirling little dervishes of polychaete worms rise up off the bottom and dance and spin in the water column. But they are tiny, too tiny for the rays to eat. Then we tried feeding them larger worms that lived in fouling communities, tearing up barnacles, oysters, and hydroids and picking out the three-inchers. Our fingers ended up a mass of cuts, stings, and infections. We knew we'd have to find a better way. It was becoming clear that even if we had armies of people roving the flats, it would be a struggle to keep a hundred rays fed. And from their gut contents, we knew they could eat eight to ten small worms at a sitting.

Until we figured out how to grow worms, a subject that Anne was researching, or found a reliable economic supplier of live bait worms, it was back to the mud flats.

If you took Florida's coastline with all its bays, estuaries, meandering creeks, and bayous and stretched it out, there would be roughly eleven thousand miles of tidal lands. And if you took shovels and buckets and screens in hand, and declared war on them, there would no doubt be metric tons of worms living down in the mud that could be caught, but it would require the funding of a public works project.

That night I was after plumed worms, *Diopatra cuprea* and *Onuphis magnum*, all-purpose worms that are large, easy-to-find, and, once removed from their heavy, shell-covered tubes, readily eaten by electric rays. They make a tube of parchmentlike material by secreting mucus and mixing it with sand. Most of the tube that lies beneath the surface is clean and white, but the section that sits above the substrate like a periscope presents an untidy array of shell and debris stacked one on

Nights were spent on my "Living Dock," holding a light above the water dip-netting Nereis pelagica *worms.*

top of the other. The shells adhere to the tube by a sticky glue secreted by the worm, and added to it is a hodgepodge of dead sea grass, bits of detritus, and anything else the worm can stick on.

The worm peers out of its opening, writhing its tentacles about and picking up bits of plankton and detritus. Its leathery casing and debris afford an excellent fortress, camouflage, and place to hide from the marauding crabs.

I jammed my digging fork down beside a plumed worm's tube and pried hard, ripping up the bottom. The tube came out easily.

Taking it in both hands, I pulled firmly, stretching it out like a rubber band. Finally it broke and I could see the parchmentlike lining, but no one was at home. The worm had obviously crawled out, found a new tube, or died.

That was what I was afraid of. Most of these tubes would be empty, and I'd have to walk out further on the flats to find live ones. I felt the wind at my back; I didn't like the mist and the stickiness, and the wisps of fog moving across the flats. I didn't like being out there digging for worms at all, when it would be so much easier in the daylight. But the rays were starving, and the lowest tide was at night. So there I was.

To get to the flat where the plumed worms abounded, I waded into the gulley before me, watching the water rise almost to the top of my rubber boots. Any minute now, I expected to feel the chilly water flooding my toes. But there was more than wet feet to worry about.

Stingrays, disturbed from their sleep and prowling the bottom, flapped their wings and fled before me. I moved cautiously—even boots wouldn't protect me from a lash of their poisonous tail. But boots would certainly keep me from feeling the jolt of an electric ray. This was a particularly good area for catching *Narcine*, right next to the beach, where there was a slough filled with soft mud and an abundance of worms. Only a week ago, when I was out beachcombing, I happened upon some shrimp seiners who were dragging electric rays up on the beach.

Even from three hundred yards away, I had recognized the portly frame of Earl Smith, supervising his four sons who were doing all the heavy work. The old man was practically a fixture on the beach, in his faded coveralls and suspenders, working the tide from dawn until dusk, as rivers of white shrimp left the rivers and migrated along the shores of the barrier beaches.

Earl's grandfather once owned the entire Alligator Point Peninsula, where we were standing, all three thousand acres of it. He bought it for ten dollars and a hound dog and twenty years later lost it in a poker game. Land didn't mean much back at the turn of the century, but now it was worth a fortune. Earl knew he would have been rich, but he didn't seem to grieve over it.

His four sons were straining against the small-meshed beach seine, coming ever shoreward. When they were dragging the three-hundred-yard seine up onto the shallow part of the flats, Earl bellowed out, "Hold the lead line down, boys, don't let them shrimp out."

Wheezing and puffing with asthma, he hurried down the beach and grabbed some webbing and threw his girth into it. I was right behind to help, and together we strained backward. A crowd of weekenders and beachcombers hurried over to see what the latest strike would bring. Rapidly the two-hundred-foot semicircle of webbing shrank, as the wings of the net were pulled up onto the beach, packing a great number of very distressed and harried creatures into the center. Some mullet were fortunate enough to leap high into the air and clear the cork line to freedom. Blue crabs and horseshoe crabs were gilled up in the webbing and dumped on the beach in a great tangle.

When the great squirming bag was heaved up onto the dry sandy beach, we all dived in and started picking up the big white shrimp, their tails gleaming emerald-green in the sun. The fishermen left behind all the other creatures, the anchovies, spots, whiting, catfish, skates, and rays, lying on the shore in windrows to parch and dry in the sun. Sea gulls flocked to the beach and gorged themselves, leaving their white droppings to stain the sand, and ghost crabs popped out of their burrows to tear and wrench the windfall of flesh with their scissorlike claws.

While looking for rays, I hurriedly kicked the dying gasping fish back into the sea to let them go free. No matter how many years I was around commercial fishing, I could never get used to the careless waste of life.

I was rewarded for my efforts by finding nine big electric rays in the catch. Their spiracles opened and closed laboriously as they thrashed around. Several had regurgitated their dinners of long pink polychaete and sipunculid worms. Hurriedly I waded out into the surf to get a bucket of fresh seawater to keep them alive.

The crowd of weekenders and bathers watched me fight with an irate electric ray in the net. It kept flipping around, presenting the front of its charged disk to me, electric organs bulging through the skin. I wished I had brought rubber gloves and was trying to grab hold of its tail, where it supposedly could not shock.

Earl left his boys picking the shrimp and came over to watch me, his hands on his wide hips. His face was wrinkled and weathered by the wind, but he always looked pleasant and ready to laugh. "You better watch it, Jack; they'll shock the fool out of you. Tell you what we used to do with them, back when I was a boy fishing; we'd have the best time with them shocking fish. Used to be back before they built all these houses on the beach, there weren't nothing but prickly pear cactuses and dog flies and wild hogs out here.

"And those piney woods rooters would bother the devil outa us. They'd make life plumb miserable," he reminisced. "You couldn't shoot the damn things; shooting a man's hog was worse than running off with his old lady. They'd raid our camp, steal our food, and scatter the fish all up and down the beach—aggravating things.

"But it'd tickle us to death when we'd catch a bunch of those shocking fish. Them hogs would run down, grab them, and go to shrieking and squalling like they was being roasted alive. We'd just stand there and laugh. And you know, they never did learn: each time they'd pick up one, they'd drop it and pick it up again."

William, Earl's youngest son, threw down the net and came over to look. "What you gonna do with all them shocking fish?" he asked blandly.

The old fisherman answered for me, "He's gonna send them to the nuthouse so they can shock crazy people back to their senses, like I'm

The wings of the net were rapidly pulled up on the beach, packing a great number of distressed and harried creatures into the center.

gonna do to you if you keep on standing around. We need to get that net back out there while the shrimp are running."

"Is that true?" the boy asked innocently, ignoring his father's order.

"No, they don't do that anymore. They used to, actually, as far back as the Greek and Roman times. Now they use them to study Alzheimer's disease." I had another empty bucket and was trying to nudge the ray into it, but it wouldn't cooperate.

"Alzheimer's disease," one woman in the crowd repeated. "Exactly how are they used? You see, my mother's dying of Alzheimer's. She won't eat anymore, she's going downhill every day, and the doctors say there's nothing I can do for her. I've been reading everything I can on the disease. I go to all the support group meetings."

When I saw the suffering look in her eyes, I stopped trying to catch the ray and explained how the electric organs have high concentrations of acetylcholine that is accessible to biochemical analysis. In Alzheimer's the nerve cells stop producing acetylcholine, the disease destroys the mind, and there's loss of memory and the victim's family suffers months, or even years, with an invalid until death results.

I went back to that recalcitrant ray, tired of it, grabbed it by the tail, and tried to toss it quickly into the bucket. It wasn't supposed to be able to shock through the tail, but a numbing jolt went through my body, right to my elbow. I let out a loud yelp and dropped it, and everyone looked appalled.

Earl laughed and shook his head. "Son, don't you know what they say about them shocking fish? All the old-timers used to tell us when we were seine fishing not to touch 'em 'cause they'll mess up your mind, make you crazy. You'd better watch it!"

"What?" I studied his face to see whether he was serious.

"That's right, I ain't a-joking; they say it'll mess up your mind. Make you crazy."

I thought about his remark that night as I roamed the tide flats, wading through the water looking for worms to feed our starving electric rays. Maybe Earl was right.

Killifish were attracted to my gasoline lantern and flurried and darted around my feet as I moved on, stirring up microfauna in the mud, which they dove down and gobbled up. How easy it would have been if *Narcine* would eat them: one pull of a minnow seine and I could have thousands, and they'd live in the tanks until the rays ate them. I thought wistfully of *Torpedo*, electric rays that eat fish.

Although *Torpedo marmorata* occurs in the vast depths of the Gulf of Mexico, they are too rare and difficult to catch routinely. Except for being larger, broader, darker, and lacking the vivid blotches of the common lesser electric ray, they looked almost identical.

Biologists have studied the behavior of *Torpedo californica* of the Pacific coast, where it lives in shallower depths. In a bizarre Star Wars of the kelp beds, these slow-moving fish rise high above the rock ledges at night to meet mackerel in midwater and shock them to death. They wrap their wings around the stunned fish and gulp them down head-first, while administering up to two hundred volts that shatters their spinal column.

Our smaller, worm-eating, warm water-loving *Narcine* should live better, but when we first put the spotted pancakes into our large concrete tanks, they battered themselves against the walls until the margins of their round bodies were raw. They seemed unable to learn the limits of their confines as other fish did. All those expensive rays, obtained with such difficulty on shrimp boats, perished from abrasions and infections. In a panic we drained the tanks, nailed plastic and styrofoam padding to cushion the surface, refilled it, and added a new batch of rays.

To our delight, we solved the problem, but for the wrong reasons. The plastic didn't cushion their impact, but the rays no longer hit the walls. They learned to avoid them. In all probability they navigate the oceans by emitting a weak electrical field, and wet concrete is an excellent conductor of electricity. Hence, they didn't perceive the wall and

The giant red hermit crab (*Petrochirus diogenes*) is the largest
hermit crab in the western Atlantic. It often festoons its portable
home with flowering pink sea anemones, white slipper limpets,
and purple barnacles. A host of equally colorful porcelain crabs
live inside. (Photo courtesy of Anne Rudloe)

The calico crab (*Hepatus epheliticus*) is found on sandy sea bottoms from North Carolina to Brazil. They spend much of their time buried down in the sediments, coming out at night to feed. They are a favorite food of the Atlantic ridley sea turtle. (Photo courtesy of Anne Rudloe)

Opposite: A pair of copulating horseshoe crabs are digging down into the sand. Beneath the sand, the female exudes large bluish eggs and the male fertilizes them. It takes about a month for the eggs to hatch. (Photo courtesy of Anne Rudloe)

Horseshoe crabs (*Limulus polyphemus*) come to the Florida beach at high tide during spring, summer and fall to lay their eggs, timing their arrival to high tide and the full or new moon. (Photo courtesy of Anne Rudloe)

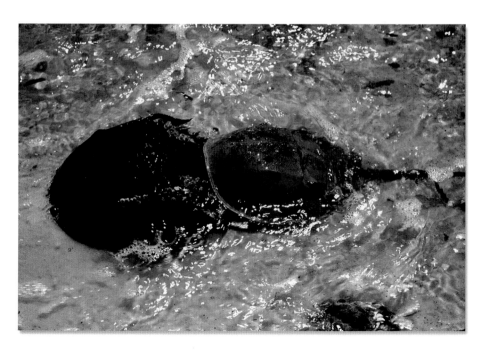

Newly-hatched leatherback sea turtles *(Dermochelys coriacea)* scurry seaward. Only a small percentage of them will survive to adulthood. Although these hatchlings have emerged in daylight, many baby sea turtles make their run for the ocean at night when predators are fewer and less active.

One of the smallest loggerhead sea turtles (*Caretta caretta caretta*) ever found in North American waters. Only in the eastern Atlantic, around the Azores, are turtles of this size normally found, indicating that they may be children of the Gulf Stream. (Photo courtesy of Anne Rudloe)

Opposite: This green sea turtle has come ashore at night to her lay eggs. She will use her front flippers to excavate a chamber above the high tide line, then deposit about a hundred eggs. After she has covered them with sand, she will return to the sea.

A large American alligator (*Alligator mississippiensis*) basks on a Florida riverbank. Both fresh and brackish waters are home to alligators, living fossils that have remained virtually unchanged for 60 million years.

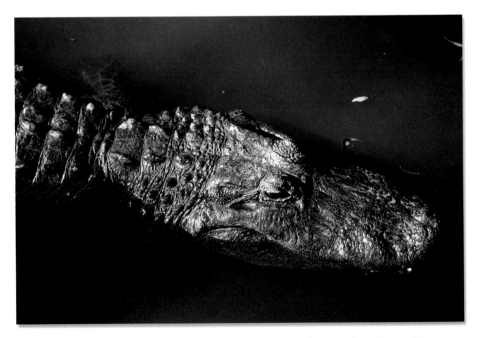

Acute hearing, excellent vision, an enormous mouth armed with needle-sharp teeth, and an almost impenetrable hide make the alligator a formidable predator. Webbed feet and muscular tails make alligators adroit swimmers, but they also attain impressive speeds on land for short distances, sprinting after prey at up to 11 miles per hour.

Mullet fishermen strike their nets in the quiet waters of Apalachee Bay off Panacea, Florida, sometimes catching thousands of pounds of the delicious black mullet that is considered a delicacy among native Floridians.

A rare photograph of the left-handed whelk (*Busycon contrarium*) caught in the act of laying eggs. One end of the accordianlike string of disked capsules is anchored into the sand, and each cell may contain as many as two hundred young. (Photo courtesy of Anne Rudloe)

The giant sea roach (*Bathynomus giganteus*) is the largest of all isopods. Here, author Jack Rudloe smiles happily after a successful expedition out into the Gulf of Mexico to capture them for the New York Aquarium. (Photo courtesy of Joe Halusky)

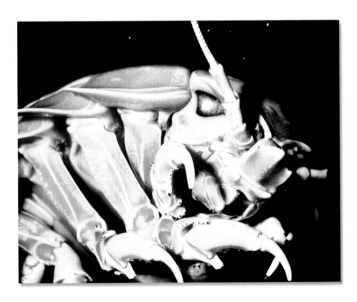

Holothurians like this red-footed sea cucumber (*Pentacta pygmaea*) may be found swimming among sea grasses, burrowed into mud flats or crawling along sandy bottoms in shallow-water coral reefs. (Photo courtesy of David Norris)

Opposite: The giant sea roach has bizarre triangular eyes sensitive to infrared light, even though these wavelengths can't penetrate the ocean's depths. But in perpetual darkness, the isopod's multifaceted lenses may have amazing light-collecting abilities that enable it to pounce on bioluminescent organisms and devour them. The largest of all the pill bugs, its eerie white, segmented body almost rolls into a giant ball, making it a true minimonster. (Photo courtesy of New York Zoological Society, Gen Mitchel)

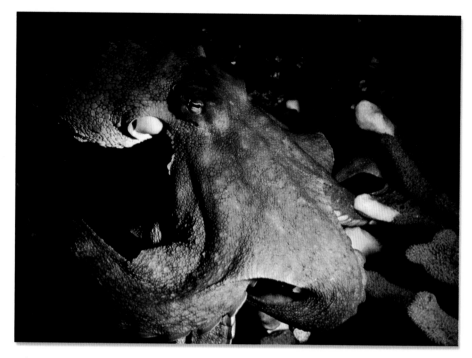

The common octopus (*Octopus vulgaris*) demonstrates an amazing amount of curiosity and intelligence for a short-lived invertebrate species. (Photo courtesy of David Norris)

The dwarf octopus (*Octopus joubini*) is more ill-tempered and reclusive than its relative the common octopus.

Oyster bars, exposed at low tide, at St. George Island off Apalachicola. Oysters (*Crassotrea virginica*) provide food and protection for a vast number of fish and crabs that dwell within Florida's shoals and estuaries. (Photo courtesy of Anne Rudloe)

The fish hawk or osprey (*Pandion haliaetus*) builds its large
bulky nests of sticks and twigs. Widespread spraying of DDT
almost caused the ospreys' extinction in the 1970s, but in recent
years they have been making a dramatic comeback.

Opposite: Cannonball jellyfish strewn
upon a Florida beach. Carried ashore
by wind and current, they then
become stranded when the tide falls.

Commercial net fishermen consider cannonball jellyfish (*Stomolophus meleagris*) a nuisance, but they provide nourishment for many other creatures, including sea turtles and crabs.

Juvenile spiny lobsters (*Palinurus argus*) have characteristic stripes that enable them to blend in perfectly with the mats of algae that grow densely on the grass flats of the Florida Keys. (Photo courtesy of Anne Rudloe)

Researchers observe a long chain of young spiny lobsters marching on the sea floor. Groups of between two and sixty lobsters march single file together, often for many miles. Why they do this is unknown.

Often seen over grassy flats in bays and inland waters, smooth butterfly rays *(Gymnura micrura)* may grow to nearly two feet across.

The chemical acetylcholine is used by the nervous system of the lesser electric ray *(Narcine brasiliensis)* to create a potent electrical charge.

The sawfish (*Pristis pectinatus*) plies coastal waters, river mouths, estuaries and sandbars. Some say it uses its elongated, toothed rostrum to slash at schools of fish, others that it roots clams and worms out of the sand with it. (Photo courtesy of Catherine Winter.)

Oyster toadfish (*Opsanus tau*) are found in the Atlantic from Cape Cod to Miami. The male's mating song is a series of high-pitched beeps, hoots and grunts. Once he has attracted a female to his nest, he fertilizes her eggs and protects them from predators until they hatch. (Photo courtesy of Wildlife Conservation Society.)

swam into it time and again. The plastic covering served as an insulator; then they quickly learned their boundaries or recognized that they were there.

The electric rays showed their contentment by burrowing down into the sandy filter beds that lined the floor of the tank, leaving only their disked impressions in the sand. They could sit there for days like that, the only sign of life being their spiracles, the holes on the tops of their heads, opening and closing, as they pumped water through their gills. Perhaps they were charging their batteries.

For a long time we wondered whether they were really eating the worms we gave them because they seldom moved during daylight, even when we poured worms on top of them. Anne suggested that we wait for night and observe them under red lights. We assumed that, like most marine animals, they might not see red in the visible light spectrum. We put in scarlet bulbs, and the laboratory looked like a house of ill repute. But under the dark shadowy glow of the overhead bulbs, we introduced several dozen *Nereis* worms from the crab corks and watched the buried electric rays pop abruptly out of the sand. The smell or movement sparked activity. We watched a ray homing in on a worm. It slid over the bottom in little hops, moving from side to side. With its eyes on the top of its head, looking up, it couldn't see the worm; it could only sense or smell it.

The sinuous invertebrate crawled desperately along the sand, trying to make a run for it and find some dark cover to hide in. It started to dig in, but the ray headed for it. We stood there with bated breath, hoping that it would strike. But the clumsy fish slid right over it, pushing itself along on its back fins, casting about as if it knew there was food but unable to locate it. It wanted food. It was starving. But the messages weren't quite right.

Then it swam back toward the worm. Suddenly it seemed to get its bearings. It stopped and began searching around for its prey. It found it and lunged forward, its pancake body completely blanketing the sinuous, invertebrate from sight. The delicate margins of its body began to flutter, lifted up, and then it struck. Water and sand sprayed out of the spiracles, the gill openings on the top of its head. "He's got it," I cried. "He's eating it."

But then to our disappointment, the worm came spinning out behind the ray in a benumbed shock. Obviously the jolt had been administered, but the ray had missed its quarry and moved on.

"We're missing something," Anne said with despair. "They're just not getting the right signals. Look at the species of worms they eat: they're not ones you find crawling on top of the sand. It's burrowers; you can see how their mouths are tubular, designed to slurp worms out of the ground."

"Let's try these," I said, having picked some plumed worms out of a nearby tank where they were being held for a polychaete order.

When I cut them out of their tubes and threw them into the electric ray tank, they immediately started secreting mucus, pushing against the sand grains, and inching their way down and out of sight. Again with the smell of new worms, the rays began prowling. We watched one moving over the bottom, lurching ahead in short movements, casting back and forth, fussily checking out the bottom.

Our ray perched over the freshly burrowed worm. We again watched it with bated breath. This time it struck and came up with the worm clamped in its jaws. It yanked it out of the sand like a robin pulling up an earthworm, but at the same time its body hunched up into a spasm. Up, up it swam with the writhing worm held in its mouth, gulping it down. Then the ray settled back down to finish off its prey. At last we had learned the secret.

We were overjoyed, but our jubilation soon turned to worry, with the thought of digging up thousands of burrowing worms, to feed hundreds of rays. Fifteen rays a week had to be shipped to Massachusetts General Hospital. All had to be fat and healthy, or their acetylcholine levels would be low.

As I waded across the gulley, I was wondering how to contact the people who sold sea worms for bait. I remembered fishing with large pink worms on the Coney Island pier in Brooklyn where I grew up as a child. They had millions of little pink legs and ominous black jaws that bit. Worms were sold by the dozen, or the piece, but where did they come from?

I was almost across the gulley, walking up the gradually sloping sand flat, when I spotted a worm eel swimming in two inches of water. It was six inches long, green and slender, moving with gentle, carefree undulations. Now there was a creature that electric rays loved, because for all practical purposes it looked and acted like a worm. They stay buried most of the time, and only once in a while stick their heads above the sand to feed or look around or go on swimming excursions. Hastily I set down my bucket and crouched over it, prepared to strike.

It came into range, my hand shot down, and I felt its muscular body writhe through my fingers, escape, and dive back onto the damp sand. Then in a blink it tunneled its way through the substrate tail-first and was gone. It disappeared through the almost-solid substrate out of sight.

But how could the rays direct their electrical discharges down into the sediments and so precisely locate burrowing animals? It was another grim reminder that electric rays were far better at feeding themselves out in the open ocean than we were at roving the flats with shovels and buckets.

Possibly the rays emitted a low voltage that vibrated their prey out of the ground, the way worm hunters "grunted" earthworms out of the ground. Commercial bait dealers often used a low voltage electrical discharge from a car battery to make earthworms leave their burrows. The lesser electric ray, *Narcine brasiliensis*, possesses a unique auxiliary electric organ that *Torpedo* rays lack, which emits low-frequency shocks. Exactly what this organ does and how it relates to the ray's behavior are unknown. It could have some relation to their schooling behavior, signaling other electric rays as electric eels and electric catfish do in fresh water. But it may also help them locate the worms and eels buried in the mud. Very possibly the vermiform prey down below distorts the weak electric field, and the ray homes in on it as a bat uses radar.

Some months earlier, Dr. Robert Johnson showed us this specialized vibrating electric organ when he was working at Florida State University's marine laboratory. Each day we were bringing him a dozen rays, and he and his team were stockpiling frozen electric tissue for a biochemical experiment to be performed back in Boston.

An anesthetized ray lay on a bed of ice, on a black-topped laboratory table next to a sink. We watched his technician busily excising two large oval electric organs from the rounded wings. He pulled up the mottled hide with forceps and expertly sliced away the connective tissue with a scalpel. They used a new blade for each ray because their rough hides dulled steel quickly.

There at the base of the two white spongy electric organs was a little cluster of thickened tissues, barely separated from the rest of the organs. That was the auxiliary electric organ that made *Narcine* different from *Torpedo*.

The electric organs are derived from muscle tissue that in all animals is capable of generating electricity in small, almost immeasurable amounts. In the electric rays it accounts for one-quarter of the fish's total weight, and when the hide is cut away it appears as clear gelatinous masses easily distinguished from the darker surrounding muscle tissues.

"Do you know how they keep from shocking themselves?" I asked Robert as he chopped the electric organs into little cubes and dropped them into liquid nitrogen. At –180 degrees Fahrenheit the soft mushy tissues changed to white smoking stone.

"No one knows," he replied, handing the smoking Dewar flask to his technician, who dropped the organs into a mortar and pestle and began grinding them down into white powder. They would be put into a refrigerated ultra-centrifuge that would spin the tissues down into their biochemical components. "The electromotor nuclei and medullar part of the brain might have something to do with it. I'll show it to you."

I looked around the room with the dead rays lying on ice, their skulls opened and brains removed, and the cavities filled with blood. Each ray had two giant gaping holes in its wings, leaving very little else behind, except trunk, tail, and viscera. It was a grim reminder that all the rays we caught, and worked so hard to keep alive and fed, ended like this. Why is it that the animal rights advocates that picket medical research laboratories for their vivisectional practices show no interest in fish? Cats, dogs, and monkeys yes, but not the lowly invertebrates or the clammy wet pisces of the deep. Perhaps it's because their forms are so alien to us, or perhaps it's because we all love broiled shrimp and mackerel. Somehow it seems OK to feed our stomachs, why not our minds?

I thought a lot about that as I wandered over the nighttime tideflat with the wisps of fog moving in: all this work to keep them alive and healthy to sacrifice on the altar of science. I wasn't going to fool myself; I shared in that responsibility. Sure I had to make a living, but I was also curious. I wanted to know the secrets of how those living batteries work, and why a mere slimy fish should have the power of the gods locked up in its tissues. If that meant killing some, so be it. And if it meant getting wet and tired digging worms, so be it, They had to be fed, to keep up their energy and the levels of acetylcholine in their electric organs. If they starved, their voltages declined and their electric shocks became weaker and weaker.

My mind was not where it should have been. Abstract thought is best done while sitting on a dock watching the sunrise on the bay, but not on a tideflat at two o'clock in the morning. The water was rising and rising fast. I had felt the change in the wind that kept the sea pushed back, and I hadn't paid any attention to it. The water moved over the rippled sand in a sheet flow and spilled into the holes I had dug. That was the usual signal to start moving back to the shore and get ready to go home.

But when I gathered up my bucket I instantly became aware that I had become disoriented. All I saw was darkness, ground, fog, and water in all directions, and a trace of fear went through me. Hastily I gathered up my buckets, digging fork, and lantern and started walking, following the long sandbar that ran roughly parallel to the beach. I knew that all that separated me from the shore was a gulley several hundred yards across.

But the shoreline was hidden in pitch darkness: there was no difference between the land and the sea. From where I stood there were distant lights, but they were on the opposite shore, down the coast. And as the south wind grew in intensity, the bit of land upon which I stood shrank away. With each passing minute I watched the water devour the dry sand flat and the sandbar submerge. And here I was, caught out in the middle, not knowing which way to go.

"Don't panic," I ordered myself. "Panic is stupid." But calling raw fear names didn't help. I paced back and forth on the shrinking tideflat like a caged animal trying to get its bearings. I realized the gasoline lantern was blinding me, so I hurried over to the highest part of the sand knot, where it was still dry, and put it down. Then I moved away from its glare and tried to discern the landmass against the darkness. But I still couldn't see, and with the warm south wind blowing across the chilly water, sea fog was building and rolling in with the waves.

Somewhere downshore there was a disembodied light, but it was surrounded by water from all directions. Either it was a shrimp boat or a distant beach house. I decided to take a chance and head for it.

I felt the icy water swamp into my rubber boots and the chill of water as it rose into my groin. It was too deep there, too quick. Desperately I searched the sky looking for the big dipper, for Polaris, the North Star, to give me at least one point. But I couldn't find it; all I could see were clouds.

Again and again I strained to see through the growing fog and focused at that dimmest light. It wasn't moving. It had to be a beach cottage, but it could be miles away, and because of the way the shoreline of Alligator Point curved around, heading for it could be a fatal mistake.

Terror rose up and engulfed me. I felt my throat tightening and I cursed myself for not paying attention to what I was doing, for wandering around at night with my head in a quandary over electric rays. Never again would I go out on a tideflat at night without getting my bearings, if there were another chance, that is.

The current was pushing hard against my legs as the water surged in with the wind. I knew this area well from shrimping; it had currents strong enough to sweep me out to sea. Before I knew it, the water was up to my stomach, and still the bottom kept dropping as I headed in the direction I hoped was the beach. Uncertainly I backed up, getting up onto shrinking, higher ground and looking around desperately through the darkness. That was clearly the wrong way, light or no light.

I tried to envision the same area in bright daylight, the shoreline with its wild dunes, the tideflat, the gulley, the sandbar, and the Gulf beyond it, but it was of no help. The water had now swallowed up all but a tiny portion of the sandbar, where my lantern still burned. I slogged over to it and picked it up.

It was time for a decision. I had to choose a direction, or any decision would be taken away from me by rising water. I would go at right angles to the light. I closed my eyes and took a deep breath to quiet my pounding heart and my trembling hands. Mich way? Which way? I asked the deep inner reaches of my mind. And from somewhere came not an answer in words, but a pull, a draw.

I moved slowly forward, feeling the cold water rise above my belt, drawing the heat out of my stomach, and then up to my chest.

"I will not panic," I ordered myself. "If I'm wrong, then I will not fight the current. I will remain calm.

"If the water comes up to my chin, I will throw down my lantern and buckets. Then I will hold my breath, sit down on the bottom, and wrench off my boots.

"And then I will try swimming, but only for a few minutes. If I still don't hit the landward side of the gulley, then I will know I have made a mistake, that my directions are wrong. Then I will drift with the current; I will not fight it. I will allow it to take me somewhere." But I knew that I had no life vest, no flotation, unless I could trap air in my bucket somehow.

There were no shrimp boats out there tonight to pick me up, only the dark horizon, black and misty, except for that ever-receding light. I felt the water rise up above my shoulders, almost to my neck, and still I moved forward, following that draw, heading in a direction I thought was north, north up to North America, all the way to the vast corn and wheat fields, the mountains, and the forests that lay safely above the sea. Dry places like Iowa and Wisconsin, anywhere but here.

All of a sudden I realized the bottom was shallowing, that I was headed shoreward. I kept going farther faster, and feeling the water level drop on me. Suddenly, I was gasping with relief; there was hope. The fact that the water was now back down to my shoulders meant the world was coming back under control. Still I was shaking, even though the water was now down to my waist. I could feel the cool air of the sea wind at my back. Now the full weight of my body was firmly planted on the mud beneath me.

I hurried forward, not thinking or caring about what I might step on buried in the sediments, and I felt the bottom firming up. I was up to my knees now, and then with a rapid burst I was coming out of the water. There before me was the wild sand of the beach; I could see the outline of the dunes. I stumbled on it, and collapsed, and sat there shaking, feeling its blessed dryness.

I had survived. For a long while I sat on the dry sands, wrestling with the fears and shaking them out of my body. But then I turned and faced the misty Gulf, and I knew I would have to go back on the next tide. I could not be afraid of the ocean. Respect it, yes, but live in abject fear, no. I had to live with it, because it was part of me.

Besides, the rays were still hungry and we needed worms. But next time, my mind would be on my bearings.

7. The Elusive Sawfish

As our fiberglass boat bounced over the chop, heading out into the Gulf off Carrabelle, I sat somberly on the stern holding the ashes of a friend, a man who had spent his life on the sea or trying to get to it. This was obviously not a routine collecting trip, although we were going out to look for barnacles on ropes of abandoned crab traps. Elwood A. Curtis wouldn't have it any other way. In his book, *A Wet Butt and Hungry Gut*, he detailed his life on shrimp boats and snapper boats, describing a Florida of fifty years ago that I had never known, a time when panthers roamed the beaches and crews of hungry beach seiners dragged manatees up onto the shores and ate them. He had nearly starved trying to become a commercial fisherman and had ended up selling ads and doing other unrelated jobs.

Always he gravitated back to the water, someplace where there were grass beds with sea trout and sandbars, where the redfish gathered. Old and sick, he spent his last days fishing on docks, messing around oyster shoals, and wading out into the marshes.

And it was his last wish that he be cremated and his ashes scattered at sea.

Ahead, at the far end of the channel, the turbid waters broke on a sandbar, and its yellow shallows rose up from the sea bottom. I directed Doug Gleeson, our chief collector, to run the boat in that direction.

I sat on the stern, next to our scallop dredge and buckets and the little velvet box that contained the ashes of a man who had loved the sea. A stiff wind was blowing, making the water choppy and pushing in the tide, giving it the appearance of the rolling ocean. Today it was the south wind blowing, pushing saltier and bluer water over the tideflats. The Gulf of Mexico had moved in on top of the estuary, with rolling swells and whitecaps and a refreshing stiff breeze.

It was time to unpack my friend. I opened the sealed box and pulled out the can that held the cremated remains. Strange, I thought, here was a human being I had known and talked to only a few months ago, and now he was ashes. I pried it open, and looked with a morbid fascination at the white crushed bones and dust packed so densely inside. It looked like seashells, not much different from the rubble that lined the bottom of the channel or was cast up on the barrier beaches in fragments and shards. Simple calcium carbonate, the fabric of life, just like the limestone and the foraminifers.

There was nothing to say, no ceremony, for the sea said it all. I motioned Doug to slow down and putter along the edge of the shoal, and I up-ended the can. The white bones poured out, and the dust took to the air. I watched the heavy particles sinking down through the waves, spinning, churning like pennies falling down a wishing well, down to the brittle stars below, down to the speckled sea trout he loved so much, the shrimp, the squid—life, abundant life.

I put the can and wrappings overboard too. A purist might cry pollution, but I figured the sea could handle it. A toadfish or stone crab would probably make its home in it, and Curt would approve of that.

Suddenly, my philosophical ruminations were interrupted by Doug's cry, "Hey, look at that!"

He was pointing to a large, flat shape moving slowly on top of the sandbar. He speeded up and headed for the elongated brown carpetlike creature that moved like a shadow. Even from the distance, it was obviously some kind of ray, but it was huge. Three triangular fins broke the surface, big, brown, and rough, like sandpaper. It was a sawfish, one that was easily ten feet long, a rare sight. It stopped and squatted on the bottom, and we watched it in all its awesome size. Doug throttled down the motor, and we puttered forward to get a better look.

What a great reward for scattering my friend's ashes, I thought. It was a gift just to see it. I regarded the sawfish as a harbinger of good fortune, as the Japanese shark fishermen consider the hammerhead shark a messenger from the god of the sea.

Before I made the trip, I reread his book and chuckled at his recollections of catching a sawfish and peddling its bill to the tourists in a Jensen Beach bar.

There must be some inherent reason that mantelpieces around the world are adorned with the stuffed trophies of sword-bearing fish. Most of those fighting marlins, sailfish, and occasional swordfishes look more like replicas popped out of a manufacturer's plastic injection mold than the living creatures they once were. Perhaps we make trophies of sawfishes and swordfish because of some inherent fascination with the sword. Excalibur, King Arthur's legendary sword, is ingrained in our mythology, a story told down through the ages. What better feeling is there than to hold a well-balanced rapier in one's hand?

I watched the lightest dust particles of Curt's ashes float away on the surface, rising and falling with the waves as we turned back to shore. I knew the Creator, who cooked up the whole mess in the first place, used some of the same ingredients to make both man and billfish.

Every year people spend millions of dollars to go out and catch these streamlined masterpieces. The billfishes are true fish, with bony skeletons, that inhabit the open oceans. Commercial longliners travel the Gulf Stream from the Caribbean to Canada in search of these hydrodynamic wonders that think nothing of speeding from six-hundred-foot depths up to the surface to strike bait and skewer it on their rapiers. They have a tight network of blood vessels surrounding their brains that enables them to function in great depths, keeping their brains and bodies warm. Swordfish feed down in the depths on squid and then rise to the warmer waters of the surface to digest their meals.

Although the sawfish is a peaceful animal, and has never deliberately attacked anyone except when harpooned or caught in nets or on hook and line, there are records of swordfishes ramming swords up through the bottom of boats, and even a few people meeting an end with a spear in their bellies. The submersible *Ben Franklin* encountered a swordfish. They were drifting six hundred feet below the surface following the Gulf Stream in 1969 when they were surprised by an assault. Their log entry read,

> It was really an attack, short, precise. The swordfish was about five or six feet long. Another one was waiting for him at the limit of our visibility. The combatant rushed forward and apparently tried to hit our porthole, missing it by a few inches. Then he circled around several minutes close to the boat. Content that his domination of this portion of his realm was not threatened, he joined his friend and left, never to be seen again. What courage for such a fish to take on a 130-ton submarine.

The smaller sailfish have been photographed off the east coast of Florida herding swarms of pilchards, little herringlike fishes, together in a tight bunch and skewering them. "Balling the bait," it's called. With their long fanlike dorsal fins raised to make them look even larger, they

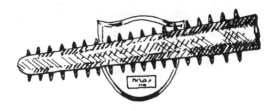

Perhaps we make trophies of sawfishes because of some inherent fascination with the sword.

continually circle the panicked, glittering little silver fishes forcing them into a tight mass, almost like sardines in a can. Then they come crashing in, a nightmare of spears, leaving the maimed and wounded bait fish to sink, swooping down and swallowing them whole. They whittle away at the packed mass of little fish until it becomes smaller and smaller. Meanwhile, sport fishermen cruise above, snatching their lines and lures, reeling up the fighting billfish one right after the other, until the wind switches, the seas become choppy, and the minnows disperse along with the sailfish.

The sawfish, *Pristis pectinatus*, does not frequent the open ocean as billfish do; it is a creature of coastal waters, river mouths, estuaries, and sandbars. Its saw is very different from the sharp, pointed rapier of the billfish. It is a large flat blade with lateral rows of protruding toothlike spikes. Exactly what it uses its vorpal sword for isn't really known, and there is some dispute about it. Sawfish are said to swim through a school of small fish, making hard lateral sweeps, impaling some on their saws, and leaving the hacked-up mutilated bodies of others to tumble to the bottom, where they swallow them whole. Some ichthyologists doubt this and believe the toothy rostrum is really used to root clams and worms out of the sand. But for all we know, it may also be an elaborate antenna for picking up electrical fields in the ocean as well.

The sawfish is so rare that virtually nothing is known about its natural history. I watched this large prime specimen heading for deeper water and freedom with mixed feelings. On the one hand, I wanted to see it go free, to procreate, and make more sawfish, and hoped it would slip past the phalanx of commercial fishermen's nets and the lines of anglers. But there also went a valuable creature, much in demand by oceanariums. Two hundred dollars a delivered foot was cruising over the shallow sand bottom like a great moving carpet. We needed the-money to pay salaries and support the laboratory, and therein lay the conflict. I saw nothing wrong with collecting marine invertebrates and fish that rapidly recolonize the environment and produce copious offspring. We essentially were one more predator that did not impact the population. But a slow-growing sawfish might be different; it might leave a gap.

The sawfish does not appear on any endangered species list, neither are there laws against catching one. They are not listed as "rare" or "threatened," but perhaps they should be. They seemed far rarer now than when I began working on the Gulf Coast. As I watched it move, I was glad I didn't have a net on board.

The sawfish must have read my avaricious mind and speeded up. Its triangular tail swished back and forth, propelling the long flattened body toward the deeper water. And just before it disappeared I had a wild thought of leaping on it, tackling it, and dragging it into the boat. But fear and common sense, and some firsthand experience with the saw, kept me from it. Twenty years ago in Madagascar it was only by a whisker that I wasn't maimed or killed by a blow from a twenty-foot sawfish.

As part of their cultural and scientific programs, the French government in cooperation with the Malagasy Republic were instituting a fisheries program. The research vessel *Ambariaka* traveled around the northern coast of Madagascfar taking oceanographic measurements of salinity, dissolved oxygen, and temperature and gathering plankton samples. In addition to two French technicians, the crew consisted of six Sakalava natives and five Comorians, who worked on the grounds of the Centre d'Océanographie. In addition to cutting grass and performing maintenance jobs, they sorted plankton and were trained to take oceanographic measurements. As a participant of the International Indian Ocean Expedition, I was invited to make the maiden shrimping voyage of the vessel because of my background of shrimping in the Gulf of Mexico.

To my knowledge no one had ever shrimped the northwest coast of Madagascar. Years later it was to become a booming shrimp grounds, but until then no net had ever churned the bottom. With too many hands helping, we spread out the net, fed it out behind the R/V *Ambariaka* until it stretched wide like a proper funnel. Then we hoisted the doors over the side with Michon, a French technician, translating

Sawfish are said to swim through a school of small fish, making hard lateral sweeps, impaling some on their saws, leaving the hacked-up bodies of others to tumble to the bottom.

my suggestions, holding them by the towropes until they spread the net, and allowing them to sink.

In a few moments the little diesel-powered boat came tight on the ropes, and we were fishing virgin bottoms. The *Ambariaka* strained ahead, towing the heavy nets, chains, and doors. I could feel the wind blowing hard in our faces, and the boat began to rock. Soon the wind picked up even more, and the sky darkened, heavy with rain clouds, and lightning flashed on the shoreline followed by a clap of thunder. We all got into our raincoats and held on.

Hollering, "Heave, heave, heave-ho!" the crew hauled back the ropes, piling them up on deck. With much groaning, they lifted the heavy doors up out of the water.

The net was gorged. I grabbed the webbing along with everyone else and hauled back with all my might. I felt the cords of crisscrossed nylon cutting into my fingers as I lifted my share and inched the wings up. Again, I wished I had a real shrimp boat with a real winch and hoisting equipment out here.

But sixteen strong backs and hands can do their share, and the mouth of the net emerged. Feeling seasick, and being less attentive than

I should have been, I bent over and looked down into the mouth of the great funnel. And there was a large pair of primordial yellow eyes staring back at me, a great raylike creature. What was that thing?

At the same instant something jolted me; something sharp and exceedingly painful slammed into my shoulder. The pain was excruciating. I glanced at my side, saw what had caused the blow, a huge brown tooth-studded saw sticking straight up from the webbing, and I jumped backward just as it made another swipe.

The crew went wild, yelling, gesticulating, and pointing to the monster in the net. It was a huge sawfish, the largest thing I had ever seen. And it had clobbered me. How fortunate I was that its saw was heavily wrapped up in the webbing, impeded from getting up much of a sideways thrust. Looking at those rows of two-inch-long teeth, rising up and out of the net, I knew how close I had come to being killed.

Two of the crew members had seen me absorb the blow and, with a look of concern in their eyes, asked how I was. There was no need of translations here. "*C'est bon,*" I said, shrugging it off. "No problem."

I didn't want anybody to say a thing about the stupidity of my sticking my head and shoulder down into the net. With my shoulder throbbing, I backed away as they went on hauling up the net by hand. They had a block and tackle wrapped around the fish and were groaning and straining and hoisting it out an inch at a time. Fearfully I unbuttoned my shirt and looked. I saw a series of ugly red marks up and down my arm. The skin was broken, and the pain was terrible, but the wounds weren't deep and I would recover to tell the story.

At last they got the sawfish up on deck, still encased in the net. It instantly went wild, thrashing around, slamming its saw back and forth into the mast, the deck, everywhere.

We were thankful that most of it was still encased in the net. Disaster could occur at any moment. At one point, its big brown sandpapery tail bowled over a crewman and sent him sprawling across the deck.

He responded with a quick fury, grabbing a club and delivering a crushing blow to the sawfish's head, which caused it to gyrate even more frantically. Captain LaBarse ordered everyone to get away from it, so it could die and we could safely approach the rest of the catch in the net. Sadly, it took a long time to die, feebly moving its huge body, its yellow belly turning red and hemorrhaging, as its life slowly passed away. Finally, the saw was lashed to the mast. The drama ended.

I had forgotten entirely about being seasick, but now that the drama was over, I was beginning to feel wretched again.

For hours, as we worked through the night, I felt that we had somehow offended the god of the sea by destroying such a creature and at one point suggested that we throw it back. "Oh no!" the French scientists said. "No one has ever seen such a big sawfish before. The saw will make a fine trophy for our museum."

I thought of the Malagasy's belief in propitiating the various gods of the sea, such as the dugong, the whale, and sea turtles, to render fishing favorable. Theirs was an animistic religion, and having watched this great creature expire, I felt we had violated some taboo. But as the net was coming up again, and I had seasickness to fight and specimens to take back to the Smithsonian, I soon forgot about the huge creature.

Suddenly there was a hot burnt smell coming from the engine. Down in the motor hole the pounding pistons began to labor and wheeze and sputter. Black smoke poured out of the stack where only a continuous puff of gray smoke filtered out before. Two crewmen rushed down the ladder to the small engine room to check the gauges. The temperature had soared to two hundred degrees.

Captain LaBarse immediately ordered the engine shut down. For a moment we drifted, with only the creaking sounds of a hot engine. "Has the *Ambariaka* ever had this problem before?" I asked.

"No, never," replied Michon. There were only silence and quick exchanges of knowing looks among the crew in the dim light.

Even if I couldn't see it, I could feel the barren teeth of the mountainous landscape, the mangroves, and the bleakness out there in those sharky waters where monsters like this sawfish cruise the shallows. Although the stench of diesel made me retch, I followed Michon down into the engine room and looked at the mechanical heart of the vessel. The water had been circulating rapidly through the engine; there was no apparent blockage of the cooling system. The motor had been sputtering as if the fuel filters were clogged, but when opened, they appeared to be fine. The engine had used a quart of oil, but there was no sign that anything was drastically wrong.

While we were waiting for the engine to cool down, I inquired, "What happens if we get stranded out here?"

LaBarse shrugged. "I am not sure. We might have to run the boat up on the shore, get out, and hike back to the Center, but it's a long way." Looking at it from a mile or two offshore, I could imagine slogging through that muck, crawling in and out of the tangle of mangrove roots with clouds of mosquitoes devouring us.

"There is a village twenty-five miles back. From there we could get a pirogue and proceed another twenty miles or so to the Centre d'Oceanographie," Monsieur Michon said.

I held on and gazed at the bleak mountainous coast of northwest Madagascar. The shoreline looked burned, uninviting, inhospitable. It was by far the most desolate and remote shoreline I had seen, a land of erosion where the rains washed the red clay mountains into the muddy Mozambique Channel. Mile after mile of dense, thick mangrove swamps covered the shoreline, mangroves full of crocodiles and hungry sharks. A lot to look forward to!

At last we cranked the engine, but the clatter was not reassuring. The Comorian engineer and a helper stayed down in the engine room, squirting oil on every moving part and keeping a constant eye on the temperature gauge. The engineer was sweating and half-asphyxiated, but with great dedication he nurtured the ailing engine.

And so the *Ambariaka* with its giant sawfish clattered along slowly, a full ten hours back to the Centre d'Oceanographie. We never had to make that trek through the mangroves, but cutting the trip short was quite a setback. I had limited time in Madagascar and had to return with a load of specimens. Save for a few small sharks, and a handful of invertebrates, all we retrieved was the sawfish. The crew of the *Ambariaka* were treated as conquering heroes with this incredible twenty-foot monster, a relic from the strange world of the distant past.

With great ceremony the creature was measured and photographed for the museum's records before the admiring eyes of the French scientists' families and the staff at the Centre d'Oceanographie. The severed bill alone measured seven feet, with its two rows of three-inch-long spikes. Everyone passed it around, admiring its weight, and a few of the natives performed a fearsome war dance with it, swinging it about against imaginary opponents. The same design has been used in warfare before. The Aztecs made swords that looked just like the sawfish's blade by embedding sharp spikes of black obsidian along a flat board. Had the idea been inspired by one of these great creatures?

The crew of the *Ambariaka* were given the meat, and they divided it up for their families and for selling in the marketplace. I was offered a large chunk, but turned it down. Over the years since I have tried sawfish. Various books laud their flavor and say how prized young sawfish are. I'm afraid I've always found it much too strong, full of urea. It can be made to taste edible, but it takes work that isn't worth the effort.

Because of the confusion between swordfish and sawfish, more than a few people have been duped into buying sawfish meat. But, as one fish peddler found out, it is a far cry from the succulent flesh of the big sleek oceanic swordfishes broiled with lemon-and-butter sauce. Once a fourteen-foot sawfish was caught in a shrimp net and hauled to the dock at Panacea. There it hung, halfway up the mast of the trawler, its great girth pressing down on the ropes, cutting into its flesh. After everyone came by and took photographs and cut off the saw, the shrimpers were mulling over what to do with it. If they threw it overboard, it would rot and stink up the dock. Yet they didn't want to go to all the trouble of untying the boat and hauling the carcass out into the channel.

And then a miracle happened. A fish peddler who was new to the business came by. Seeing this great prize he jumped at the chance and offered the fishermen three dollars a pound for the dressed meat and fifty dollars for the saw. Happily they butchered it and loaded baskets full of meat into his truck.

The peddler promptly paid them over three hundred dollars and sped off with the meat to an exclusive restaurant to offer them fresh swordfish. It was put on the menu as a special. But a few days later the irritated fish peddler angrily returned to the docks, having been berated by the restaurant and forced to take back all the uncooked meat. He learned the hard way the difference between elasmobranchs, the rays and sharks having a cartilaginous skeleton, and the teleosts, the bony fish that include billfish that do not accumulate urea in their body tissues.

As the years passed, I saw fewer and fewer sawfish. They move too slowly to outrun shrimp trawls, and their toothy blades tangle up in almost any size of gill net. And no sport fisherman will turn one loose when he catches a sawfish on a hook and line. It's considered to be an international game fish, though I don't know why. The legend and confusion that sawfish are good eating—not that people who say it have ever tried one—persist along the Gulf Coast.

Several months later, Johnnie and Edward Keith, two of my best collectors, came driving through the gate blowing their horn, with two six-foot sawfish in the back. Then came my dilemma. If I were a real purist I would have refused to buy them. Or if I were rich, I would have paid them for their struggle to keep them alive, after they caught them in the gill net, loaded them into the boat, then turned the fish loose after tagging them.

Instead, I was happy to get the pair and hurried to make room for them in our tanks. As we slid them into our largest tank, and watched the big toothy rays swim around the circumference, exploring the boundaries, I rationalized that it was really a big ocean, that we really didn't know whether the scarcity in recent years were a function of a reduced population or some long-range environmental change such as a change in the Gulf Stream, a shift in the magnetic flux of the earth's field, sunspots, or any one of a thousand other variables that often regulate fish populations.

As we watched the two sawfish settle down, Johnnie and Edward recounted how they struck a school of mullet, never dreaming there was anything unusual going on. And when the net began jerking and snatching, they knew they had something big. Moments later when a severely tangled saw popped up, they knew what it was. The big surprise was the second sawfish. Knowing they were valuable, and hoping to lessen damage, they cut the ball of webbing away from their bills. Thus they freed the saws by severely damaging their net.

As I watched the sawfish on the bottom of my tank, slowly, rhythmically moving their gills, swimming now and then and stopping, I wondered whether they were a mated pair. The large one was a male, with two long claspers hanging down behind the anal vent, and the other lacked them, thus was a female. Part of me said they should be out there in the ocean, making more sawfish. Another part said that in this age of asphalt and need for environmental sensitivity, it was better that people get a chance to see and appreciate these incredible wonders behind the glass walls of an aquarium. Seeing them alive would be a once-in-a-lifetime experience. And maybe, just maybe, they would give birth, and the aquarium could raise them up and release the surplus young into the wild. The only hope for many endangered species of reptiles, birds, and mammals is captive rearing. Why not rear such fish?

Of course, I knew that I was putting forth a biased argument. The truth was that I was going to sell them to the highest bidder, and that made all my rational arguments suspect. I kept all this concern to myself. After all the trouble my collectors went to, I didn't think they would appreciate hearing it. Another part of me said that this was a great gift from nature, from God or the Great Turtle Mother and I should rejoice—probably the same thing the caveman said as he hurled his spear into the now extinct woolly mastodon and the North American camel.

Several days later we were preparing to ship them to the New York Aquarium. Nixon Griffis really wanted a deep-water sawshark, a creature from seven hundred fathoms. The curator in charge of the exhibits was delighted with the idea of receiving not one, but two of our shallow-water fish, even if they were rays. The sawfish is a bactoid, more of a ray than a shark. Even though it has a long sharklike body, the gill slits lie on the undersides, whereas sharks have them on the sides. But since they appeared to be a mated pair, Nixon Griffis was consoled with the idea that we might have the first live birth of a sawfish in captivity. That gave him the prospect for the impossible that he so loved. Up to twenty-three sawfish have been born alive from a fifteen-foot female in the wild.

We kept them for a good two weeks before I finally got around to shipping them. I needed that much time to acclimate them properly, to induce them to eat in captivity, and to make sure they were in prime condition. But the truth was that I had grown fond of these great lumbering beasts with their long tooth-studded saws protruding from their sandpaper-skin brown bodies. Word got out, and people came from all over the area to see them. If ever there were monsters in the sea they were manifest in these raylike creatures.

They had their own personality. Nothing bothered them inside their new competitive and crowded environment. We had rock bass, grunts, sea catfish, and sea turtles snapping down food as quickly as we dropped it in. The slow-moving sawfish had a hard time competing during the feeding frenzies. But they compensated by swimming in the midst of the fish, slashing their saws from side to side, and causing all others to flee. Watching them, I had the feeling that the saw was far more than a mere weapon for bludgeoning. It was an extremely sensitive sensory organ. Just the touch of a herring or piece of fish with the tip of the bill makes the sawfish jump into action. It leaps forward and engulfs its meal in one or two gulps. Then, with full stomach, the sawfish sways back and forth and roots out the gravel, making a comfortable nest in the bottom.

We stopped feeding them two days before shipping so that they would travel on empty guts. The truth was that we had never shipped sawfish before, and I was nervous about it. A lot of money and effort were tied up in those two fish. It was a risk and a big challenge.

There was only one direct flight from Tallahassee to New York, with a stopover in Atlanta. The trouble was that it left at seven in the morning. We had to start packing at four.

The blaring alarm clock shattered my sleep, and I groped for it to avoid waking Anne. My collectors were coming in to pack at five. I had the coffee going, but barely had my eyes open. I was still in a deep fog, the kind in which you don't want to do anything. It was pitch-dark out and cold. The lights of my neighbors who go fishing at dawn had come on. Stars shone down in their lonely darkness. It was four-thirty, and it seemed more than enough time to go down, pack two sawfish, and have them at the airport by eight. I was beginning to feel better about the situation after coffee and with eyes open.

I had planned the packing strategy with my helpers, Leon Crum and Edward Keith, days before. We had done a thorough job of building the shipping containers. All day long saws screamed as they sliced through new plywood; hammers rhythmically tapped away, nailing it against the framing. Styrofoam sheets were cut out and inserted for thermal insulation and cushioning. The giant heavy-duty plastic bags were inserted, filled with filtered seawater. All that was needed were two sawfish to go into them with their bills wrapped to prevent them from perforating the bags.

I walked up the street to the laboratory in the chilly November air. I met my helpers coming to work, Leon with his coffee mug in hand, awake and anxious, Edward silent as usual, wearing his Caterpillar cap, his bushy hair protruding from beneath it.

We flicked on the lights of the wet lab, making us squint in the sudden artificial glare. All the creatures in the tanks were moving about, the two ridley turtles immediately swam over expecting food, and fish rose up and looked expectant. The spiny lobsters were out prowling away from their rock ledges. It's called crepuscular activity, in the sea or in the aquarium, animals' moving about during dawn and dusk. During the day they are quiet, and in the middle of the night activity shuts down. But now they were in full swing.

Both sawfishes were on the move. Call it ESP or whatever, but they seemed to know something was up from the time we entered the building. Day after day they lay there sluggishly, hardly moving a few inches until it was time to feed. Perhaps it was the vibrations of dragging the shipping crates over to the tank, or the lights' being suddenly turned on after total darkness, but they were gliding over the bottom, swimming a good four inches above the gravel, cruising around the circumference of the tank.

Edward watched them. "They look nervous or something," he said, yawning, trying to get the sleep out of his eyes.

"I reckon they got a right to be," Leon said with his usual enthusiasm. "You ready?"

"Let's get the female first," I said, as the flat brown carpet of fish with its protruding toothy bill cruised toward us. "She's a little smaller. We can practice on her."

Edward plunged his arms into the tank, grabbed her by the tail, and tried to jerk the fish up. But she swung around with her bill to get him, as he jumped away. Leon then grabbed at her middle, but the power of that animal was incredible. She again twisted from side to side and wrenched herself loose. I managed to get a slippery hold on one of the three dorsal fins, but she was already free. The great armored ray bolted around the tank in a fury, slammed into the opposite side, and came charging back. I tried to work up the courage to grab her again, but looking at that ominous tooth-studded weapon made me hesitate.

Again the image of that monster on the boat off Madagascar flooded my memory.

The male cruised past us, and because the female was still in a wild frenzy we decided he'd be easier. "Here goes," cried Leon. His bare arms shot into the tank and caught it around the middle. "Catch the bill!" he cried, pulling backward with all his strength. "Catch the bill!"

We rushed over to help him. Edward and I grabbed the head, to prevent the bill from swinging back and forth, and wrestled it down. Cold water splashed up and cascaded over us. "Get the tail! Get the tail!" Leon cried.

Edward released for a moment to step around him, and the sawfish gave a mighty thrust. I felt it wrench out of my headlock, the thick sandpapery hide scraping and abrading my skin. "Let go!" Edward cried. "We've got him." A cold wet shock went through me as the tail delivered a walloping slap to my face. Leon bellowed as the toothy rostrum struck him and splashed back into the tank. A second later it was back in the water, churning the tank, free again.

"God almighty damn," my wounded collector shouted. "He's ruined me." He held up his arm, showing a series of small holes trickling blood. "That varmint's a whole lot stronger than I thought he'd be."

"You all right?" I asked, ineptly getting to my feet, feeling the sting and bruise.

"Yeah," he muttered, glowering at the fleeing sawfish. The whole tank was in turmoil: fish were swimming frantically in all directions; sea turtles were paddling as fast as they could, going around and around the tank.

For a moment we stood by watching the sawfishes bolt to and fro, trying to collect our wits. I glanced at my watch: five-thirty, dawn was breaking. We should have had one in the box by now, ready to start the next one, and they were just as far from being caught as when we first came in. "Maybe we should postpone this until we figure out a better way to catch them."

"Yeah," agreed Edward, vexed. "Like drain the whole damn tank, and then get them out."

I considered it, but that would take all day. All the other fish in the tank would have to be moved.

"No," Leon said stubbornly, "he's done made me mad now. I'm going to get him into that box if it has to be in little pieces." I knew from long experience that it was useless to argue with him when he took something personally. We would have to try again.

"All right, but if we don't get one in the next try, we'll have to postpone. I should be booking the shipment right now. We're way off schedule."

The male came swimming past me. Gathering courage, I pounced on him, and instead of trying to haul him out, I pressed him down with all my might. He squirmed and fanned his tail, sending gravel flying in every direction. At the same time, to my chagrin, he was rubbing his soft yellow underbelly down into the gravel. I didn't want to hurt him, which is easy to do by causing internal hemorrhaging, but I didn't want him to hurt me either. "I've got him; I've got him; come on, grab him quick!"

Edward had a firm grip on his head and saw, I had his middle, and Leon gripped the tail. In one mighty heave we hoisted the 150-pound fish out of the water, and with grunts and gritted teeth, wrestled it down to the concrete floor and jumped back.

The sawfish went wild, gyrating back and forth, swinging its, saw. "Throw water on the floor," I yelled, "or he'll scratch his belly."

Seawater cascaded down on the concrete floor from our five-gallon buckets until the sawfish was practically swimming again. Now there was nothing to do but stand back and let it fight itself out. After a good five minutes it began to weaken, the flurry of activity stopped, and again we tackled him. Only this time, in the world of air, we had the advantage.

While I sat on its back, knees pressing the ground to take my weight off, my helpers wound the bolt of cheesecloth around its bill, filling in the spaces between each of its twenty-two pairs of teeth, covering the sharp points until the entire saw was rendered harmless.

All during the bandaging, the big creature let out loud snorts, its gills opened and closed, and occasionally it gave a feeble wave of its fan tail. Its huge eyes seemed to be looking up at me with recrimination.

Nevertheless, we hoisted it into the waiting shipping crate, and I watched it lying in the oversize plastic bag while the oxygen was being jetted in. Once that majestic spiked nose caused terror to all at sea, and now it looked silly. We couldn't help laughing at the absurd sight of his huge bandaged nose.

The fish swatted his covered bill against the plastic, trying to shake it off, but the box was built so he could not turn around and had only enough room to move his saw slightly from side to side.

Leon took a deep breath and leaned up against the tank to rest. "I'll tell you one thing. I pity the poor SOB who has to unpack him on the other end."

Panting, tired, soaking wet, I looked at my watch and the numbers frightened me. "It's six-twenty!" I cried. "We've got to get the other one packed up in thirty minutes or we'll miss the plane. Maybe we should just ship this one."

"No, we can get 'em," said Edward. "I think I know how to do it this time."

He climbed up on top of the tank, then jumped into the water, wading rapidly across the tank holding a dip net. Without choice, we all jumped in and followed him, charged with adrenaline like soldiers going into battle. We waded over the gravel bottom, pushing sea turtles out of the way, rock bass, catfish, and sheepshead fleeing before us.

We knew this was dangerous because we were on the sawfish's turf. First it ran. Then, when cornered by our big stomping feet, it turned to fight. Edward's dip net snagged the approaching teeth, and before the fish could wrench it loose from his grasp, we dove down on top, pressing the female to the bottom, getting our arms beneath her, our hands on the bill. The smaller female managed to get in a few good slaps with her tail, and a few jabs at our hands with her teeth, but within the allotted time we were proficiently bandaging up her two-and-a-half-foot bill.

"You know," Leon panted, "we're getting better at this. Too bad there aren't any more sawfish to practice on."

Cold, drenched, and sore from our wounds, we hoisted each box into a separate pickup truck and sped off for the airport. I managed to call ahead, and they were waiting for our last-minute arrival.

Sawfish are sold by the foot. But it was never possible to get an exact measurement. Once or twice we tried putting a yardstick on the bottom of the tank. When they pounced on a piece of fish, and stopped to gobble it, we figured that the male was seven feet and the female about six-and-a-half. We planned to get an exact measurement when they were removed from the tank but ran out of time.

However, John Clark, the curator of the New York Aquarium, disagreed with our measurements. Not that he bothered to measure them either, when the staff unpacked the fish. He was chagrined. "Good Lord, did they have to wrap them up like Christmas presents?"

The entire staff of the aquarium, clerical help and visitors alike, clustered around to watch the curator trying to unpack the monsters, snipping the cheesecloth away from their bills.

At last they slid them into their largest tank and watched as the sawfish descended to the bottom, swimming around discovering the new and larger parameters of their confinement. Then they settled to the bottom and sat there opening and closing their gills. Within a day they were feeding.

The time had come to pay our bill, and John decided to settle the measurement dispute. He put on his wet suit and scuba tank and slid over the side, tape measure in hand, and approached the larger male.

Suddenly to his surprise he was under attack: the vorpal sword went snicker-snack! He was in a nightmare of teeth, coming at him from all directions, violently lunging. He bolted from the tank and scrambled out with the sawfish charging from the rear. The female was right behind him.

After that experience, we easily settled on a compromise price. For ten years when I periodically went up to New York, I sat beside the tank, watching my sawfishes with no little pride as the crowds pressed past. Of all the people staring at them, I felt uniquely blessed to see more than a strange-looking fish in an artificial environment.

The story had a sad ending. The mated pair lived together for seven years in the same tank, until a new curator took over. He was going to change things. The sawfish were dull, lumpish things, he declared, that always sat on the bottom—not a good exhibit. He demanded that they be separated. The male died almost immediately; the female perished several months later, some said, of a broken heart.

8. The Great Turtle Rescue

When the tide falls in St. Joseph Bay, on the northern Gulf Coast, it looks as if someone snatched the plug and all the water has run out.. Right before one's eyes, sandbars pop up, the tips of turtle grass leaves emerge, and whorls of large fishes and rays can be seen across the water. Sometimes six-foot sand sharks get stuck in the tidal depressions and must wait for high tide to escape. The fifteen-mile-long, five-mile-wide bay is like a giant tepid bathtub during the summer, most of it shallow with a large deep channel leading in from the Gulf of Mexico.

We had a group of Earthwatch volunteers collecting horseshoe crabs, towing canoes over the two-foot-deep sand flats, searching for trails in the pitted sand. Periodically we would stoop and yank one of these hoary old living fossils out from their repose in the sand and dump it into the canoe. Horseshoe crab blood is being widely used in pharmaceutical institutions as an indicator of endotoxins, which are toxic products of some bacteria. Because endotoxemia is often a lethal disease, anything that goes into the human body must be certified free of this foreign substance.

The horseshoe crab blood is a sensitive indicator of endotoxins, clotting with the most minute concentrations. As a result, thousands of crabs were being harvested and bled around the Atlantic coast and then released. The blood, used to manufacture a test for endotoxins, is widely used in bioindustry and research. We were conducting a study, funded by the U.S. Food and Drug Administration, to see how well the crabs survived after being bled. Hence, half the creatures had a third of their blood drained out. All of them were tagged, measured, and released.

Now and then we picked up a crab that had a shattered shell that had healed and grown back together. I explained to our volunteers that it was probably bludgeoned by an irate commercial fisherman when it tangled up his net, and he tried to destroy it so he wouldn't catch it again. But the amazing clotting agents in the crab's blue blood kept it from dying. It congealed into a thick, sticky jelly that hardened with an epoxylike seal that prevented the crab from bleeding to death.

"Here's one that was bitten by a loggerhead sea turtle," I explained, holding up one with a big V-shaped plug bitten out of its carapace. The old wound had small purple-striped barnacles growing over the leathery scar tissue. "It was one of the lucky ones that got away. Most of the time turtles flip them over and tear out their gills and legs and leave only a hollow shell. There are a lot of big turtles in this bay."

That didn't make the two women who had just arrived from the Midwest for their first encounter with the wilderness coast of north Florida feel any easier. They were a little nervous, especially because walking that tideflat was something like a hike in a minefield. There were hundreds of stingrays. Often they radiated out before us, sent into flight as our shadows passed over them. "They're more frightened of us than we are of them," I said reassuringly. "Just move slowly, drag your feet along, and you'll flush them out of the sand." Sure enough, the diamond-shaped brown rays would emerge and glide gracefully over the sandy ribbed bottom and once again rebury themselves.

I didn't want to scare our new arrivals to death, but neither did I want them or me to make a rush trip to the hospital. The rays' "stinger" is a large hard movable spine made up of dentine, attached midway down their long slender tails. In some species it can grow to six or eight inches long, a veritable dagger, but in the small stingrays that abound on the tideflats of St. Joe Bay it was only an inch or two.

But that was long enough. If stepped on, the ray swings the tail over its back, inflicting a lacerating wound with its saw-edged spine, at the same time introducing venom through two long grooves. The result is agonizing pain, swelling, and a horribly slow-healing wound.

Over the years I have carried a number of people to the hospital screaming in pain, clutching their groins, as the lymph glands became inflamed. Few commercial fishermen along the coast haven't been stung by this otherwise unobtrusive fish at one time or another, inadvertently stepping on one while pulling a seine up on the beach or while taking it out of the net.

As we moved along, keeping an eye out for them, we pulled more horseshoe crabs out from the sand and tossed them into the canoe. Suddenly, right next to Conch Island, an old Indian midden overgrown with palms and marshes, something broke the surface. In that momentary glance I decided it wasn't a fish and probably was too big for a blue crab. Its movements were all too erratic.

Again the water was disturbed, the glassy sheet broken as something scaly and reptilian popped up and submerged.

Abruptly all the weariness of the weeks of collecting, bleeding, and tagging nearly ten thousand horseshoe crabs vanished. Before me was unquestionably one of the smallest sea turtles I had ever seen foraging on top of the sandbar in a foot of water. It looked almost small enough to be in the "missing year"-size category, the size at which their whereabouts are a total mystery. No longer did I feel the sunburn, the heat, the cumulative fatigue of working day and night with teams of volunteers, punching tags into scrabbling, pinching horseshoe crabs until our fingers were raw. This was a find.

I had to catch it.

I dropped the rope of the canoe and started rapidly sliding my feet over the sand, hoping to sneak up on it, trying to keep an eye on the bottom for stingrays. If I could get between the turtle and the deeper channel beside the sandbar, maybe I could maneuver it up onto the tideflat.

Several stingrays were disturbed and swept off over the tideflats like brown shadows. Several other stingrays unburied themselves, scurried off, and reburied a few feet away with only their eyes, spiracles, and part of their tail above the surface, otherwise blending all too perfectly with the bottom. Two or three flaps of the wings, and even these features disappeared beneath settling sand.

I was closing the distance, and still the little sea turtle hadn't noticed me. I knew it would, sooner or later, and I would have to make a flying leap to catch it. Then suddenly its dark head popped up, peered around warily, and the turtle became aware of me. It bolted, and I was after it at a dead run, hoping to cut off its direct route to deep water. If I failed to turn it, the chase would be over and this valuable turtle lost to science.

The thought vaguely entered my mind that if I ran fast enough, I could escape the lash of a stingray's tail if I stepped down on one. But instantly I dismissed that as nonsense. My mind flashed back to an incident years ago when I accompanied some boys on a "stingaree hunt." One young man took off after a large fleeing ray with gig in hand, trying to hurl it onto its back. Suddenly he leaped high in the air and landed with a big splash and a gut-wrenching scream. A small pale brown ray, one that totally matched the bottom, was attached to his foot by its

It was a baby loggerhead, the smallest I had ever seen.

three-inch serrated barb. We had to yank the ray off and listen to his scream all the way back to shore, and then to the hospital.

As I ran, I prayed to the Great Turtle Mother that that wouldn't happen to me. But I had no choice, turtles were part of my life. I got in front of the fleeing creature and cut it off from the channel. It turned, realizing that it was heading in the wrong direction. The little turtle arched around, desperately beating its yellow flippers, winging rapidly away from me, trying to get back to deep water. But I was right behind it, with dangerous leaping strides.

All thoughts of danger vanished when I got a good look at it. It wasn't the endangered ridley, born of Mexican shores, as I first thought. That would be a find in itself, but this turtle was even more valuable. It could help solve one of the greatest puzzles in biology, the mystery of the "lost year." It was a baby loggerhead, the smallest I had ever seen, distinct with its reddish-brown shell, yellow scaly flippers and head.

I put on a burst of speed. My quarry seemed to be tiring, but so was I. Running through water is exhausting, and I was panting and gasping. But the hunter instinct was upon me. As I sprinted to close the gap with the foot-long zigzagging turtle, a flood of thoughts went through my mind. Atavism—how many times had man found his dinner by leaping on a fleeing turtle and catching it with his bare hands? Then I was on top of the little loggerhead. I tried to push thoughts of belly flopping on a stingray out of my mind. I leaped through the air and landed with an explosion of water, felt myself come down hard on the sand, and felt my fingers close over the hard turtle shell. I felt the turtle trying to wiggle itself free, turning its head and trying to bring that sharp beak down on my fingers. With all my might I pressed it into the sand, leapfrogged ahead, and was on top of it.

I pressed my weight down to immobilize it, and then triumphantly lifted it out of the water. With a desperate slap, slap, slap, the little loggerhead flailed the side of its brown shell with its winglike flippers. Even though it was scarcely eight inches long, it wasn't easy to control. Again and again it tried to use its sharp jaws, hissing menacingly, ready with mouth agape, showing a pink tongue. The little loggerhead kept arching its head around, trying to bite me, and I was trying to keep my fingers clamped on the rear of its shell and not drop it. But no matter what it did, I wasn't going to let go.

I was exhilarated. It was possibly the smallest loggerhead on record in the Western Atlantic. Normally the only time one sees a turtle this size is when it's raised in an aquarium for a year. Where they live in nature is the great mystery.

By this time my helpers had shuffled over to see what their madman leader was doing. And the bright-yellow-skinned little turtle with its brown shell got an audience of "oohs and ahs."

"How very strange," June Keiser, one of our volunteers, commented as she came up to me towing the canoe, "we kept seeing you running, and then I saw you dive through the air. It didn't make any sense, knowing how shallow it is. Well now, now that you've caught this turtle, what on earth are you going to do with it?"

Gratefully I placed it in the bow of the canoe away from the pile of scrabbling, flexing, spiny horseshoe crabs.

As we headed back to camp, I explained why this turtle was such a find. Over the years scientists have carefully protected the eggs of nesting loggerheads on beaches throughout the Southeast, watching hundreds of thousands of three-inch-long hatchlings kick their way out of their sandy nests and frantically flipper their way down to the water's edge and disappear. They have protected the eggs from raccoons, chased off predatory ghost crabs, shooed the birds away, and prosecuted poachers. When the hatchlings hit the water they disappear and are not seen again until they're the size of a dinner plate, somewhat larger than the turtle I was carrying.

Professor Archie Carr of the University of Florida was the first to ponder this great mystery when he was a lone herpetologist wandering the Caribbean back in the 1930s. But now sea turtles have been "discovered," and there are armies of scientists and conservation groups roaming every turtle beach in the world, relocating eggs and tagging every nesting female that crawls ashore, and still most of the mysteries are unsolved, especially the missing year.

And that gap of time, from when the hatchlings first scurry into the surf until they're seen again by humans, isn't just restricted to green sea turtles at Tortuguero, Costa Rica, or Atlantic ridleys from Mexico. It's all sea turtles, all over the world. It's baby leatherbacks digging out of their nests on the black sandy beaches of Surinam, or Pacific ridleys in Sri Lanka, or green turtles in Hawaii, or baby hawksbills in New Guinea. No one knows where they go. They all crawl to the edge of the sea and vanish. The next time anyone sees loggerheads, they're about five times larger, weighing anywhere from thirty to fifty pounds. The big ones that come up on the beach to nest can weigh three, even four hundred pounds. But this one scarcely weighed more than two pounds, and to my knowledge it was the only one of that size thus far reported in American coastal waters.

Only in the Azores, smack in the middle of the Gulf Stream off the west coast of Africa, did anyone regularly find juvenile loggerheads this size. In fact, they were appearing in the nets of commercial fishermen there with such regularity that scientists at the National Marine Fisheries Service were beginning to believe that little loggerheads spent their lives in the eastern Atlantic, thousands of miles away from their natal beaches of the southeastern United States. And the so-called missing year may be far longer. They may spend up to five years drifting about in the North Atlantic gyre near the mid-Atlantic ridge and the vicinity of the Azores, feeding on jellyfish and other pelagic organisms. By the time they return to the American continental shelf and coastal habitats they are almost half-grown.

We triumphantly carried this missing-year turtle back to base camp, drilled a small hole in its shell, and shoved in one of the same tags we were using for horseshoe crabs. I told the volunteers what little I knew of the natural history of loggerheads. The Gulf of Mexico is not their primary habitat; there are far more of them along the southeast coast of

Florida. Nevertheless, right out in St. Joe Bay, during a particularly bitter winter of 1978, one shrimper dropped his nets down in the fifty-foot-deep channel and loaded down with loggerheads. He was looking for white shrimp, which aggregate in the muddy bottoms that are warmer than the surrounding water column. Instead he had a dozen turtles on board in a one-hour tow, and they tore his nets to shreds, so he left, pitching cold-shocked turtles overboard.

"Why do you suppose they bury up in the mud?" one of our team asked, after we carried the little loggerhead back down to the beach, watched it swim off with the yellow tag in its shell, and returned to tagging and bleeding horseshoe crabs.

"That's a good question," Anne replied, as she measured the carapace of a fighting, flexing crab. "No one really knows. At first scientists believed it was to get away from the cold. The mud is always two or three degrees warmer than the ambient temperature, but in Port Canaveral where the great concentrations of turtles are found, they bury in the summer as well as the winter."

"The shrimpers say they come in there to hide from sharks after they've been bitten or chopped up in a boat propeller," I added. "They say the mud helps heal their wounds, and they rid themselves of barnacles. Those anaerobic sediments will smother the barnacles in a few days, and then they'll drop off their shells when the barnacles are dead."

Several years ago when the South Florida Water Management District opened its control gates to prevent flooding after months of intensive rain, fresh water and heavy sediments roared out into the Atlantic and smothered coral reefs off Palm Beach. Up to three feet of mud settled over the bottoms, destroying coral and altering the ecological balance of the reef. However, divers observed a number of loggerheads moving in and burrowing into the mud that had never been there before.

Their attraction to mud was only one of the many unsolved mysteries concerning sea turtles. Dr. Joseph Kirschvinc at the California Institute of Technology Rock Magnetism Laboratory discovered a number of years ago that sea turtles, like a wide array of other migratory creatures including homing pigeons, porpoises, and yellowfin tuna, have ferromagnetic crystals in their brains. There are millions of them, so tiny that they can only be seen under an electron microscope, far smaller than the magnetic mineral grains in the electric ray heads. The crystals were first found in 1972 by Dr. Richard Blakemore at the Woods Hole Oceanographic Institution, when he was examining bacteria from marsh mud under a dissecting scope. He noticed that they persistently swam to one side of the microscope slide: north. Upon his rotating the slide, they moved back in the same direction. When he held a magnet over them, they rose up out of the sediments, and when he reversed the polarity they went back down.

He called them *Aquaspirillum magnetotactium*. They actually have built-in compasses, chains of internal submicroscopic ferromagnetic crystals that arc with the torque of the earth's magnetic field. The bacteria have an amazing ability to concentrate vast quantities of iron around their cell walls and to form them into perfect crystals of magnetite.

Because they are anaerobic bacteria, living in stagnant mud, exposure to oxygenated water means death. So if the bacteria are kicked up by wave action, they must get down to the mud or die. But they are too small to settle by gravity, so they follow the vertical component of the earth's magnetic field, in the Northern Hemisphere by swimming downward.

I couldn't help but wonder whether the loggerhead sea turtles, each one with its skull packed with millions of ferromagnetic crystals, were drawn to the mud by some magnetic response. Dr. Kirschvinc found the sediments often contain high levels of fossilized biogenic magnetite.

He also discovered that loggerheads migrate between magnetic anomalies on the seafloor. And although these "magnetic mountains" are the result of subsurface deposits of iron and not the residue of dead bacteria or magnetite-coated chiton teeth, they exert a profound influence on the movement of whales and sea turtles.

Fishery biologists have learned that loggerheads migrate northward following the Gulf Stream, veering away to their nesting beaches along the Florida, Georgia, and Carolina coasts.

They travel all the way up to New Jersey and New England waters to feast on horseshoe crabs and attack lobster traps, and before the cold weather comes, they return to the South. When the turtles are returning, swimming just inside the Gulf Stream, they navigate within magnetic corridors created by magnetic anomalies on the seafloor. These are areas of intense magnetic fields, several hundred times stronger than the earth's background magnetic field. They are called magnetic mountains because on a chart they look like concentric lines of a topographic map.

The turtles migrate along the magnetic minima, the weaker parts of the field, almost as if they were avoiding the stronger areas. And off the east coast of Florida, there are a number of magnetic hot spots that might have had some relation to the turtles' flocking into the Cape Canaveral shipping channel. When a shrimper from the Carolinas dropped his nets down into the busy Port Canaveral shipping channel in 1969 on one cold winter morning, he made scientific history and started a far-reaching controversy. His net came into contact with hundreds of loggerhead sea turtles, all but paving the bottom, one of the most unusual concentrations ever seen. For some unknown reason, they had gathered in the channel and dug down into the mud.

When the National Marine Fisheries Service learned there were hibernating sea turtles present, they declared the Port Canaveral navigation channel to be a critical habitat and closed it to shrimping. That made a lot of commercial fishermen angry because the channel's deep, relatively warm water was one of the few places where white shrimp could be caught in cold weather.

The concentrations of loggerheads that paved the bottom of the Canaveral channel became even more unpopular when their presence threatened to shut down the Corps of Engineers' channel maintenance program.

Suddenly, conservationists were locked in dispute with industrialist, shipping, and military interests. There were rumors of hundreds of loggerhead sea turtles being sucked up into the dredge, and we were rushed over to cover the story for *Sports Illustrated*.

With torturous metallic groans, the immense drag arms of the four-hundred-foot hopper dredge *Sugar Island* were lowered to the silty bottom of the Port Canaveral shipping channel. Pumps roared as the colossal seagoing vacuum cleaner began sucking up the fluid muck and speeding it through a twenty-four-inch pipeline into the middle of the ship.

Tim Claughborn, a graduate student, walked around the grated railings wearing ear protectors, intently watching for a glimpse of sea turtle remains amid the reeking, black slurry that formed and boiled in the hoppers. He had been hired by the National Marine Fisheries Service to determine the impact of the Corps of Engineers' dredging operation.

"Our final estimates of how many turtles are killed are going to be very conservative," he shouted above the screaming dredge pumps. "We know we're missing turtles. If you see a carcass, that's one. Two days go by and you find a flipper and intestines, that's two."

When the hopper was full of muck, the dredge moved off to the dump site five miles away, swilling its muddy cargo. After reaching its destination it stopped, and like a malignant black duck relieving itself, split open and squatted on the face of the sea. Abruptly, all the sludge dropped to the bottom, turning the water black and turbid. There was no telling how many shredded turtles went with it to lie on the mountain of silt as shark and crab food. Then it turned back for another load.

When the Corps of Engineers had announced plans to widen and deepen the channel, the National Marine Fisheries Service (NMFS) went into action. Charged with protecting marine endangered species, they promptly notified the Corps that the bottom was carpeted with threatened loggerheads, and it wasn't long before the Port Authority, the U.S. Army Corps of Engineers, and the U.S. Navy all wished they would go away, especially when NMFS prohibited any dredging.

The Corps had become increasingly sensitive to environmental issues, particularly ones involving endangered sea turtles. "If this were just a navigation channel and we knew all those turtles were there," Jon Moulding of the Jacksonville Corps' Environmental Branch had told us, "we probably would have delayed action. But this dredging was for national defense."

A giant basin was under construction to load and off-load missiles on Trident subs. The Navy wanted the channel cleared, and the Corps found itself between the military's rock and the Endangered Species Act's hard place. Meetings were held in Washington, letters were sent back and forth, and the dredging remained in limbo.

Finally, the argument of national defense prevailed. The Corps was given the go-ahead to dredge with the stipulation that if the dredge started killing turtles, they would have to shut down or hire a trawler to move the turtles out of harm's way. NMFS brought on observers to monitor the dredging.

Before long NMFS's worst fears were realized. Turtle parts appeared in the spoil overwash. Paul Raymond, another graduate student, photographed turtles torn in half and others with their shells cracked.

He photographed the drag arm raised out of the water with the front half of a big loggerhead hanging limply from the draghead's mouth. The dredge crew tried to help him pull it out to measure and describe, but the turtle was so tightly wedged that they had to give up. Down went the draghead, and once again the vessel rumbled as the six-foot-high pumps began roaring and the turtle was sucked through with the raging torrents of mud, blasted into the hopper, and lost in the morass.

Soon mutilated turtles began washing up on the beaches. Newspapers called it a scandal. PORT DREDGE KILLING TURTLES, read the headlines of Canaveral's *Today*.

The public outcry was becoming intolerable. Finally, a law officer from NMFS's Charleston office boarded the dredge and inspected the grisly remains. Then he climbed the metal steps that led to the wheelhouse, and there in the quiet air-conditioned instrument room, he explained the penalties for violations of the Endangered Species Act to the captain and first mate. The captain could be thrown into jail, the $30 million dredge could be confiscated, and/or the contractor could be fined up to $20,000 for each destroyed turtle.

Finally, the Corps' environmental division in Jacksonville ordered the contractor to hire a shrimp boat and get started dragging the sleeping turtles away from the dredge.

But finding a shrimp trawler for hire in Port Canaveral wasn't easy. At best, shrimpers are a tight-knit group, suspicious of outsiders and people doing anything but shrimping. They were still angry about the Canaveral ship channel's being closed to them because of the turtle concentrations. And few would risk their boats and gear dragging a channel full of hangs and snags—sunken barges, cables, and general debris.

Finally, Captain Glenn Buffkin came to the rescue. Weathered from years of standing behind the wheel of a seventy-five-foot shrimp trawler, *Miss Natalie*, Buffkin stood six feet tall, filling out his salt-stained blue jeans with muscle and resolve. Each evening he headed out into the busy channel with a boatful of government biologists, observers, and crew members—something few commercial fishermen would countenance.

As soon as Anne and I stowed our gear aboard, we could tell that it was going to be a very different trip from others we had taken. Glenn Buffkin was more open and talkative than most shrimpers. The Corps of Engineers had told him we were coming, and that was OK with him: we were just one more set of observers.

It didn't take long before we were talking about friends we had in common and about ports and bars. We discussed the conflict over the Canaveral channel and shrimping's being closed.

"Shrimpers don't think sea turtles are becoming extinct," he told us as we left the jetties behind and headed out into the rolling Atlantic. "No matter where they drag they catch one or two every now and then. Snapper fishermen see them in ninety feet on the hard bottoms, and swordfishermen see the little ones way out in the Gulf Stream floating in seaweed. No one wants to catch the doggone turtles," he said a shade defensively, "most shrimpers throw them back alive, but no matter how you try to save them, you drown one now and then."

I knew that the decision of whether a turtle lived or died was made by the captain and crew regardless of any laws and fines that might be imposed. At three o'clock in the morning, twenty miles off shore in rough seas, no marine patrol or Coast Guard officer would be there when a loggerhead or endangered ridley was plopped out on deck. For that reason, when my book *Time of the Turtle* was published, I solicited the aid of the Chelonia Foundation in Arlington, Virginia, to buy and distribute several hundred free copies from boat to boat along the Florida coasts.

"Got any good recipes?" one shrimper joked as he took his book. Overall, the reactions were positive. Shrimping is grueling work, dragging nets all night, culling shrimp, icing them, and working on torn nets. By day they sit at anchor, sleep, read and reread the same thumbworn girlie magazines and paperback novels. Almost any new book was welcome.

And the book paid off. "I want you to know you done good," another shrimper told me. "Last trip we caught three ridleys (the most endangered of all turtles) and we only ate one. We let the other two go, and that's real conservation. Before you come on the scene we would have butchered them all."

It was the best I could ask for. Little is known about turtles at sea, and I regarded the shrimpers as storehouses of untapped knowledge. It was unfortunate that so little rapport existed between them and the scientific community. Glenn Buffkin was one of the few men who bridged both worlds.

"When I heard the Army Corps wanted someone to drag these cooters out of the channel, I thought I'd check it out," he said as we cruised along.

He turned the wheel as the channel took a sharp turn, putting the trawler on automatic pilot. "I'd been fishing up in the Carolinas," Buffkin continued, "and was getting pretty tired of staying away from my family for nine months out of the year. It was a chance to stay home, so I give 'em a price and they took it."

"Why do you think there are so many turtles in this channel?" I asked him as we headed past the flashing buoys.

"I don't know. I've been shrimping for twenty years. Each year I work all the way from Charleston to Key West chasing shrimp. And I've caught turtles all up and down this coast. But not like this! Something draws them into this channel."

Some scientists believe the lack of current and sloping contour of the Canaveral channel draw in the turtles as they migrate along the coast. It is a man-made ditch, cut through a long barrier island, built in the 1950s. Unlike other channels on the south Atlantic seaboard, which are kept open by rivers flowing out to sea, no current comes from the Banana River into the Canaveral channel except what the Corps permits to escape through its gates when it locks barge traffic and light shipping in and out of the Intracoastal Waterway. Because there are no currents to keep the channel swept out, it acts as a sediment trap for silt carried down the Florida peninsula by longshore currents. Frequent dredging is required to keep the channel open.

Moving along rapidly was a large ship heading down the channel blowing black smoke. "Here comes the dredge," said Buffkin, while turning the wheel to edge us over to the side of the channel. "He dumped his load and is coming back for another. We'd better get out of his way 'cause he's a heap bigger than us." The *Sugar Island* traveled past at seven knots, throwing an enormous wake that made the rigging on the little *Miss Natalie* rattle and shake.

In spite of myself I was fascinated with this mud-sucking monster. With its screaming pumps, its slurping drag arm, and its belly that bulged with noxious-smelling mud, it seemed the crowning culmination of all machines that devour the earth.

"This job ain't as easy as some think," the captain said, adjusting the Fathometer that etched out a graph of the channel bottom. "You risk getting run over by tugboats and barges all the time. It's dangerous out here, a lot worse than regular shrimping. We have to stay right in the channel. When we first started, they made us stay right close to the dredge where the bottom was all tore up and full of mud lumps. One time we mudded down and caught the net in the wheel and almost went up on the jetties. A time or two when we bogged down in the mud, I thought we were going to get sucked into the dragheads. But now they

There were turtles here and turtles there, beating their flippers with fury and thunder and trying to bite.

let us drag up and down the channel, and we catch even more turtles and fewer get killed."

As the dredge disappeared from view, the crew set the sixty-foot otter trawl overboard. Brett Adkins, Buffkin's fair-haired teenage son-in-law, released the brake on the winch, and the two ironclad doors splashed into the sea dragging the funnel-shaped net behind it. With its especially equipped mud rollers, it trailed three hundred feet behind us swooping up everything in its path.

Buffkin towed for only thirty minutes, because longer drags might drown the air-breathing turtles. Some nights they caught only one or two a tow, such as bright moonlit nights when the turtles could see the

trawls coming. But on dark nights the *Miss Natalie* often bogged down in loggerheads.

"All right, boys, let's wind her up and catch us some cooters," the captain drawled when the alarm clock rang in the wheelhouse thirty minutes later.

Paul Brown, an observer for the National Marine Fisheries Service, and Larry Evans, the Corps' biologist, put down their notebooks filled with capture data and headed for the back deck.

The two crewmen, wearing yellow slicker suits, engaged the winch, and the old shrimp boat began vibrating as the drum spun around reeling in hundreds of feet of steel cable.

The otter doors rose from the dark, starlit sea and crashed together. Paul Brown looked down at the webbing that hung heavily down in the black water. "We either got a load of mud or a load of turtles."

Glenn hurried back to the stern and inspected his net. "We got 'em this time! We're flat loaded down with turtles."

The revolving brass cathead groaned; the blocks overhead vibrated as the hoisting ropes stretched under the strain. Slowly, inch by inch, the gorged net was raised out of the sea, showering water on the deck. There, veiled in the webbing, were yellow skins and barnacle-covered shells of loggerheads, too many to count.

There were turtles all the way from the bottom of the net to the very top, high above our heads where they hung from the lifting boom beneath the deck lights. Even in the pitching sea, with all the danger and strain on the blocks, they looked preposterous, like turtles roosting up in a tree.

Glenn didn't think there was anything funny about it. He braced himself and tried to grab the release ropes. But the rolling Atlantic snatched them from his hands as the immense, gorged bag rocked to and fro. All five men tried to tackle it, but with each roll of the sea it would wrench out of their hands and bash into someone.

"All right, let it down," Glenn shouted to Bobby, "before the damn thing kills someone."

The great webbed sock plopped to the deck with a squish, and the shadowy, bulky forms of turtles and fish looked out from the criss-crosses.

The captain put a whip line around the lower reaches of the net, gave a thumbs-up sign, and once again the machinery strained, lifting up a section. With violent snatching of the release ropes, the bag knot broke loose, and sea turtles tumbled out on the deck. There were turtles here and turtles there, beating their flippers with fury and thunder and trying to bite. And still more big hulking turtles toppled down from the wings and landed on top of each other. Some were caught sideways in the webbing, and Glenn had to shake them. Soon more turtles lay on deck.

The captain glanced up. "Oh, hell," he muttered, "here comes one of those Air Force tracking ships." Off in the distance was a stack of blazing lights. "OK, drop her out," he called as he ran back to the pilothouse.

Once again the nets splashed into the sea, and the drum spun madly as the cable whipped through the blocks and the *Miss Natalie* surged ahead.

"All right," Larry said, stepping over a barnacle-encrusted female and trying to keep his balance as the boat pitched and rolled, "let's do this in an organized fashion. Hey!" he called to Bobby, Glenn's sixteen-year-old son, who was dragging turtles out of the way and trying to shovel the trash fish off the deck. "Watch your leg." The deckhand glanced down and hastily moved away from a big three-legged male loggerhead lying on its back with its mouth agape. The jaws, capable of crushing through the armor of whelks and horseshoe crabs, snapped shut, missing him.

"So far no one's been bitten," Paul said reassuringly, "and we've had nearly a thousand turtles on the boat. One night one grabbed me by the boot, but all he got was rubber."

The newly arrived loggerheads first had to be tagged, measured, described, and weighed. Like a champion weightlifter, Paul used his girth to grab a turtle by its front and rear flippers and lift it up. Hastily Bobby affixed metal tags through the margins of each of its fore flippers with special heavy pliers. Calipers were used to measure the carapace.

Above the moan of the wind and the throb of the diesel, voices called out, "Tag Number AA308 and AA309, length 65.3 centimeters [25$\frac{7}{16}$ inches]; width, 28.5 [11$\frac{1}{8}$ inches]." Then Paul shouted out the description to Larry, who jotted it down on a clipboard.

The Canaveral Turtle Rescue Operation was providing an invaluable by-product of scientific information into the movements and behavior of turtles at sea. For years, all that scientists knew from breeding beach tagging is that sea turtles came ashore, laid their eggs, and disappeared back into the surf. Faithfully, a few returned two years later, often to the exact spot, to nest again. Almost nothing was known about the males or subadults, which never came ashore. Most of the turtles netted on the *Miss Natalie* were relatively small, averaging less than a hundred pounds. A few two- and three-hundred-pounders had been hauled aboard.

Weighing them was a major operation. One by one the angry, hissing, snapping turtles were encased in a webbed sack, and Glenn's crew members struggled to lift them up to the hanging scales. All the while the rolling Atlantic lifted the *Miss Natalie* up and dropped her down.

"Hold it! Hold it!" cried the Corps' biologist, throwing his clipboard aside and joining the rest trying to steady an encased turtle. It broke loose and swung around like a drunk punching bag, knocking Brett to the deck. He scrambled to his feet and tackled it. Paul hollered above the wind, "Weight 125 pounds. Let her down!" The turtle was gently lowered to the deck and dragged out of the way. "OK, bring the next one."

By the time they were finished, it was nearly time for the net to come up.

Brett sat wearily on the tail end of a large overturned female, resting his head in his hands and watching the towering lights of the tracking ship as it bore down on us.

Glenn was at the wheel, looking grim. "I'm fixing to get out of the channel," he declared, watching the four-hundred-foot military ship steaming straight at us.

As the titanic gray vessel passed in the night, bristling with antennae, cranes, and a huge radar saucer, sailors looked down at us from three levels of lighted staterooms. The loran plotter, which the Corps of Engineers had placed aboard the trawler to record where the turtles were taken, etched out a diagram of the *Miss Natalie*'s jog outside the buoys.

The captain breathed a sigh of relief when the ship had passed and teased, "I'd hate to catch that one in my net."

All through the long night, squeaking, groaning machinery repeatedly hoisted up another turtle-filled net until it too swung back and forth from the boom above the rolling Atlantic, showering marine life on the deck. Brett snatched the release ropes of the gyrating bag until it opened and disgorged its load yet again.

More and more large loggerhead turtles tumbled onto the deck amid avalanches of trash fish, flounder, crabs, and shrimp. They lay there, relics of the dinosaur age, forlornly waving yellow flippers. The deck lights gleamed off their belly shells, which expanded each time they filled their lungs with air and exhaled.

Like brown-shelled bulldozers, those that landed upright plowed their way through the pile of grunting croakers onto the paint-worn deck. The measuring and tagging resumed, but after six tows, there was no place to step. The deck had become a carpet of turtles. Finally, Larry Evans, the Corps biologist, declared, "OK, that's enough for one night. It's getting too rough to work."

With the nets aboard, the *Miss Natalie* surged forward, past the blinking sea buoys, unencumbered for the first time, plowing through the waves as if she were delighted to be rid of the burdensome yoke. It was time to set the tagged turtles free.

How unhappy and out of place those creatures looked sprawled all over the deck. They are cumbersome out of water. Even when the females go ashore to lay their eggs, they look awkward, breathing heavily, covered with sand, tears running down their faces. But underwater there is nothing to compare with a turtle's grace and beauty.

Several months earlier we had been diving with Norine Rouse, who operates a dive shop in Palm Beach, several hundred miles south of Canaveral. Almost every day for the past twenty years she has traveled out to the edge of the Gulf Stream and taken groups of divers down to count and observe sea turtles. The Stream comes closer to shore along the southeast coast of Florida than any place in the world. Off Canaveral it sweeps along sixty or seventy miles offshore, but at Palm Beach its blue transparent waters sometimes wash over the very beaches.

"Invariably the turtles show up on the north end of the reef and work their way down to the south, against the current," she told us as we headed out on her dive boat, *Loggerhead II*. "The loggerhead females come here in summer, usually from April to July, and the males come from December through February and then they leave.

The hawksbills always come a month later. Greens we see erratically, but no ridleys."

The cluttered shoreline of Palm Beach dropped away, and a vivid blue, blue sea with puffy white clouds appeared ahead of us. Right off the famous Breakers Hotel we splashed overboard for a drift dive in the Stream.

Down, down, down through the blueness we went, until the limestone coral outcrops eighty feet below reared up from the bottom. This was a very different environment from the coral reefs hundreds of miles to the south or the sea grass beds on the Gulf Coast. Here the coral was dwarfed: temperatures were too unstable to achieve reefs. But it was a fairyland nonetheless. As we were swept along in the Gulf Stream, Norine stopped to touch a spiny, yellow burfish. We had entered the underwater world, wearing compressed air on our backs, not as invaders, but as friends and observers.

Angelfish darted into crevices; mounds of brown lumpish stony coral and pink and yellow patches of soft corals carpeted rocky ledges. The swift current swept us effortlessly along, past lobsters crouching in their burrows with their antennae thrusting out. Yellow snappers schooled, moving against the flow, and green moray eels stared out from under the rocks. We were carried along by the moving Gulf Stream, covering more than a mile on a single tank until we approached a great loggerhead turtle that had wedged itself halfway under a limestone ledge. It raised its hoary old head and stared at us curiously. Its back was covered with moss, and a metal tag Number 5840 was embedded in its flipper. That told us that in all likelihood it was a female, because most of the turtles that are tagged are nesting females. We pulled her flipper out to get a better look at the tag, and scribbled the tag number down on our slates. Finally the great turtle grew annoyed with us and swam off. Later we learned that it was tagged on a nesting beach forty miles north of there at Hobe Sound two months earlier.

Norine knew many of the big loggerheads by the pattern of the barnacles on their shells and wounds from shark bites. When we surfaced, she remarked, "It's very rare for us to find tagged turtles. If we're lucky we see three a year. Last year was a bumper year for turtles. We saw a total of 143 loggerheads and only a couple had tags on them." She added, "I think tagging them makes them shy; they're much more reluctant to have humans come near them than untagged loggerheads. And how can you blame them?"

In the next five years, Norine found three turtles that had been tagged on the shrimp trawler off Canaveral.

Sitting on the deck of the *Miss Natalie*, watching the stars above and the lights of the Kennedy Space Center on shore, I reminded Anne of our Gulf Stream dive.

She shook her head in amazement. "There must be thousands of turtles out there. When you think of all the tagging programs on the Atlantic and Gulf coasts, the hundreds that are tagged each year on the beaches, all this work off Port Canaveral on the shrimp boats, and how few tag returns there are you realize how little we know about their populations."

As we headed five miles down the coast riding the Atlantic swells, I looked at turtles with flippers bitten off, or chunks of their shells gouged out, the tale of shark attacks. Paul pointed to a tarnished tag on a badly chewed smaller female. "This is an old friend, probably the third time I've personally caught her. Maybe 20 percent of the turtles we haul off and release turn right around and come back to the channel. We get some bad-looking turtles here. They get chopped up by boat propellers. Some of them look like the pirates attacked, but they're really tough."

All the turtles that came aboard that night were healthy, but periodically sickly, emaciated specimens were caught. Those who want to hasten the maintenance dredging at any cost claim that the channel has become a turtle boneyard; that they go there to die and it doesn't matter whether they drown in shrimp nets or are ground up in the dredge pumps.

But healthy and sick, large and small, there almost seemed to be a waiting list to get in. As fast as Glenn Buffkin trawled them up and hauled them away, new turtles arrived. I sat on the deck, buffeted by the early morning wind, watching the endless flat Florida shoreline glittering in the darkness like diamonds on black velvet, and pondered the puzzle. Never in all my years of knocking about the Gulf Coast and the southeastern Atlantic had I witnessed such quantities of turtles caught in shrimp nets. Even during the height of the breeding seasons off the Georgia coast, the most I witnessed was three or four turtles caught in a full night of dragging. Yet here each night the deck was covered with loggerheads. Sometimes thirty or more came up in a single tow.

Surveys were made up and down the Florida, Georgia, and South Carolina coasts looking for concentrations of hibernating turtles in the deep muddy channels. Nowhere, except in the Port Canaveral ship channel, did they find any. At first, scientists thought the turtles came to Canaveral to hibernate during the winter, but they found them in the summer too, buried in the mud.

Ahead of us was a submarine headed for the military base. With a light blinking from its mast pole like an evil red eye, the black sub moved past us in the night. I couldn't help wondering whether a man-made electronic device was drawing the turtles. Perhaps it was some low-frequency vibration coming from the submarine communications system or the Kennedy Space Center. We needed to find out, but nobody was talking.

And there was some evidence that it was just coincidental. Across the continent in the Gulf of California, on the Twenty-ninth Parallel, large numbers of torpid green turtles were discovered in the mud during one particularly cold winter. Cedar Keys, also on the Twenty-ninth Parallel on the Gulf Coast, is a picturesque fishing village that once supported one of the few commercial turtle fisheries on the Gulf Coast. Before it became illegal, fishermen caught greens, loggerheads, and ridleys in special wide-meshed turtle nets. In spring they caught the mud-encrusted turtles as they came out of hibernation.

It was all very perplexing. If one follows the Twenty-ninth Parallel across the ocean, one comes directly into line with the great pyramids of Egypt. As Cayman Island turtlers have remarked, "Green turtle very mysterious, mon"—by which they could mean any sea turtle.

The engine of the *Miss Natalie* slowed, and Glenn stepped out on the back deck. "OK, let's chuck 'em," he said with a yawn. "Another night, another load of cooters."

Happily, Brett grabbed up a turtle by its fore flipper and heaved it over the side. Then everyone joined in hurling turtles, one after the other. I stood on the railing, getting splashed, trying to absorb one of the weirdest sights of my life. Heavy-shelled, flippered reptiles sailing through the air out into the darkness: for a brief moment with their winglike forearms, they soared like birds, then landed like an avalanche of boulders.

When the deck was empty, we headed back to the Canaveral Harbor. Glenn Buffkin's gaze picked up the missile tracking ship moored at the Air Force base. "They're going to fire off a missile tomorrow night," he yawned. "That ship will be downrange to track it. You ought to hang around and watch it go. It's a pretty sight when it lights up the whole sky."

Suddenly, I was struck by the irony of all these ancient sea turtles dating back many millions of years, sleeping in the primordial mud at the foot of a space center. Probes for life elsewhere in the universe are launched from barren concrete slabs on what was once a mangrove swamp teeming with wading birds and aquatic life. Great numbers of these ancient reptiles nested on the sandy beaches then. Now a relative handful remain. And yet, the great sea turtle rescue operation was a success. After great effort the dredging equipment was eventually modified so that it kills far fewer turtles. Maybe the worst is over in Canaveral and the long climb back for sea turtles lies ahead.

The Corps of Engineers' turtle clearing project was deemed a success. By the time the dredge sucked up its last cubic yard of muck a month later and steamed away, the *Miss Natalie* had caught and relocated 1,249 sea turtles. Fewer than a hundred had been destroyed by the dredge.

Eventually the U.S. Army Corps of Engineers switched to a clamshell dredge, which cut the mortality down to almost nothing.

In the years that followed, the tag recoveries showed two patterns of behavior: local turtles that bred and nested on nearby beaches of the Canaveral National Seashore and Merritt Island Wildlife Refuge, and long-range recoveries of migratory turtles that worked their way up to the coasts of North Carolina and Virginia to breed, no doubt following the Gulf Stream. Very few returns came from south of Canaveral, perhaps because no shrimping industry existed to the south and the opportunity for recapture was much less.

Results from tagging studies are slow coming in. They come from a shrimp boat here, a nesting beach there. The sea works against the metal on the tags, and many fall off. But every return is a nugget of information helpful in piecing together the movements and migrations of these mysterious creatures.

With the observers, charter fees, special nets, and navigation equipment, the Corps spent several hundred thousand dollars to minimize the destruction of an endangered species.

Maybe that little loggerhead we caught in St. Joe Bay would grow up someday and reproduce. Four months after we released it, it was recaptured exactly in the same spot where I first ran it down, off the old Indian midden island. We received our makeshift horseshoe crab tag in the mail: the mullet fisherman and his wife who caught it said the tag fell out in the net, and they turned the turtle loose. Somewhere along the great wilderness coast of west Florida, it may still be out there.

9. Trail of the Spiny Lobster

We launched our small aluminum skiff in Key West, headed out into the Gulf. It was hard to believe that these tropical waters with their sea grass meadows and patch reefs were all part of the same Gulf of Mexico as our windswept pine-forested shores at home. Instead of the open expanses of marshes found in the Panhandle, the shoreline was a walled horizon of red and black mangroves with tangles of prop roots. And the sea was filled with colorful tropical creatures that loved clear sunlit waters and couldn't abide our harsh winters, muddy oyster reefs, and estuaries.

The Florida Keys are a crescent of fossilized Pleistocene islands and reefs. The concave side holds back the green waters of Florida Bay and the Gulf of Mexico. The convex side is the rolling Atlantic bounded by the ever-flowing Gulf Stream. It is this giant ocean river, fifty miles wide and fifteen hundred feet deep, that brings tropical warmth to these waters and allows living coral reefs and all their biological riches to flourish. We had reached the only piece of tropical reef in the continental United States and the southern boundary of the Gulf of Mexico. For twelve hours we had bounced along interstates, making our way down from Florida's Panhandle past the crowded interchanges of Orlando and Miami.

But at the sight of the blue tropical waters, the great patches of limestone and coral, the mangrove swamps and sea grass beds, our road weariness disappeared. Even with the commercialization of the Keys in recent years, there is still magic in this tropical fringe. Enormous bridges, one seven miles in length, connect the islands where currents race between the Gulf of Mexico and the Atlantic.

We had come to this ocean paradise to search for baby spiny lobsters, which we planned to take back to our laboratory in Panacea. It was a test program, to see whether they could be commercially grown, for Florida crawfish are among the most sought-after of the seas' wealth.

Each year over 5 million pounds are landed from Miami to Key West, a dockside value of nearly $12 million.

We had timed our visit to meet the baby lobsters as they came swimming through the island passes. Every month they sweep through the gaps along with bits of sea grass, sargassum weed, pulsating jellyfish, and boards covered with gooseneck barnacles. The force of the currents between the islands is strong. The water shoots through like a river in flood, spinning off whirlpools.

Today, we were searching for some of the few remaining "Witham habitats" to find larval lobsters. Years before, Ross Witham and nine state biologists discovered that hanging squares of Nomad or artificial turf on buoys fooled the larvae into thinking they were hiding in mats of algae so that they took refuge in them in large numbers.

The flood of new baby lobsters is pumped up by the Gulf Stream, probably from the reefs of Honduras, Yucatán, and limestone outcrops far out in the Gulf of Mexico. Like most marine organisms, the lobsters begin life as microscopic floating eggs swept along in an unending plankton soup. The creatures number in the billions of trillions: copepods, tiny jellyfish, radiolarians, fish eggs, and so on. Among them are spiny lobsters that have undergone twelve very different stages of metamorphosis, changing forms and shapes as they are carried by the currents through the Caribbean for almost a year before they turn into tiny lobsters.

Under a microscope the newborns look like transparent spiders with monstrous jaws. As they rise to the surface, waving their froglike legs, they are scattered by surface currents. By day the tiny lobster larvae sink several hundred feet down into the greenish-blue depths. Then, as the last rays of light fade, they kick their way upward to the surface amid the luminescent protozoans and diatoms. When the sun rises above the horizon, the spidery little waifs submerge again into the cold deep abyss.

For most coastal fishes and invertebrates the ocean is an impossible barrier, the distances too vast for larval stages to survive thousands of miles of ocean-current travel. Most of the shallow-water forms, like oysters and shrimp, must complete their larval stages in a few weeks and hurriedly rejoin the community of their birth or be swept to oblivion. But not the spiny lobster. It rides the Gulf Stream, the great oceanic highway, along with schools of sailfish, yellowfin and bluefin tuna, swordfish, sharks, marlin, and sea turtles to their little-known destinations.

As the months pass, the lobster larvae develop, all the time adding mouthparts and digestive organs to their fragile bodies, sensory hairs, and muscles. Moving in the Stream, or entrapped in the huge circular eddies that spin off in the Gulf of Mexico and out in the Atlantic, they live in a world of high mortality. From birth, untold thousands are devoured by ravenous arrowworms, each scarcely a tenth of an inch long. Anchovies, the equivalent of m to the microscopic lobsters, dart through the plankton, their mouths open, straining them out. Larval kingfish and tarpon, with dazzling silver bodies, enormous teeth, and gleaming green eyes, snap them up one after the other. Billions of larvae are born and billions die within a few hours or days after their creation.

To many of these developing tropical animals, the Gulf Stream may be a streetcar to oblivion. There is no telling how many bright shiny tropical creatures meet an icy death out in the North Atlantic. But for a vast amount of life including huge pelagic sharks, whales, and big game fish, the Gulf Stream serves as an ocean highway.

Yet every year the deep reefs off North Carolina are repopulated with tropical larvae swept up from Florida, perhaps from the Gulf of Mexico. Mixed in with the queen angelfish, and other hardy tropical animals living at the extreme edge of their geographic range, are a few spiny lobsters. North Carolina is probably the only place where both tropical spiny lobsters and New England clawed lobsters live in close proximity. In many ways it is a mixing zone between northern temperate fauna and southern tropical forms.

The Gulf Stream flows around the Atlantic in a giant clockwise gyre, spurred on by the trade winds. Its center is the Sargasso Sea, which is lighter, higher water—at least one foot higher than the surrounding ocean. The stream runs around it like water circulating around an upturned bowl.

It takes about nine months for the current to complete the cycle, about the same time it takes for a spiny lobster to grow from egg to the advanced larva stage.

As we saw the buoys growing larger on the horizon, we hoped that we had picked the right time to come. The collectors floated at the surface, or just under the water. The Witham habitats had been in the water for a year now and were so encrusted with seaweed, sea squirts, trumpet worms, and the like that it took both of us to hoist one into the boat.

Every new moon, a new flood of baby lobsters leaves the Gulf Stream and swims into the dense matrix of prop roots and waxy leaves of the red mangroves. Throughout the mangrove coast of the southern Gulf and from the wilderness shores of the Everglades and the Ten Thousand Islands north, they pour in. Whether the lobster larvae come from far Caribbean islands or the fossilized reefs of the Florida Middle Grounds ninety miles west of Tampa is unknown.

Although from time to time the tiny transparent larvae appear as far north as Tampa Bay, and may even drift into Florida Panhandle waters, their northern appearances are rare. Florida Bay and the Everglades are their habitat, amid the mangroves and the turtle grass beds.

No longer microscopic and spiderlike, the larvae are pushed by the tides, driven by the winds and currents through the island passes. Three-quarters of an inch long, these crystal-clear lobsterettes have elongated shrimplike bodies and well-developed legs. With their antennae stretched out before them like spears, they swim strongly, forever heading toward the estuaries, moving against the swift tidal currents like salmon swimming upstream. No longer planktonic animals, they are ready to make contact with the right object, be it a mangrove prop root covered with red algae, a buoy, or a wharf piling heavily fouled. Bushy red algae is the key: they seek out clumps of it and hide.

Danger is all about them, as swarms of squid, mangrove snappers, grunts, and speckled sea trout roam the waters. Many who have survived all those months in the plankton are snatched up even before they make it through the passes. But by daylight the survivors have found refuge in the dense forests of algae. They cease eating at this stage of their life cycle. They are designed to swim, streaking forward at the rapid rate of a foot a second.

Anxiously we approached the first weathered buoy of the Witham habitats, overgrown with barnacles, hydroids, and algae, and with our combined weights and lots of grunts and groans, we hoisted the water- and mud-sogged collecting device into our boat and flipped through the "pages."

And what a collection of life abounded in those sheets of woven fabric! Flattened porcelain crabs, purple with white stripes all over their bodies, darted away to cover. Ruby-red cleaning shrimp with bright candy-cane stripes rained out from between the pages, and we eagerly grabbed them up to take back to our laboratory. Pink and yellow snapping shrimp were there also, not the drab green and brown species that one finds in north Florida, but living jewels of the tropics. There were hairy orange brittle stars and large tube worms that made spirallike tubes of calcium carbonate plastered to the collector, along with an amazing number of clams that attached with byssus threads. We delicately picked out golden arrow crabs with long spines protruding from between their eyes, and scraped off a treasure of orange, red, blue, and golden sponges that encrusted the pages of the collector.

"Look at this," I said, pointing to a large spiny oyster, *Spondylus*, that adhered to the woven mat with a thick calcium secretion. "I thought it took years for them to reach this size and that they grew slowly. But here they are only a few months since they were planted and they're almost full-grown. Isn't it amazing how fast mollusks can pull dissolved calcium carbonate out of the water and turn it into structure?"

Anne was less enthusiastic as she scrutinized the pages of the book, observing the mats of bryozoans and clumps of white sea pork. "The only things missing," she said glumly, "are the lobsters."

We dropped it back down with a splash and steered our boat to the next buoy.

It was equally heavy and should have been loaded with larvae, but again all we found were red cleaning shrimp hopping about, unhappy brittle stars, and more flattened porcelain crabs disturbed by the light and exposure, frantically trying to run away, but no lobster larvae.

"Maybe the moon isn't right," moped Anne, "or the leaves aren't attracting the right kind of growth this time of year."

"They're supposed to catch year-round," I said. "Let's keep looking."

We moved on to the next, and the next, hoisted them into the boat, shook them vigorously over a dip net, and finally we found our first baby lobster. It looked like an oversize grass shrimp. By the time we had run all fifteen traps, we had collected a grand total of six.

We examined our six little PLs (as the puerulus stage larvae are known) with disappointment. We needed several hundred to take back and put into our tanks. If a large dependable supply could be found, there was a chance the mariculture project might succeed. Raising PLs into mature lobsters is a far simpler problem than trying to keep the earlier stages alive as plankton.

When they undergo their last molt and enter the bays, they become tolerant of lower salinities, variable temperature, and silty water that would be lethal to the younger phyllosome larvae. The puerulus larvae can be raised to mature lobsters ready for the pot in two years or less.

Not bad considering the lobsters of New England, where people talk in terms of five years before a harvest can be made.

"We're not going to get the PLs here," Anne said, inserting the oxygen hose into the bag of larvae and inflating it. "We'll have to start looking in seaweed and other places. Maybe we ought to try the boat basin in Key West. They say that up to two hundred have been caught in a single night."

"Well, we're here, so let's go and try to find some juveniles at least, some very young ones, and take them back and see what kind of growth we get," I said, trying to sound encouraging. "Maybe we'll get lucky and see some PLs hiding in the algae mats on the bottom."

We dropped anchor where the current wasn't too swift, put on our scuba tanks, masks, fins, and snorkels and dove into the warm blue waters, a short distance from a mangrove island where large white herons meandered along the shore looking for minnows.

Over the side we went, into the familiar shallow world of waving green sea grass meadows, sponges, and tall purple trees of soft coral. Through our masks we viewed a patch reef rising up from the bottom like a miniature mountain in twenty feet of water with swarms of brightly colored festive reef fish spinning and flashing about it.

In an effort to find tiny lobsters, we turned over every clump of algae, looked beneath every rock. I all but stood on my head to view the underside of a coral head and suddenly found myself inspecting the dentition of a huge black-and-white reticulated moray eel. Somehow I managed to perform a semi-backflip out of there and saw Anne's derisive grin through her mask and snorkel. The large moray hung half out of his den, regarding us malevolently, continuously opening and closing his huge jaws in a silent eerie warning display.

We moved away and swam to another coral head a hundred yards away, a large intricately patterned chunk of brain coral. Some of these big mound-building corals have grown slowly for centuries, biologists had learned by coring them and examining growth rings. It is the soft-bodied polyps that are the architects.

Around the rock and coral edges, black sea urchins, *Diadema antillarum*, vigorously waved their long needle-pointed spines as we approached, keeping us at bay like antiaircraft guns. Moving around them was a hazardous undertaking because the spines produce extremely painful wounds. Carefully we examined every spot before

I suddenly found myself inspecting the dentition of a huge black-and-white reticulated moray eel.

placing a hand on it. But they are one of the protectors of lobsters, who can hide among them with impunity.

Slowly we made our way over the grass beds, half-crawling and half-swimming, parting the dense strands of turtle grass hoping to see the antennae of transparent shrimplike lobsters. They were probably there; it's just that our eyes were not trained to find them. Multitudes of creatures hide down in the turtle grass. With their broad leaves and rhizomes, this flowering plant traps sediments and detritus and provides a food base for everything else. With plenty of sunlight for photosynthesis, the sea grasses grow and grow until wave action eventually tears them off and sends them drifting out into the ocean, sooner or later to pile up on beaches and rocks, decompose, and recycle their nutrients back into the bay.

It is called turtle grass because green sea turtles love to graze on it, munching away like cows with specialized serrated jaws. From the clear horizonless waters of the Ten Thousand Islands below Naples to St. Marks far up into the Panhandle, one of the world's largest submarine meadows of sea grasses abounds in shallow water less than thirty feet deep. In addition to turtle grass, it also includes Cuban shoal grass and manatee grass. If there is a true cradle of life, it is the grass beds. For here life not only envelops the blade of grass, but heavily encrusts it with tubes of calcareous serpulid worms, bryozoans, and algae. Down among the protective network of roots dwell sea worms, tiny clams, and other burrowing animals. Giant conchs graze the turtle grass meadows as well.

As we swam about in the clear shallow waters there was a scattering of small fish that seemed to follow us, picking at the organisms we dislodged in the grass. Two small barracuda watched us curiously, but there wasn't much else to be seen.

Then out of nowhere another barracuda materialized. At least eight feet long, a silver and black torpedo, it swept around us twice and disappeared. Anne looked at me with eyes that reflected my own alarm, and quickly we moved closer together. Then it was back, circling us from about a hundred feet, coming perceptibly closer on each pass. Its wonderful set of teeth held my attention. Holding our diving knives before us, we were fully aware that they would be almost as much help as a baby's rattle if it decided to strike. Then it was gone again.

Anne waved to a coral head, and we swam to it and huddled under an overhang. Suddenly I saw the world as a lobster crouching in its den might see it: defensively. But I wasn't a lobster. If the fish pinned us there too long, we'd run out of air. I checked my gauge; there was still 1,000 pounds of pressure, and Anne was at 1,200 pounds per square inch (psi).

Five minutes and still no barracuda. That one must not have read the books that say barracudas don't attack, but only follow from a safe distance. Anne pointed to another patch reef that was closer to our anchor line. I nodded and we swam for it. Still no barracuda. We watched there for another minute. No fish.

A little way beyond, the anchor line reached to the boat and our world. The water that had seemed crystal clear now seemed like a dangerous blue fog. Then one more long swim and we were back at the boat and in.

"Well, now what do we do?" Anne yelled, unstrapping her tank.

"What do you mean, 'what do we do'? We pull anchor and leave," I said, already snatching it up.

We sped off, the green meadows beneath the hull racing past. On the other side of the mangrove island, I cut the anchor. "What do you think?"

"I think we need lobsters," Anne said. "Besides, that was a territorial display. If he was hungry, he would have just struck. Instead he let us know that he was there and we were trespassing. He's still back where we left him. Who knows, maybe he's feeling very pleased with himself. Let's go get some lobsters."

We anchored, put on our tanks, and dove in again. After a moment Anne began waving me over to her. And there they were, a cluster of long, spiny, waving antennae emerging from a multicolored sponge-encrusted cement block. There must have been twenty little lobsters, six inches or less in length, packed into the discarded block that someone had once used to anchor Witham habitats. Lobsters that couldn't squeeze in crouched against the sides. As we watched, a small French angelfish moved over from another block and entered the den. This generated some shifting around, after which the fish was evicted and retreated to its original block. That cinder block, though apparently identical to the one serving as a den, was shunned by the lobsters.

The spiny lobsters were brownish in color and had none of the bright markings of the adults. One came out to investigate us, bolted backward, and vanished into the grass before we could bring our dip net down on top of it. We caught the rest and swam on but failed to find others.

If one had to depend on wild stocks of tiny lobsters to harvest from the grass beds to grow to maturity, it would be hopeless. The more we swam about, the more we were discouraged about the entire idea. We would have to become at least as good as the multitudes of fish and crabs that dine on these tasty crustaceans.

The little lobsters are also voracious predators, stealing out of their hiding places at night, pouncing on worms and minuscule clams, unmercifully tearing them apart with their powerful little pincers. Nighttime was probably the best time to be looking for them, when they roamed among the pink sea urchins that graze on the encrusting algae that grows on grass blades.

All these creatures, the queen conchs, the big lumpish brown sea cucumbers, the barracuda, the wrasses, and lobsters depend on these dense strands of submerged flowering grasses. Yet few actually eat it. Hordes of little shrimp are there, bright green and camouflaged so perfectly that they escape all notice. Only by sweeping our dip nets through the grass, lifting the nets out of the water, and examining the strands against the small mesh webbing, did we find any. Only now and then,

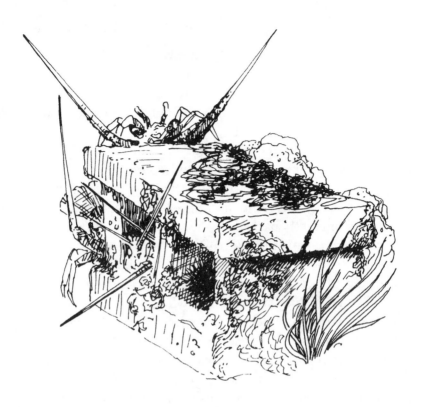

There they were, a cluster of long, spiny, waving antennae emerging from a multicolored, sponge-encrusted cement block.

nestled down among the leaves, flipping madly and trying to escape, was there another lobster.

We sighted a number of larger lobsters, but they were bigger than what we were looking for, what the fishermen and the law call "shorts," with a carapace under three inches. We wanted only the very little ones.

For two years after the larvae first arrive in the grass flats, the little lobsters spend their lives in the protective shelter of the turtle grass, foraging among the tangle of mangrove roots and flats at night, bunching together in dens by day. Being social creatures, a dozen or more cluster together beneath coral heads.

Swimming along, we came upon more of these living mountains of coral with their feathery sea whips and schools of brightly colored fish. Abruptly the carpet of grass ends and is replaced by a zone of coarse coralline sand mixed with shell rubble and the majestic living rocks themselves. There, crouched down beneath the base in caves, were the antennae of large spiny lobsters, much too large for our research.

This barren fringe of sand, shell, and fragments of algae surrounded the reef like a moat. Seen from above, flying near Key West, the "fish haloes," as they are called, are obvious. They are caused largely by long-spined purple sea urchins and fish cropping away at the grass and algae. When they leave the protection of their rocky crannies they seldom venture far as they move out into the open. The urchins emerge from beneath the crevices of the coral to gnaw at the algae during the night and return when the first rays of daylight penetrate the sea. In the daytime, their enemies—the triggerfish and parrot fish that can snatch them out by their spines, flip them over, and tear into their soft undersides—are on the prowl.

Yet *Diadema* is a great protector of the little lobsters. They crouch among the spines without harm while a prowling barracuda hovers nearby, unable to get at them. Sometimes we dislodged the urchins and scattered the little lobsters to catch them. But often the urchins were too thick, adhering to the rocks. The young lobsters moved back amid the spines, knowing we could not follow.

We spotted what looked like a dead lobster washing back and forth in the wave surge. We knew that it was an empty carapace and that somewhere in the inner reaches of the den one of the lobsters had just molted.

Small lobsters like these molt more frequently than adults, shedding their small shells at least once a month. It is a slow process, leaving the lobster at its most vulnerable. Any fish or crab, or creature of any sort, no matter how small, becomes a menace when the lobster peels out of its shell, soft as a jellyfish, nearly helpless and capable of only the feeblest movement. The molting process begins when the lobster absorbs water. Then, between the joints of the thorax and abdomen, it splits apart, and the large flabby crustacean emerges. It hides deep in the inner caves, protected by the thorny antennae of the other lobsters that look outward, hardening its forming new shell as fast as it can. Usually only an hour or two passes before the newly armored lobster is tough enough and strong enough to reemerge.

Behind the coral head, an almost legal-size lobster ventured curiously to the mouth of its lair and looked boldly at us.

That was the only legal one with a three-inch carapace we saw on the reef. All the larger ones had been stripped out. Every year during July, the state of Florida permits a special recreational lobster season that we had come to call "Lobstermania." Fifty thousand people swarm down to these limestone rocks known as the Florida Keys, cram the highways, restaurants, and motels, and pile into boats to roam the reefs. The value to the local economy is beyond estimation, but it is devastating to the lobsters. If the lobsters that are harvested in Florida had to replace themselves, instead of getting larvae from afar, the fishery would have been long gone, stripped out by overharvesting.

Not that many Florida crawfish ever manage to reproduce. Virtually every spiny lobster that survives its predators and grows to legal size ends up in a wooden slatted lobster trap, according to biologists at the Florida Department of Natural Resources. Wherever you go in the Florida Keys, with the exception of the Everglades National Park, the Looe Key Sanctuary, and the Fort Jefferson National Monument, the ocean is peppered with buoys.

One old fisherman told us, "Twenty years ago there used to be about forty or fifty fishermen down here who made a good living fishing. But now there are five hundred and each one has about two hundred traps." And the state's biologists support this statement. In 1968 there were 90,000 traps, by 1975 there were 500,000, and by the mid-1980s there were more than a million traps.

Amazingly, we learned from fishery biologists that the landing of roughly 5 million pounds over the years has remained stable. But the "catch per unit effort" has greatly declined. Fishermen are using more, bigger, and faster boats and are covering more territory than ever before while saturating the sea with traps. It takes more effort and energy to produce the same amount as before. And, of course, the price is higher.

As we turned over rocks and concrete blocks and looked over log-gerhead sponges while finding only an occasional small lobster, I couldn't help recalling the days when we made routine collecting trips to the Keys and saw an ocean full of waving whiskers that once carpeted the seafloor. Now, at the end of the lobster season, there were only a few undersize ones that were hanging on, dodging traps and divers.

It was hard not to come across a lobster trap while swimming because they crisscrossed the bay. Often there would be a number of small lobsters imprisoned inside with their antennae protruding from the slats. Only some of them may have crawled in there of their own volition; the rest were jammed in. With so many traps being set, there wasn't enough bait available. Fishermen had learned that putting a small live lobster into the trap would attract others and used them as lures until they starved to death.

We had made a modest start on collecting postlarval and juvenile lobsters to begin our aquaculture experiments. We returned to the boat, I cranked the motor, and we started forward through the chop. It was time to leave.

We headed back to shore to rest before meeting with another biologist who would take us out later for a night dive. Were the little lobsters we took adding to the problem or perhaps helping to solve it in the long run? Someday, if the fishery could be managed and the habitats protected, we would once again see forests of waving lobster antennae protruding from every rock and ledge. After all, a million eggs is a lot of eggs.

10. Octopuses I Have Known and Loved

We couldn't have asked for a calmer, safer ocean as the twenty-four-foot charter dive boat sped over the glassy waters beneath starlit skies. The mangrove islands of the shoreline disappeared behind us, and soon we were out at sea about to explore the living coral reefs off the Florida Keys.

The purpose of our dive was twofold: to see whether there was a "premigratory buildup" of spiny lobsters, and to look for several octopuses to take back to our laboratory. We were far more likely to see these nocturnal animals on a night dive. By day, they remain hidden in dens in the rock.

For the past ten years, Anne's former mentor Dr. Bill Herrnkind had been studying the bizarre migrations of the spiny lobster. Anne had traveled to Bimini with him and other students aboard the Florida State University research vessel *Tursiops* to witness the odd migrations called "marches" in which spiny lobsters move over the seafloor in single file, sometimes in the thousands.

Although such migrations had been observed in Mexican waters, in other parts of the Caribbean, and occasionally in Florida waters, it was best known off the coast of Bimini, where it usually occurs in the fall of the year as the first cold fronts come sweeping down and spread their chill into the shallows. The lobsters begin to assemble, massing together and milling about, the great mobilization before the march.

Swaying back and forth on their long jointed legs, they finally leave their lairs and march together in single file from two to sixty lobsters at a time. Over the featureless sand bottom and patch reefs they go, the antennae of each overlapping the tail of the one in front. They march for miles in an undulating chain that looks like an enormous bristling serpent marching day and night. Exactly why they do this is a great mystery.

They are not sexually reproductive animals about to shed their eggs or mate. Most of them are late juveniles or recently matured animals.

Few creatures attack the formidable marching crustaceans. The chains stop periodically, and the lobsters form a defensive circle with all sharp antennae facing outward. And then the march continues. Over the horizon they go, down the edge of the Bahama Bank to the warmer waters of the Gulf Stream.

For several weeks before the actual migration begins, the lobsters pack together in certain ledges and dens in the coral. As many as twenty to thirty may crowd together in a spot that would be ignored at any other time of the year. This premigratory buildup is the best indication of migration about to begin, and Bill Herrnkind asked us to check for it while we were in the Keys.

It was four miles offshore to those reefs at the edge of the Gulf Stream. By day you could see them rising up like fingers from the bottom. But at night we had to rely on the Fathometer to find them. Jerry Caldwell, the captain, watched his loran flashing out numbers marking our position. "We should be right on top of it," he said uneasily, but the Fathometer still etched out a flat straight line that indicated sand bottom. Then abruptly the graph began to rise. We had found live reef bottom.

Suddenly a ghostly yellow loggerhead sea turtle popped up in front of our bow and loudly expelled air from its lungs, a fellow air-breather in that watery world. There was a large white barnacle on top of its scaly head, and the turtle watched us through wise old eyes. The top of its brown barnacle shell emerged briefly from the blue water. Then it vanished.

"They always say a loggerhead will mark a reef," I remarked, "and there's proof. Back in the days before electronic positioning equipment, the old snapper fishermen looked for schools of fish and watched for sea turtles to come up. They found the rocks that way."

The captain studied his notebook and nodded with satisfaction at his loran that was flashing our exact position on the earth in illuminated digital numbers. "We're right on the money. I'll stick to my newfangled equipment, thank you."

With a noisy rattle of chains, the anchor plummeted out of its chute, and Jerry backed down hard until the hook caught in the sand. "We always make sure we avoid anchoring on the reef itself," he explained. "Don't want to damage the coral."

We put on scuba gear and dropped over the side together with several local divers who were familiar with the reefs.

Pulling ourselves down the anchor line through blue oceanic water, we passed through schools of flashing silvery minnows, so thick they looked like a solid wall. Golden amberjack swam above us, inspecting these peculiar intruders with black rubber skins and plumes of bubbles that flattened like silver jellyfish as they rose to the surface.

Down, down through the black waters we went until the lantern on the surface disappeared from view. Slowly but spectacularly the living reef rose up before our dive lights. The massive stony bastions marked the true underwater limit of the Gulf of Mexico. Beyond the reefs were the cold black depths of the Atlantic Ocean.

Nothing is more beautiful and more exciting than a night dive in the tropics. We were at one end of a rock ledge and planned to work our way up its spine. The lights of the other divers showed like fires blazing in the warm clear waters. When we encountered a solitary lobster out foraging, we cut off our lights and watched it in the dim glow of a single red light. Many crustaceans do not see by red light and are undisturbed by it.

In the darkness plankton flashed all around us like a sky full of stars. Every move we made was outlined in blue bioluminescence. And with a ghostly glow of diffused light our exhaust bubbles rose to the surface. The lobster sat there patiently sieving sand for small worms, clams, or whatever else was edible. And when we finally turned our lights back on, we attracted minute crustaceans and glittering tiny red and blue fish that flashed around the beam like bugs orbiting a streetlight.

There was no way this quest could fail for we had already found the mystery and beauty of the reef at night. We could just sit here making the water glow with blue fire by waving our hands, disturbing the plankton and the twirling sea walnut jellyfish sweeping by in the current.

To me they were among the most beautiful creations in the ocean; not even diamonds and faceted stones could compare with living ctenophores. For in the daylight they caught the white light from the sun's rays, refracted it with their interminably working zipperlike comb plates, and broke it into a spectacular changing array of greens, reds, blues, yellows, and pinks. By night the beating zippers phosphoresced into a cold blue fire when I touched them. For all we understood, these watery blobs of jellyfish could be disembodied souls moving free and

Swaying back and forth on their long jointed legs, the spiny lobsters leave their lairs and march in single file over the featureless sand bottom, each one's antennae overlapping the tail of the one in front.

radiating light. If water is the essence of life, then these watery jellyfish and their kin are the epitome of life itself.

By day the coral reefs that bound the Gulf of Mexico are among the most impressive creations of the ocean world, mighty stone fortresses of elkhorn and staghorn coral reaching up from the bottom and resisting the enormous forces of waves and currents. But at night they are even more impressive. In the gin-clear waters a diver can see that the reef is truly alive.

Out from their limestone cups the soft anemonelike polyps of the coral expand. Each armed with tiny stinging cells that filter microscopic food from the water, the tentacles spread out their web of death, ready to immobilize and capture any planktonic passerby. Swimming among the reefs at night and looking up at the walls of ornate coral polyps was

like being in a living canyon. Our lights provided quite a bonanza for them. Like moths swarming around a light bulb, amphipods and other tiny crustaceans followed and clustered about us.

As we swam along the bottom peering into the crevices and crannies and looking for lobsters, we could feel the wave surge washing back and forth, back and forth. All kinds of creatures adjust to the surge—crabs, lobsters, horseshoe crabs, and fish—using the steady movement as a directional reference, an oceanic compass.

When darkness came a very different set of creatures took over the reef. From beneath the crannies and cracks the lashing arms of brittle stars snaked their way along the bottom. A leaf-shaped speckled flatworm fluttered across the coral, swimming in midwater. They are so beautiful in their speckled rainbow hues that the most jaded of marine biologists would just sit and watch in wonder.

A smooth cowrie shell with its tapestry of colorful mantle tissues lapped algae from the rocks. And down on the sand bottom, a few yards away from the caverns of coral, felted purple sand dollars and heart urchins worked their way across the coarse sand bottom plowing up a dinner of microscopic creatures.

I was engrossed in watching the cowrie, when I suddenly felt Anne's pull on my arm. She was pointing upward, toward the moonlit surface. A six-foot shark was circling overhead, keeping a respectful distance, watching us curiously. It gave no sign of interest, none of the fins-down, tail-up, aggressive posture. It was just another creature of the night, minding its own business.

Nevertheless, after it passed, concentrating on the benthic inverte-brates at the base of the rocks wasn't so easy. I decided to become a sea turtle mentally and banish sharks from my mind.

I was inside a turtle's armored shell, with my own bone-crushing jaws that could bite through a conch shell or crush a horseshoe crab and do a number on a shark if necessary. I extended my arms and stroked against the current, seeing them as powerful yellow flippers with a thick leathery hide. I told myself that there were a great many hoary old sea turtles like the one we saw at the surface that had managed to survive the sharks, even great whites and tiger sharks.

And because I was one with the ocean, no shark would bother me. I concentrated on finding lobsters and looking for this great multitude gathering before the migration. I hoped to spot a gravid female. A full-grown female that weighs three to five pounds and is five years old, a rarity in the shallows of the Florida Keys, can lay up to a million eggs. Heavy with dark ripened eggs attached to the underside of her tail, she moves to the outer limits of the reef. Twice, possibly three times in her life, she spawns. She moves deftly, ready to dart away should the sharks that are cruising far above her draw too near or should a grouper attack. With the moon gleaming down upon the reef, the gravid lobster begins spewing forth her eggs into the water. With each vigorous flip of her tail, the membranous egg casings are ruptured, and the tiny phyllosome lar-vae are hurled into the open water, unfolding from their egg casings and free for the first time.

This scene has been witnessed by only one or two divers over the years, and the accounts of it are sketchy. I have never seen a fully mature gravid female while diving, but years ago I saw a shrimp boat in the northern Gulf come into Apalachicola with a couple of them caught on the Florida Middle Grounds.

The Middle Grounds are extensive fossilized Pleistocene coral reefs that rise up from the west Florida shelf approximately ninety-five miles south of the Florida Panhandle and one hundred miles west of Tampa. Their steep-profiled escarpments rise precipitously 35 to 50 feet from the surrounding sand bottoms, which average 110 to 120 feet in depth.

These ancient reefs flourished during the last Ice Age. They are now huge limestone ledges covered with a thick layer of invertebrate growth. Far removed from the estuaries, their ledges and canyonlike walls are covered with hard and soft corals and tropical algae that provide superlative fishing grounds. Grouper, red and gray snapper, scamp, grunts, and sea bass browse among the crannies. The Middle Grounds receive fish from the shallow inshore flats as well as Caribbean species transported by upwellings of the Gulf Loop current, which is a branch of the Gulf Stream.

Looking out from under a coral head, as if trying to make up its mind whether to venture out on the bottom, was a strange looking creature that was found much more commonly in the northern reefs. It was a slipper, Spanish, or bulldozer lobster, *Scyllarides nodifer,* closely related to the spiny lobster. Its orange-red body and white striped pointed legs made it look like some incredible beetle creeping over the coralline sands in my light beam.

The shrimpers in north Florida had named them "bulldozers" from their squat reddish-brown bodies with two rounded flaps on their heads, which looked like the blade on the earth-moving machines. The flaps are modified antennae that raise and lower like aircraft wing flaps.

Contrary to what the shrimpers believed, they don't use them to plow their way through the sand. When we introduced them into our seawater tanks, we learned that the pointed sharp legs are used for clinging to the craggy surfaces of limestone rocks. They crawled over the bottom like bulldozers, eating spiny oysters and almost any other clam they could find. Squatting over some hapless clam, a lobster pries the valves apart with infinite patience, even if it takes all night. When the clam's muscles can't take any more and the shells gape, they insert their hind walking legs and with knifelike edges slice away at the meat.

We learned that the bulldozers tolerate crowding and even seek each other out to huddle together under rocks like colonial animals. Only now and then is there a standoff. When two bulldozers meet head-on, one moves the flaps on its head up and down. The other flaps back for a moment. They stand there holding their ground, and then through some unknown signal or dominance hierarchy, one steps aside and lets the other by—a most civilized method of settling a dispute.

During the course of her two-year aquaculture study, Anne learned that slipper lobsters were an excellent candidate for mariculture, perhaps even more so than spiny lobsters. They were high-priced and could be grown to commercial size, twelve to fourteen inches long, from two-inch juveniles in just eighteen months. They were not cannibalistic, like New England clawed lobsters, and they didn't use up all their energy by running hysterically around the tanks like their spiny lobster cousins. They just sat there, ate clams, and grew fatter. Best of all, they never seemed to develop any diseases, a characteristic practically unheard-of in high-density aquaculture.

Only one thing kept our bulldozer project from being an investor's dream: the fact that once again we hadn't found any puerulus larvae. Although we could get female lobsters with eggs during the summer months, no one had succeeded in raising hatchlings for more than a month or two. Like spiny lobsters, they were believed to spend six to twelve months at sea, and nobody could duplicate the open-ocean environment in a tank.

In its own way the bulldozer's life history is as great a mystery as where the little sea turtles go after they leave the beach. There were thousands of lobsters below, enough to support a small commercial fishery, and no one had ever seen the first of their transparent larval forms. The smallest we had seen from shrimpers were already two inches long.

It was worse than the spiny lobster problem. People had caught spiny lobster larvae with Witham habitats and in clumps of red algae, but virtually nothing was known about baby slipper lobster ecology. We had looked through shell rubble in dredge hauls from hundred-foot depths off Apalachicola where the adults were.

The handful of two-inchers that shrimpers brought us were bright red. Maybe that coloration had some relation to the place where they were hiding, we thought, so we tore apart piles of red sponges, looking in their canals. We found the usual lots of pistol shrimp, hairy brittle stars, and amphipods, and we got our fingers full of glasslike sponge spicules that itched for days, but never any larvae or juveniles.

The only clue was a single observation several years before in the Bahamas of a similar larval lobster riding the Gulf Stream north, perched on top of a moon jellyfish and one or two caught in plankton tows by researchers off St. Petersburg.

I lay flat on my belly, so I could be on eye level with the slipper lobster that had just crawled back into its lair, and shined my light down into the crevice. I was hoping I would find some of the baby red lobsters there, or maybe really get lucky and discover one of the transparent slipper larvae hiding in the crannies, but to no avail. All I saw were slate pencil urchins, and more snaky, hairy brittle stars, and the mystery continued.

Down here in the Keys, washed by the margins of the Gulf Stream, the modern living reef seemed like a study in nature's purity, its clear water bustling with life and activity. Squirrelfish with big red eyes were out and moving. Usually we could catch only a glimpse of them during the day, hidden back in their crevices. Green morays cruised along the bottom or swam in the water column going about their lethal business, ready to turn and sink their sharp fangs into anyone or anything foolish enough to disturb them.

Between the spurs of stony corals, sand washed back and forth with the wave action, scouring away the surface and preventing new corals from forming. Periodically, hurricanes sweep in and scour away all rubble from the overhanging walls of these living spurs, making the characteristic sand-floored canyon formations found all along the outer reefs of the Florida Keys. Sometimes these "living spurs" and abutments can extend as much as two hundred feet into the incoming seas. The same species of coral found landward of the reef in more protected waters are not oriented to the waves and may be dashed to pieces when the storm sweeps in.

We came upon a lobster out on the open bottom, foraging away from its den. Stunned and motionless, it stood there in the glare of our underwater lights. The shadows made it look like a huge insect, and I was reminded of a story a seafood dealer told me.

An old Kentucky senator was retiring and a testimonial dinner was held for him with the most lavish of fixings. Fine wines were served, but the main attraction was the broiled spiny lobster placed before him. That was back in the 1930s when lobsters weren't on most menus.

His speech began, "Ladies and gentlemen, I have sacrificed and worked hard to serve my constituents. I haven't minded, I worked day and night, fought in the legislature, I done this and I done that but there's one thing I ain't-a-gonna-do for no-one: Eat this damn bug!"

The open-sea bottom is a dangerous place for a spiny lobster, especially by day. Triggerfish lunge in and peck out their long-stalked eyes, blinding them first and then picking them apart. Sharks and grouper sweep down and gobble them up, and loggerhead sea turtles love them so much that they actually dismantle heavy wooden lobster pots with their powerful jaws to get at them.

Their biggest natural enemy is the octopus. From this tentacled mollusk, no rock ledge or bed of sea urchins is safe. It steals into lobster traps, slipping through the cracks with its long fleshy arms, flattening its body and slipping in to get at its prey. Old conch fishermen in the Keys learned long ago that the way to flush lobsters out of their deepest inner sanctums is to thrust a dead octopus on a stick down into their burrows. Terrified, the lobsters come tumbling out.

The moment an octopus approaches, lobsters begin loud frightened stridulations, filling the sea with their cries of terror. Tentacles lash out, and the lobster is surrounded. Despite desperate efforts to break free, the hundreds of octopus sucker disks hold tight. The octopus gives off a puff of black ink and drags its prey to its cave. Engulfing the crustacean in its arms, covering it completely, the octopus bites through the carapace with its hard, sharp parrotlike beak. All motion stops as the octopus poison does its work. A few hours later scattered bits of lobster shell, spines, legs, and antennae are cast out for the foraging wrasses and smaller fish that cluster around the mouth of its burrow.

I have no idea whether octopuses attack bulldozer lobsters in the wild, but they won't touch them in captivity. We found that they eagerly latch onto blue crabs and stone crabs in our tanks, and if they're hungry enough they'll reach up and grab a fish. But the rough-hided brick-shelled bulldozers can live side by side with octopuses unbothered for months. Perhaps the bulldozer exudes some repellent.

If it does, its chemicals have no effect on grouper, which gobble down both bulldozers and octopus like vacuum cleaners. The octopus also has its share of other predators: large nurse sharks love to swallow them and sea turtles will grab them, but their main enemy is the moray eel. Hence a curious symbiosis has developed between the spiny lobster and the big green morays. Frequently, lobsters and morays share a den, looking out on the world like apartment dwellers hanging out of tenement windows. No octopus dares draw near and risk the razor-sharp teeth of the moray. Out streaks this great serpentlike fish and seizes the octopus in its curved jaws. Over and over it flips the inking, squirming "devilfish," biting violently, swallowing down a little more each time until the last tentacle disappears. Sometimes octopuses escape, leaving a torn-off tentacle still in the mouth of the eel. We've seen several with only seven legs.

When this eight-arm apparition moves into a den of lobsters and they begin their loud sounds of terror, the moray may be attracted to the noise. Like a green streak, it moves in for the kill. Sometimes the octopus casts out black ink containing chemicals that desensitize the eel's olfactory nerve and flees off into the darkness, leaving the eel to poke about the empty rocks.

I saw an octopus moving over the face of a rock and gestured to Anne to come over and watch. There was no rapport with this creature; it was frightened by our lights and the sudden attention we paid it. Cousteau's divers have spent long hours coaxing them out of their lairs with food and have successfully interacted with them. But there wasn't enough time for that on this trip; I just wanted to take it back home to our tanks.

My hand shot down and grabbed its squirming writhing body. I felt the tentacles wrap around me with tremendous force, the suction of the white disks all over its arms. But with a puff of ink it released its hold on me, slithered out of my grasp, and vanished beneath a coral boulder.

I lay down on the sand floor and beamed my light into the crevice, but I could see nothing. I considered reaching down under there, but the thought of ramming my fingers into the needle-sharp spines of sea urchins, or worse, the mouth of a moray eel, kept me from doing so.

Most of my experiences with octopuses came from pulling up crab traps or from encountering them on shrimp boats. There are few scenes in nature that are stranger than watching twenty or more suddenly displaced, angry, frightened octopuses squirming on the deck of a boat, blushing red, spurting black ink over everything, and heaving their bodies along the deck in an attempt to escape. They drag themselves away

With a puff of ink the octopus vanished beneath a coral boulder.

from everything else with their sucker disks until they hit the vertical gunwale and move along the side of the boat.

But a surprising number head directly for the scuppers, as if they knew their freedom lay just beyond the square holes cut in the side of the vessel. Whether it is due to luck, following the slope of the deck, or thinking the black hole is the mouth of a den, if the scuppers are not blocked off, one after the other slips through and dives to freedom. Years ago the shrimpers just let them crawl off, leaving all the shrimp, fish, and other creatures to writhe and gasp their lives away in the alien world. But Americans are discovering what the rest of the world has always known, that octopuses make a delicious repast, and now few are permitted to get away.

Of all the creatures that swim and crawl through the ocean, if I had to pick my favorite, it would unquestionably be the octopus. Even

though humans malign them with such names as "devilfish" and tell preposterous stories of enormous octopuses that reach up and wrap their tentacles around divers or boats and drag them into the depths, they are extraordinary animals.

From the moment we bring them into our laboratory they begin losing their fear of people, especially when presented with live crabs to eat. Over the years, when I have had time to spend with them, I have developed a rapport with octopuses. And I've always found it hard to accept that these intelligent and responsive creatures are classed in the same phylum as the lumpish clams, oysters, and whelks.

Studying octopuses objectively in the laboratory is difficult because they have a habit of studying you. An octopus is a curious animal. Often when I happened to put my hand into the water, an octopus's tentacle would reach up and hold hands with me. The strange sensation of the sucker disks' caressing my fingers, investigating them, touching and sensing, is an odd yet calming feeling. If I relaxed, the octopus would often pull down my hand, wrap more tentacles around it, and draw it closer to its mouth.

I was playing with an octopus in the tank once when it suddenly reached up and fastened a tentacle around my hand and forearm. I instantly recoiled, and almost as if it understood my fear, it released its grip and looked up at me with an expression I can only describe as baleful. It was almost as if it felt guilty for giving me a scare.

I have learned to trust them, and they have returned my trust. All I had to do was offer my hand slowly as one does when first patting a strange dog.

But I have certainly learned to mistrust the dwarf octopus, *Octopus joubini.* Commonly found in shallow grass beds hiding in the abandoned shells of clams, cockles, and whelks, these little creatures can be mean-tempered. They deliver a painful bite by injecting a mild venom that makes one's hand swell up like a severe bee sting. They make poor pets in the aquarium, being shy and recalcitrant, hiding in their shells by day and only sneaking out at night to ambush a crab or shrimp.

The common *Octopus vulgaris,* which also have the ability to inject venomous saliva, can be a joy to be around if they are kept in a large enough tank and a comfortable enough environment. If too closely confined, they crawl out and end up on the floor, dead and shriveled. The ones I have kept learned to recognize me as their keeper and seemed to enjoy the company of those who showed an interest in them.

National Geographic's photographer Bob Sisson agreed with that observation. When doing a piece on octopuses he spent time with one at the University of Miami. He told us that he always wore a wool cap and a certain jacket and carried a camera. Whenever he went to the tank, the octopus greeted him. Sisson has gained a reputation as one of the best natural history photographers, partly because of his ability to spend endless hours with a subject simply observing it. With the octopus he was convinced the subject was observing him.

One day he had a chance to test his theory. Walking down the University of Miami's campus, he spotted a man who was his size, had a beard, and could have passed for a brother. He practically dragged the man off the street asking him to participate in the experiment. At ten o'clock in the morning, the same time Sisson appeared every day to work with his eight-legged subject, he dressed the man in his jacket, his cap, and his camera and pointed him toward the tank. The octopus saw him approach, came out of its lair, and started swimming over expectantly. Then suddenly it froze, looked the impostor over, let out a jet of black ink, and fled for safety.

Amazingly, *Octopus vulgaris* is an annual species; they live only one year. And when they are ready to reproduce and lay their eggs, all their curiosity and communication stop. They crawl into their dens, becoming sullen and unmoving. And when the eggs hatch, they die.

I have often felt that if they lived as long as we do, their intelligence might equal or exceed our own. They have been photographed dragging a shoe or other strange object along the seafloor, taking it back to their lair. Why? Perhaps because someone's lost leather shoe, down among the coral and sea urchins, is a novelty to an intelligence locked in what some would call repulsive, soft blushing flesh. Who can explain the social behavior of an octopus? When one is dying in the tank, another coils its arms around it and holds it until it finally ceases breathing, as if comforting and protecting it in its last hours. And when death comes, the protective octopus drags the corpse away to the far end of the tank and leaves it as if administering burial rites.

Because I know they are so responsive and communicative, I have a terrible conflict over eating octopuses. Truly they are one of the most delicious morsels in the sea. When the shrimpers bring us dead ones we always have a pot of octopus chowder going on the stove. In fact, Anne achieved local fame with her octopus recipe, which was published in a local seafood cookbook. But neither of us could ever kill one, not for food, and I don't think for science either. Even shipping them to aquariums is traumatic after they have become pets.

As I sat on the seafloor, shining my light into the dark crevice into which the octopus had disappeared, some words Henry Beston wrote in *The Outermost House* flowed into my mind.

We need another and a wiser and perhaps a more mystical concept of animals.... We patronize them for their incompleteness, for their tragic fate of having taken form so far below ourselves. And therein we err, and greatly err. For the animal shall not be measured by man. In a world older and more complete than ours they move finished and complete, gifted with extensions of the senses we have lost or never attained, living by voices we shall never hear. They are not brethren; they are not underlings; they are other nations caught with ourselves in the net of life and time, fellow prisoners of the splendor and travail of the earth.

Then it occurred to me that the only way I would ever know the mysteries of the octopus, or solve the riddle of the sea turtle migrations or the slipper lobster larvae, would be to die and come back as one of them. Only then could I grasp their perceptions in their underwater world. But how many lifetimes would it take to be just one of each creature in the sea? Before me was the featherduster worm, radiating out its brown florid tentacles from the coral head, next to a patch of encrusting orange sponge.

To become one of each species was beyond comprehension. There were just too many. Maybe I would take off a few hundred years and go through the life cycles of selected creatures that interested me: the lantern fishes in the deep ocean, the hammerhead shark, and the green sea turtle. Certainly I would have to answer the riddle of the ridley turtle but answer it to whom? And in what terms?

Perhaps I'd take a few hundred million years and become all of the creatures before me, all the plankters that swept by in the current, the copepods, the arrowworms, the jellyfish. And then it occurred to me, as I sat there on the sandy bottom waiting for the octopus to reemerge and breathing up my packaged container of air, that perhaps I had already done so. Maybe this human skin I was wearing was only the latest in a long list of reincarnation experiences.

Suddenly I felt the sea begin to change. There was some sort of disturbance above us. Even though we were sixty feet down, we could feel the wave surge washing us back and forth with increasing intensity at each passing minute. The gin-clear waters around us were becoming turbid, and visibility was shrinking as the bottom was stirred.

Anne and I looked at each other, knowing it was time to go. Time and air were running out, and as the bottom became more agitated, it was taking more effort and air to stay in one place.

We hung onto a ledge, watching the sea fans, with their white polyps blossoming out, sloshing back and forth, back and forth. We were relieved when our fellow divers swam over and gave the thumbs-up sign. Kicking our way through the blackness and surges of luminescent plankton, we made our way up, up to the welcome light of the skiff that awaited us. Our minds were no longer on beauty. There was worry now.

It wasn't easy hoisting our gear onto the boat without getting hurt. All about us the sea churned with rolling whitecaps, as distant lightning flashed. It was literally blowing a gale. The moment we were aboard we took off in the twenty-four-foot charter boat for the long jolting ride home.

Although fast, these fiberglass wonders must have been designed by sadists. With each slam of the waves, it felt as if my kidneys were being smashed against my shoulder blades and my spinal vertebrae were being compressed with the continual impacts.

The twenty-four-foot boat had a two-hundred-horsepower out-board, and our guides were racing wide open toward the shore, hoping to outrun the approaching squall.

Suddenly there was a high-pitched roar, as the outboard motor foot jumped forward and we were shoved up onto a sandbar. No one was hurt, but the young man running the boat quickly apologized, "The wind's so strong it's blown us off course. We're just coming into the passes."

Everyone got out and pushed with all his strength until we were floating again. It never failed to amaze me how suddenly the weather and sea can change. I was reminded that the sea is no respecter of persons. It will drown heroes, followers of Great Turtle Mother, and people who love it as well as anyone else. Suddenly there was a roar, the outboard motor jumped out of the water, and we were thrown forward as we plowed up again on another sandbar. Cursing and bruised, our guide backed us off and we were soon back out in deep water, battering and being battered by the seas.

The only thing to get our mind off the abuse and worry was to sing, and sing loudly we did. "Nearer My God to Thee" was the inevitable choice. Again we ran aground, and again we pushed off. Apparently the gale was pushing us back onto the same sandbar despite our powerful motor. Two hours later, with rain beating in our faces, we spotted the lights of the shore in darkness. When we finally docked, Anne fervently whispered the Bahamian phrase "We done reached." It was like a prayer.

11. The Creature That Time Forgot

The Everglades is a land of water and rocks, of endless sawgrass prairies interspersed with tropical forests, of exquisite snowy egrets and ancient bellowing alligators. Called Payhayokee, the "river of grass," by the Indians, it is unique in the world. Fresh water flows one hundred miles south, fifty miles wide and six inches deep in a vast sheet creeping southward from impoundments south and east of Lake Okeechobee. It moves almost imperceptibly across the face of south Florida to the mangrove wilderness of the Gulf Coast and the remote storm-swept beaches off Cape Sable.

We were on assignment for Readers' Digest Books, hoping to see some of the many endangered species that occur within the endless boundaries of the national park. Each year millions of people drive through the 800,000-acre wildlife paradise, crowd onto boardwalks, and hike along the trails.

But it was easy to get away by ourselves. We had only to park our car and take off through the sawgrass, and we met no one. Sawgrass gets its name from the serrated edges of its leaves that make nasty scratches on bare arms and legs of anyone foolish enough not to wear long pants and long-sleeved shirts.

Even less inviting is the rocky, difficult terrain that underlies a thin layer of muck. When we first waded out into the sawgrass, headed for a distant tree hammock, it was not what we expected. Instead of boggy mud, our feet were tortured with an endless bedrock platform of sharp pinnacle rock. Here and there a cypress tree popped up through the limestone, but everything was dwarfed, growing out of nearly one bare rock.

Soil formation takes more time than has passed in the Everglades, which is probably the youngest land in the United States. Repeatedly the sea has invaded and retreated, alternately submerging and exposing south Florida as glaciers have advanced, retreated, advanced, and retreated again over the last million years of the Pleistocene Ice Age, pulling water in and out of the ocean basins.

During periods of high sea level, what is now the Everglades was a vast marine shoal covered with shifting calcium carbonate sands. When exposed to air, the sand hardened into limestone, which was in turn eroded by rain into almost razor-sharp pinnacles of rock, ridges, and pits.

We struggled over the bare bedrock, too shallow for a canoe, too rough to hike, watching the sea of green sawgrass stretch out on the horizon. The sedges were unmoved by the clear water that crept around their stems and barely ruffled by the wind that swept over the prairies. It changed color with the sun, the clouds, and the seasons. It went from brown to green to yellow, with tufted seed heads standing above the three-edged razor-sharp blades. You can fly around the 'Glades in a helicopter for two or three days and never see a soul away from the highways.

Our goal was a distant hammock up ahead said to be the home of colorful tree snails. We had seen other races of the snail in the park. Some of them were spectacular, gorgeous green or yellow, or green with a red stripe coiling around their shell. They stood out from the foliage like Christmas ornaments, grazing on the lichens and barks. Some varieties are limited to single hammocks, and their numbers have become depleted by shell collectors over the years.

In the week that we explored the Everglades, we saw endangered species including southern bald eagles, limpkins, and Everglades kites, great birds with nine-foot wingspans. By accident we happened on a rare five-foot indigo snake in the coastal prairies in a place appropriately called Snake Bight.

It was a spectacular reptile with glossy black scales that glistened like polished stone in the evening sun. Feeling our presence, it stopped, tested the air, its long black tongue whipping in and out, reading and sensing its green world. Staring ahead with its coalblack eyes, it moved sinuously off into the swamp, with the majesty and power of a creature that feeds almost exclusively on diamondback rattlesnakes.

We felt honored to see it. Hoping to see more such creatures, we forged on, the price being scratched hands and sore feet.

"Mean stuff," I said, surveying my reddened hands. "I wonder how the Indians got used to it."

"They didn't," replied Anne, stepping cautiously behind me. "Archaeologists found very little sign of early man here. Most of the settlements were on the coast. The Seminoles lived in the heartlands of the 'Glades only after they were driven there by white settlement." She looked distastefully at the bloody mosquito she'd slapped off her neck.

One of our guides a few days earlier had demonstrated how the Seminoles could subsist on sawgrass. I stopped, pulled the heart out of the rest of a single stalk, and nibbled at the tiny bit of soft tip. It wasn't bad, tasteless but edible.

Anne watched me dubiously. "It seems like they'd use up all their energy pulling out the hearts trying to get enough to eat. It's no wonder man never lived here and stayed on the coast. It takes almost as much effort to open an oyster.

"Maybe they ate sawgrass when they were fleeing from the cavalry. It's a wonder they could survive the mosquitoes year after year."

The mosquitoes are the true guardians of the Everglades. They are the protectors of the tree snails in the hammocks, the wading birds, and the reptiles, delighted when fresh human meat comes into their midst. They licked off the insect repellent, like hors d'oeuvres, in preparation for the feast. We knew that without them, and their contribution to the food chain, there would be no majestic wood storks, or roseate spoonbills, or great blue herons. For their larval forms, the wigglers, provided substance for the trillions of mosquito fish that swarmed in the waters that trickled through the sawgrass. The little fish ate their weight in mosquito larvae each day and in turn provided food for the birds.

And we, in turn, by providing our blood, gave substance to the mosquitoes and made our own less than willing contribution to the food chain.

Wading along the slough and creeks was the easiest way to travel, for there the sharpest of the pinnacle rocks were worn away. We sloshed through the primordial mats of diatoms and algae that covered the rocks with a yellow-green coating. In half a foot of water billions of water boatmen, tiny insects with large paddlelike feet, exploded before us and swam down into the ooze. The wet ground was paved with tiny black cone-shaped snails, and mosquito fish were everywhere, darting among the stalks. The very ground seemed to exude life out of the crannies of wet rock, nourished and filtered by the eternal flow of clear water that forever seeped fifty miles down to the Gulf of Mexico to blend gently with the salt water.

I was inspecting a tiny scarlet mite clinging to an insectivorous bladderwort, not paying attention to where I was going, when I suddenly stepped off into a deep hole that was almost up to my neck.

"Wow! I just found a 'gator hole," I yelped and grabbed frantically onto the bank of sawgrass, hoping he wasn't at home. With great energy I catapulted myself up onto the bank of sharp grass.

Anne stepped around the hole, ready to help me out. "I think they only use those during droughts, but I could be wrong. That's all we need three miles out here is another alligator incident."

Everywhere we went in the Everglades we saw plenty of alligators, fat, well-fed 'gators, swimming along the creeks, lying in the sun, hanging in the clear water, or crossing the roads with their "high walk." Pushing their long bodies off the ground and dragging only the tip of the tail, they created a sense of being thrust back into the primordial steaming swamps when dinosaurs ruled the land. And at night, when we heard them bellow their mating calls, the whole swamp shook with thunder.

They are the saviors of the swamps during the dry season. Then they create excavations called alligator holes that fill with water. They seek out areas where the limestone bedrock eroded thousands of years ago to form pits that later filled with mud. And then, churning their bodies back and forth, shoving the mud out with their noses, they excavate pits and provide places for water to collect.

Into these excavations and low places retreat fish, turtles, and snakes, followed closely by wading birds, raccoons, deer, and other life, to pass the drought until the rain comes again. The water continues to evaporate, and soon fish parch and dry. The many wading birds time their breeding cycle to take advantage of these concentrations of food.

Wood storks, with their majestic black and white plumage, walk clumsily around the edge of the holes, shuffling through the mud stirring up multitudes of seething, desperate trapped little brown fish and gobbling them down. They hunt by touch, groping blind in the mud with their ten-inch-long bills. When they feel a fish, their beaks snap shut by reflex, closing in 1/25,000 of a second.

When there are lots of fish, they breed. When fish are scarce or scattered, they don't. The wood storks gorge themselves on minnows until the rains come and Payhayokee once again begins its flow. Rains wet the dusty sawgrasses and hammock, making them once again gleam wetly in the afternoon sun. Then the mosquito fish, which have been lying in tiny limestone depressions skimming oxygen off the surface film with their upturned mouths, are suddenly liberated. The survivors fight their way over the wet rocky floor into the depressions where mosquito larvae swarm and gorge themselves, eating their weight in wigglers each day. And so the cycle starts again.

When we arrived at the tree hammock, we came across a number of wood storks. High up in the treetops they looked like little old men with their black wrinkled bald heads doddering along, hopping from branch to branch, making strange sounds. The sounds came not from vocal cords, because they haven't any, but from the clacking of their bills.

Then suddenly several took off, ungainly at first, flapping their five-foot black-tipped white wings. They hopped, rather than flew, into the air. But when they were airborne, we saw their great power and beauty as they spread their wings and spiraled upward, seeking the air currents a half-mile above the ground.

They are not birds that take kindly to civilization. Unlike the great blue herons and certain other wading birds that do just fine wading around in front of the picture window of someone's Florida room, the wood ibis shies away from humans. Every year fewer and fewer passed over our house on the northern Gulf during their fall migrations south to the Everglades.

Their populations are tied to the water levels in the Everglades and the Big Cypress Swamp in south Florida. When the water is high and the fish are dispersed in the grasses, finding enough food is tough and they produce few or no young.

These living bird fossils breed from November through April in the dry season, flocking to the drying ponds to feast on fish. There have been few successful nestings in recent years because of artificial manipulation of water levels in south Florida's vast network of drainage canals. Since 1900 their populations have dropped 90 percent, and each year fewer and fewer take to the skies. Some say that they would already be extinct if they didn't live so long.

Before Florida was settled, when Lake Okeechobee flowed slowly and freely to the Gulf of Mexico, filtering its abundant fresh waters through thousands of square miles of sawgrass and swamps, bird life flourished. The water was the foundation of the intricate web of life. But

Mangroves: there is something primeval about them.

man's activities altered that flow. In 1962 the floodgates along the Tamiami Trail were closed, and the natural flow was blocked. For years a man-made system of canals and reservoirs controlled all the overland flow into the park.

The changes in water flow nearly destroyed the bird life and caused the rich fisheries in Florida Bay to collapse. But in our society people come first: when the cities and agriculture needed water, the Everglades dried up and parched. And when torrential rains came and there was too much water, they opened the floodgates and destroyed breeding efforts.

Now efforts were under way to rectify the problems, to let the water flow more naturally through the Everglades. But whether or not the attempt would succeed, only time would tell.

In Flamingo, we finally reached the mangroves. The sawgrass that had stretched for an eternity gradually lessened and became heavily mixed with scrubby vegetation. The crystalline aquarium-clear fresh water that flowed so gently over the face of the Everglades became brown and tealike as brackish water from Florida Bay mixed and blended.

As we hiked through the familiar salt flats, marsh vegetation, and thick tangles of red, black, and white mangroves, we stared dumb-

founded at a veritable vegetable soup. For in this transitional zone night-blooming cereus and prickly pear cactuses grew among the salt-loving bushes. Bromeliads and strangler figs of island origin mixed freely with the black mangroves, which we explored by canoe and by wading around the matrix of prop roots.

Mangroves: there is something primeval about them, their geometric tangle of aerial roots, their rich organic smells, their sounds of insects and bubbling muds. They are the base of the food chain for pink shrimp, shelter to lobsters, and a hiding place to crocodiles. Half a million acres of mangroves wrap the Florida peninsula from St. Augustine on the east coast around the Keys and upward to Cedar Keys in the northern Gulf. North of Tampa Bay they're dwarfed and mixed with marshes, but along Florida's southwest coast the mangrove forests can be truly awesome, especially at night.

They perch over silt and limestone rocks with their air-breathing prop roots lifting up. These salt-loving bushes follow and colonize new land that is rising out of the sea. A century ago much of what is now swampy, semidry land in Biscayne and Florida bays was open water. With altered water flow caused by man's drainage and the resulting erosion of beaches and deposition of sediments on the shoreline, the bays are becoming vast mangrove swamps. The sea rolls in through the tangled roots that catch and hold the silt, and the rotting leaf litter slowly releases the nutrients and detritus back into the system.

At Cape Sable we saw mangrove bushes rise up into trees, forming a thick impenetrable forest. We waded through swamps looking at the abundance of life that grew on the air-breathing roots, the brownish-green algae mats, and brown and yellow sponges that pumped water through their intricate canals. Hydroids fluffed and waved in the currents, along with barnacles and coon oysters. Schools of silver mullet moved among the shallows foraging and picking at the nutrients.

Wading over the flats, a sea hare gracefully undulated its wings, sweeping in the current past us, and we saw a few hoary old horseshoe crabs covered with moss and algae, plowing along stirring up silt.

As we snorkeled into the crisscrossed geometric tangle of mangrove roots, we looked at the decomposing leaf litter that was overgrown with bacteria and fungus making more nutrients for the system. The tired old oval leaves that were continually falling off the red mangrove trees were constantly broken down into nitrogen-rich detritus, which became food for the tiniest of organisms and formed the very basis of the food chain.

We watched white mangrove jellyfish, *Cassiopeia,* sitting upside down on beds of decaying leaves and beanlike seeds, pulsating their circulating domes. But we kept our distance, because one touch against our bare skin would bring a painful sting.

In Florida Bay we snorkeled around the mangrove roots and peered and poked at the crowded world of soft-bodied, brightly colored invertebrates, the sponges and tunicates, the hard-shelled oysters and barnacles. All hung together on the roots, all filtering their food from the rich soup of seawater beneath shaded mangrove trees. Here and there a mud crab scurried off on the gray muddy banks or a black mangrove crab made its way up the prop roots and a pistol shrimp clicked its big claw from down in the mud.

Because so many animals are nocturnal, we had to explore the mangroves after dark. Even I who love marshes and mangroves had seldom waded into them at night. A gasoline lantern or flashlight is of little use among the dense thickets and tall grass. It's easy to trip or step off into boggy ground; the foliage makes only shadows. As you move forward lighting your way, the sounds of fish and other creatures flurrying around outside the range of your light fire the imagination and fill one with apprehension.

We waded along the mud flats, past the aerial roots of the black mangroves that thrust up from the bottom like thousands of eerie spikes. Our lanterns made the geometric hatchwork of the waxy-leafed red mangroves even spookier. Things splashed and bubbled and popped out of sight of our lanterns. Things rattled and shook the branches periodically deep in the impenetrable thickets—probably raccoons, but we kept moving toward open water.

The spiderwebs kept us out of the inner sanctums of the mangrove thickets. Fighting our way through the springy roots and dense bushes in the dark, and suddenly having our faces and necks plastered with strong sticky webbing, made our neurons explode with involuntary shudders. Those same golden orb weavers that we admired so much in daylight—with their dazzling black-and-yellow markings, as they sat prominently in the center of their webs between the red mangrove branches—became a nightmare of the dark because we couldn't see to avoid them. But the real guardians of the inner mangroves were the mosquitoes. Tucked away from the sea breezes and even strong winds, they had endless places to hide.

We knew as long as we had a sea breeze blowing in our faces, rippling the water, they would stay there. If the wind died, the mangroves were a bad place to be.

A few yards distant from the prop roots, out in the open water, our lanterns caught the eyes of thousands of pink shrimp, glowing like hot little coals. Had we brought our dip nets, we could have feasted well that night, and for a while we regretted our promise to ourselves that on this trip, we came only to look, not to take.

Everyone loves shrimp. Mangrove snapper, tarpon, snook, trout, red and black drum, and sheepshead rove the prop roots and grass flats in search of pink shrimp. They render all that decaying muck, fungus, and bacteria in the mangroves and marshes into a delicious protein that delights all palates. It is said that the roseate spoonbill gets its magnificent pink color from its diet of pink shrimp.

During the spring, shrimp so tiny that one practically needs a microscope to see them, all eyeballs and whiskers, swarm into the shallows and hide in the inner recesses of the mangrove prop roots. They move in on high tides, feast on worms and amphipods and all the tiny creatures that are living on the fallen mangrove leaves, and drop out on low water.

There was a series of loud, hoarse, ungodly squawks, followed by an explosive beating of wings and a raucous bellow that faded off into the distance. It's hard to get used to suddenly meeting a blue heron at night.

Beneath the hot Florida summer sun and the endless food among the marshes, mangroves, and sea grasses, they grow and grow. By the time the first full moon in October or November coupled with the first cold front comes, adult shrimp pour out into the island passes and channels into the Gulf of Mexico. Miles out to sea, far from the sight of land, shrimpers from all over the South Atlantic and Gulf are waiting for them at the Dry Tortugas fisheries' grounds.

This enormous commercial fishery depends in part on the water-control gates in the Everglades. If the water is too salty during drought, the larvae do not settle. If too much fresh water is dumped into Florida Bay through the canals, the salinity plunges abruptly and the tiny shrimp perish.

But this was an extraordinarily good year for shrimp; everything was in balance. We watched their ghostly transparent forms bolting away from our feet, again lamenting the lack of a dip net, when suddenly there was a series of loud, hoarse, ungodly squawks that sounded as if something were being murdered. It was followed by an explosive beating of wings, and the raucous bellow of the creature faded off into the distance. I jumped backward, almost banging into my wife. "Damn, you'd think that as many years as I've been stomping around these places I'd get used to great blue herons." Anne was just as startled. "A beautiful bird like that ought to have a better voice. You know I'm aware that mangroves are productive, valuable, full of fish and all that, but I can't help it—I don't like them, especially at night. They're full of creeping, stealthy things, and there's no light. I prefer the marshes and sawgrass where it's open and you can see."

"You do get the feeling that something big with teeth is lurking in there," I said of the approaching thicket of a mangrove island that rose as a great shadowy mass before us.

"Well, the crocodiles are almost all gone. There are only a few left in the park, and our chances of seeing them when we go out with the ranger tomorrow are next to nil."

"Oh, I don't know, we've been pretty lucky so far. We've seen an indigo snake, several Everglades kites, flamingoes. We've heard a panther scream the other night…"

"We heard something," Anne put in hastily. "How do you know it was a panther?"

Ignoring her, I went on, "We might get lucky and see one. Ever since I was a child I've wanted to see a crocodile in the wild, and I've been severely disappointed. Even when I've gone to places in Africa and Madagascar where they were supposed to be, I didn't see any."

"How do you expect to do that?" she argued, at the same time trying to wave the mosquitoes away. That gentle sea breeze that kept the insects at bay had suddenly died off, and the true demons of the mangroves were coming out with their thirst for blood, ready to make us contribute our fair share to the food chain. "The park's public relations director told us that people spend years here and never see one."

I smashed four mosquitoes on my neck. "She also said a bunch of tourists saw one laying eggs on the road shoulder next to the concession stand in Flamingo last year," I said hurriedly. "Let's get out of here; the mosquitoes are terrible."

In summer the Everglades become unbearable. I have crawled on my belly through dense thickets of mangrove prop roots in Madagascar to collect hermit crabs, waded up to my neck in the freshwater swamps of Surinam for fish, and camped on the barrier islands of Honduras, but never, anywhere, anytime have I encountered mosquitoes as terrible as those in the summer in the Everglades.

The Seminole Indians, who were forced into the Everglades by white settlers, learned to boil garfish and smear themselves with ill-smelling oil to protect themselves. Smoking fires blazed into the night, but several Seminoles we talked to said that nothing did much good when the wind died down and the bloodsucking swarmers came out. One night I had to make a call from a lone telephone booth at the edge of Alligator Alley at Naples, and I had trouble breathing. With each slap on my face, I squashed no fewer than fifty mosquitoes at a time.

The next morning we were grateful for the rush of air from Officer Tom Goldbin's patrol boat as we sped across Florida Bay. The strong north wind that was blowing kept the mosquitoes at bay, but unfortunately it whipped the normally clear bay into a bluish-white froth. It didn't seem tropical that chilly day at Key Largo. We could hardly see the bottom, much less all the myriad life in the turtle grass beds.

Tom was a little reluctant to take us into the depths of the crocodile habitat in the mangrove forests of Florida Bay. "It's protected; we don't allow boat traffic in those areas." Seeing our disappointment, he paused. "But if journalists and nature writers can't get in and see them, people who can spread the experience to others, I don't know who can," he grinned. "OK, we'll go, but the way it's blowing and the way the water is churned up, I doubt we'll see any."

"How big do they get?" Anne asked, making herself comfortable on the boat cushion as best she could in the bouncing chop and spray of the water.

"Most of them are four or five feet, but there's one old monster that's about seventeen feet long up in Mud Creek. There's a lot of alligators up there. Crocs are more tolerant of brackish and salt water than alligators, and they have the same general appearance, but once you get close, there's no confusing them."

Even if we never saw one of these reptiles, the bird life was incredible. Before us great flocks of cormorants, or water turkeys, loudly beat their wings, slapping the water with their feet as they ran before us. The ranger stopped to watch a pair of roseate spoonbills that appeared as pink explosions amid the mangroves. When they took off with their long necks outstretched, he looked at them with admiration. "No matter how many times I see them, I can't get over it. I can tell you this about the Everglades: you have to learn to love it. It's not like all the other national parks where the geology and land dominate. You can't rush through this place; you have to take it slow, a little at a time. One day you'll come upon a hundred pink flamingoes; some other day, I'll see a manatee or something else."

We gazed at the flocks of white pelicans floating at the edge of mangrove islands and saw more wood storks wading along the edges of the creeks, their long bills down to grab at minnows. "People come here to see bird life and they aren't disappointed," he said, "even though there're not nearly as many wading birds as there used to be."

Here birds normally found in Central America exist side by side with North American cardinals, mockingbirds, and crows. The Everglades is a great mixing bowl of North and South American life.

We moved farther into Florida Bay, listening as the herons, egrets, and white ibis in the mangrove thickets filled the air with screams and calls. In some places the saltwater forest was so thick and dense that when our boat entered a creek the canopy closed over us. Here and there a few delicate yellow flowers graced the red-rooted mangroves and gave off a pleasant citrus odor. In September, the tropical storm season, the podlike seeds would hang from the branches, ready to break off and be carried far and wide by the winds that send waves surging into the latticework of exposed roots. Everywhere in Everglades National Park, signs remained of Hurricane Donna, a great storm of 1960 that had sent torrents of water into the swamplands for three consecutive days. Now the silvery stalks of dead mangroves stood ghostly watch, surrounded by the new growth that had taken over since.

Yet the system must have those punishing hurricanes or its productivity declines and the swamps become stagnant. After a good pounding like the great hurricane of 1935, enormous areas of mangrove forests were torn open. Trees that weren't killed outright were weakened, only to be finished off by Hurricane Donna. It seems to work on a twenty-five-year cycle. In 1965 Betsy finished off many mangroves left by Donna.

The pounding waves and howling winds open up the dense undergrowth and flush out the detritus and allow sunlight to penetrate. The seedlings sprout rapidly, and the fast-growing young trees produce and shed more leaves than the mature ones. As they grow older, their productivity slows and so does the growth cycle.

It takes some horrendous waves to dislodge the mangrove trees, for they anchor themselves by strong lateral roots that sprout out from the trunk and lower branches and form a complex network that holds the plants securely. We searched among the living and dead saltwater trees for signs of crocodiles, but saw none.

Crocodiles are elusive and secretive animals, a tiny Florida remnant of a population that may have once numbered in the tens of thousands. Now it is estimated that there are roughly two hundred within the boundaries of the Everglades National Park.

Between searching for crocs and puttering along in the patrol boat, Tom chatted with people fishing in the park, checking their catches, telling them where they could and could not fish, and handing out informational leaflets. He told the birdwatchers where they might see roseate spoonbills and wood storks and white herons.

Then we came to a derelict old fishing skiff with an old man casting fervently. He looked as if he had been out there forever with his brown-tanned skin, wrinkled with the weather. "That's Sarge," said the ranger. "I've arrested him a number of times for fishing in closed areas, but we're good friends. You'll enjoy talking to him. He probably spends more time out here fishing than any human alive."

As we headed for him, Tom stood up in the boat and surveyed the open water. "We've got to watch it; the fishermen get hot if you run through a mullet mud to get to them."

"Mullet mud?" I asked. "What's that?"

"That's when the silver mullet stir up the bottom, and the trout come in to feed on them. If you motor through a mud streak, it causes the fish to scatter and disperse, and that's about the worst thing you can do."

The ranger provided an official uniformed presence in the park. He prevented people from hiking into the interior of the mangrove islands where the birds nested, and he patrolled looking for net fishermen. A newly passed law made it strictly illegal to fish with gill nets in the park, making commercial fishermen furious.

As we approached Sarge, Tom chuckled, "Sometimes he's glad to see me because he's broken down. I can't tell you all the times I've had to tow him in. He keeps running that old motor."

We pulled up to the bony weathered old man, who had several days' growth of gray beard. He had a sunbleached cap, once khaki colored, that read, I'D RATHER BE FISHING.

"Ain't nothing biting," he said and held up one trout. "I been fishing all morning and this is all I caught. It's too doggone windy."

When Tom introduced us, and said we were writing an article, he looked at us curiously. "This place ain't overfished like some say; they just ain't no fish here." He gloried in the opportunity to protest the U.S. Fish and Wildlife's regulations.

"They got all the best fishing spots closed for them damn crocodiles. Little Madeira Bay, Taylor Run, Mud Creek, and Davis Creek are where you catch the big redfish and snapper, but this man'll arrest you if you go in there."

"You see many crocodiles?" Anne asked, trying to defuse his vendetta.

"No, hardly ever see one. Mostly there's 'gators out here, big ones."

"Tell them about your run in with the 'gator, Sarge," the ranger suggested.

Sarge lifted his salt-stained, worn khaki shirt and revealed a line of white scars running down his back and arms. "Weren't nothing to it, really. I hooked this big redfish and the 'gator wanted him and I wanted him. So when he grabbed the fish and started to come into the boat with me, I used my convincer."

He reached down and showed me his big wooden club.

"Only the 'gator did all the convincing," Tom laughed. "It was a good thing for Sarge we just happened by afterward, or he would have bled to death out there. We had to rush him to the hospital."

We said good-bye to Sarge and continued on, exploring the upper reaches of Florida Bay hoping to get a glimpse of a crocodile. We covered Joe Bay, Little Madeira Bay, and Davis Creek, where they were supposed to be, but nowhere did we even see a sign of one.

Once we saw a "'gator slide," where the big reptiles came out to sun, squashing down the vegetation beneath it. It looked like a well-traveled path. We crept along the shoreline, noting the yellow lichens on the mangroves and extensive spiderwebs.

We continued looking, but to no avail. At last we entered a narrow creek that cut through the mangroves with a heavy cable held afloat by large white corks blocking the entrance. A government warning sign said to keep out. "This is Mud Creek; it's the last possible place to see one," the ranger said. "In the nesting season, not even biologists are allowed to go in."

Anne lifted the cable. We moved into a secluded world of palm trees rising up behind dense waxy-leafed mangroves. It was shallow, and the propeller kicked up white mud and leaves. Still no crocodile. Signs were hopeful: fresh flattened grass, and saltwort where something big had lain.

"There's an old crocodile nest up on the left. Let's get out and take a look."

A bank slide had been made, worn down to the bare white marled earth, where the mother crocodile had attended her nest. They build their nests above the high water, on whatever dry land they can find. And here among the saltworts was just enough elevation to prevent the eggs from being soaked by anything short of a hurricane.

It was a simple nest, not the elaborate elevated pile of vegetation that an alligator puts down but a hole dredged out in the high mangroves. "This used to be much higher," the ranger said, pointing to the bank. "It eroded over the past year."

We stood there looking, glancing behind us at the dredged-out trail that led down to the bank of the creek, feeling as if we were violating the crocodile's privacy by entering the world of that harried animal that had been so relentlessly hunted for its hide, or often just shot for the "sport" of it. Yet we were drawn on by curiosity, and to a degree our fascination with fear.

We could feel crocodile everywhere in the dark canopied air. It was all about us in the swamp, that stealthy, eerie feeling that gnaws at the imagination. What atavistic memory instinctively distrusted and feared swamps? Was it because we are descended from a race of anthropoids that lived in trees or in the hills and knew that evil dangerous reptile-type creatures with cold green eyes, scaly hides, and teeth lurked at the river's edge or water hole? Nowadays, with man dominating everything, the fears made little sense, or did they?

After we looked at the worn-down nest, the ranger shook his head with disappointment. "Well, folks, we tried. I'm afraid that's about as close as we're going to get to a crocodile today. Maybe you can come back another time."

"It's better than nothing," Anne encouraged. "I've never seen a crocodile's nest before."

We walked back down the trail the mother crocodile had worn out. Then we pushed off, started the boat, and moved slowly down the creek, churning up mud and rotting leaves with the propeller.

Suddenly, the water before us gave a mighty swirl, and up it came, the great monster of monsters. Its craggy pointed snout was encircled with white fangs, its body the color of gray marl. It was huge, almost as long as the boat, moving slowly, ominous and malevolent. There was no confusing this hoary old water demon with the sluggish alligator. It surged ahead, its gray jagged bumps rising above the water. The full length of its back emerged. "That's the one," cried the ranger, "the old man of the swamp or I should say the old lady."

He ran the boat slowly beside it. The creature boldly cruised ahead, on the surface, with us gazing in astonishment on its immensity. No wonder the ancient Olmecs of Mesoamerica depicted the world resting on the back of an enormous crocodile in their art. We sat there speechless. This was as close to a prehistoric saurian as anyone living today is likely to get. Perhaps the species was becoming extinct, but that one surely seemed unaware of its plight.

The great reptile seemed angry at our encroachment. With a booming splash, it slammed down its craggy flat tail, sending a sheet of water cascading into the boat, and it sank into the murky marl water and disappeared.

That was our crocodile. We returned home to finish our article, now knowing there was no confusing it with an alligator. Anyone can tell the difference by looking. The alligator is black, its head broad, its manner entirely different.

Commercial fishermen in Carrabelle and Panacea along Florida's northern Gulf Coast had been telling me for years about seeing a crocodile years ago, and I had never believed them. Our home coast is hundreds of nautical miles from where a crocodile should by rights be. Yet one was reportedly captured by fishermen two hundred miles out in the Gulf Stream. There seemed to be no way such creatures would be able to survive the cold winters of north Florida.

Later I went back and talked to some of the old-time gill-netters in the Florida Panhandle who fished the offshore islands. Without exception they all said, "About fifteen years, or ten years, ago you'd see one on Dog Island, a big fellow. Couldn't get near him, though; he'd dive in and haul ass. There ain't no mistaking him for a 'gator."

I had to agree.

Sadly I learned that a year after we saw the great crocodile it was found dead, rotten and decomposed. Park authorities performed an autopsy on it and found fragments of lead shot inside. Someone had blasted away its life.

Why, is the question. As long as people try to protect wild lands and set them aside for endangered species, there will be conflicts. When the Everglades was made into a national park, commercial fishermen were run out, forced to move out of Flamingo. There were still hard feelings. When Florida Bay was closed to net fishing, anger intensified. Although no one is coming forward to say why he shot the crocodile, it probably has some connection to the U.S. Fish and Wildlife's edict. And the crocodile was a victim of someone's anger.

Yet mother nature has compensated. The great mother crocodile of them all is gone, yet suddenly there has been a small population explosion of crocs. They seem to be reproducing all over the park. Numbers of new smaller crocodiles have been spotted in the habitats where the old ones were and even in new areas.

For the first time there is optimism that the crocodiles and perhaps even wood storks may be coming back, and conservation measures may pay off.

12. On the Edge of the Abyss

Thomas Lee Mills, skipper of the shrimp trawler *Norma Yvonne*, puffed his cigarette in the darkness and turned on the Fathometer. The whirling needle noisily traced out a long, fuzzy black line over the moving sheet of graph paper. "We're at seventy fathoms [a fathom equals six feet, thus four hundred twenty feet] right now," he said quietly. "It won't be long before the bottom starts dropping off fast. I'd say that by three or four in the morning, we'll have a good two hundred fathoms of water beneath us."

We had been at sea for eight hours, moving due south off the Florida Panhandle out in the Gulf of Mexico on an expedition to find and bring back some strange, rare deep-water creatures for the New York Aquarium.

"But I'll tell you," the big skipper continued, "the way these seas have been building, I ain't so sure we're gonna be able to work when we do get there. Now it used to be that you could work this royal red shrimp territory out there in between the northerlies. But crazy-acting as the weather's been, I don't know. Last year they'd blow through about once a week; then it would clear up and even get pretty out here. But now these fronts come down one right behind the other, and I'm afraid that's what's happening."

"A big boat like this ought to be able to take it," I said hopefully, leaning back in the comfortable pilothouse chair, watching the sweep of the illuminated radar beam. We were alone; not a blip or mark of any kind showed up anywhere on the screen.

The skipper laughed sardonically. "Oh, hell yes, this boat can take it. She weighs fifty tons; she don't ride the waves, she flattens 'em. But *you* ain't gonna stand up to it. When she hits those twenty-five-foot seas and goes to flamming she'll beat your guts out. And when you got them big seas breaking over the bow and flooding down the decks, it don't take but a second for a man to get washed overboard. Damned if

I'm gonna get drowned out here trying to drag up a mess of monster sea roaches!"

Thomas Lee didn't think much of our expedition. He had agreed to run the *Norma Yvonne* for Aquila Seafoods in Bon Secour, Alabama, only because it was January, the coldest and most wretched month of the year, and there were no shrimp. His own sixty-eight-foot wooden trawler was tied to the dock, along with nearly all the other shrimp boats. He needed to make some money.

Finding a vessel large enough and well enough equipped to trawl the submarine De Soto Canyon off Pensacola, Florida, in two hundred fathoms where *Bathynomus giganteus* lived had proved an ordeal. Never before had these big, grotesque, jointed-legged creatures been placed alive on public display. Occasionally the deepwater shrimp fishermen would haul up one in their nets and bring it in dead as a curiosity.

Months earlier, we had gone from dock to dock, fishing village to fishing village, asking whether any shrimpers were fishing for royal reds. But all we got was an emphatic "No! I doubt you'll find anyone still messing with them royal reds anymore."

In the 1950s the Bureau of Commercial Fisheries first discovered the royal red shrimps. They were doing some exploratory trawling in two hundred fathoms and brought up a deckload of big red succulent royal reds, *Hymenopenaeus robustus,* previously known from a handful of pickled specimens gathering dust on the shelves of the U.S. National Museum.

The crew cooked up the shrimp, and overnight they changed from a scientific curiosity to a gourmet's delight. Adventurous shrimpers, spurred on by the discovery, had rigged up their boats to work the deep water. But fishing out there, farther than any shrimp boat had ever gone before, was brutal on equipment. The heavy seas would snatch the rigs off the bottom and tangle them. As cables were wound in, standard winches used on trawlers would often burn up from the strain, leaving the crew to haul in more than a mile of steel cable by hand, sometimes in gales. Sharks attacked the nets, and when the violent squalls struck, there was no shore to run to for safety. After a few years of trying, most skippers stopped replacing their miles of rusting cables and went back to working inshore for the traditional pink, brown, and white shrimp.

But we located the *Norma Yvonne,* one of the few boats that had been rigged for fishing royal reds. With giant hydraulic winches, she was built to last. "But I'll tell you something," Thomas Lee commented. "It damn sure don't pay to fool with them red shrimp unless there ain't nothing in shallow water. Long as I can catch three or four boxes of pink shrimp in twenty or thirty fathoms, that's where I'm gonna work! I ain't got near the expense nor the risk in getting them." Then he winked at me. "And the trash fish ain't nearly as boogerish-looking as this deep-water stuff!"

As we headed farther and farther out, we studied the National Marine Fisheries Service's printout of when and where *Bathynomus* had been captured by research vessels over the past twenty-five years. Nixon Griffis sat quietly in the galley, puffing his cigarette. A few months earlier we had had another lunch together. After describing his last trip to Africa in search of the hammerheaded bat, he had asked me, "Jack, where can we catch a monster? We need something so unusual that it will really draw crowds to the New York Aquarium. The giant toadfish was great, but I want something spectacular, something that will boost membership in the New York Zoological Society."

The only monster I could think of was the giant sea roach, *Bathynomus giganteus,* that lived deep along the edge of the continental shelf off Florida. With a length of up to two feet, it was the world's largest isopod, a flat-bodied crustacean with ten pairs of sharp-hooked legs and segmented body. Most species of isopods live in the ocean, although many are found in fresh water and a few live on land. The inconspicuous and ubiquitous pill bugs, or "rolypolies," that hide under rocks in a garden are isopods. Imagine a giant pill bug, with its jointed body, hooked claws, huge triangular eyes, and a mouth filled with cutting plates, and you've got a real monster. *Bathynomus giganteus* is also a living fossil. Common in the seas some 60 million years ago, it survives today only in a few scattered places around the world's oceans. Beyond the Gulf of Mexico it is found in the Sea of Japan and the Bay of Bengal.

Anne and another marine biologist at Florida State University, Joe Halusky, sat across from Nixon mapping the earlier *Bathynomus* coordinates.

"Latitude twenty-nine degrees, four minutes North," Anne called out, "longitude eighty-eight degrees, forty minutes West."

Joe grinned happily. "I can't believe this." His pencil made another round circle next to the tight bunch of others. "It's just too good to be true. Look at all these little rascals: they're sitting right at the edge of the continental shelf, just at that drop-off between two and three hundred fathoms."

"How about it, Skipper?" Anne asked. "Can we drop it down right here?" She pointed to the middle of the dots.

Thomas Lee grunted, "I don't know about that! I got a chart of my own in the wheelhouse, and it's got all the bad bottoms marked off. There's coral reefs out here in two and three hundred fathoms that will tear a net all to pieces. The government boat don't mind tearing up nets or losing a whole rig: they got plenty of money to replace it. All it takes is one bad hang out here and a man can lose eleven thousand dollars in nets and cable before you can say 'Don't do it!'"

A moment later he returned with his chart drawn with big red squares. "We'll put over here at the 2950 loran line, what we shrimpers call the 'edge of the earth.' I believe we caught some of them sea roaches there before." Thomas Lee flipped through our scientific reprints scattered around on the table. He contemplated a line drawing of *Bathynomus*. "I don't pay no attention to the trash that comes up when I'm out here. I'm interested in only one thing—shrimp. But you don't forget an ugly-looking critter like that."

As the evening wore on, the seas began building and the ninety-foot steel-hulled trawler pitched and rolled. Dishes flew out of the cupboard, and the two crewmen, Frankie Nelson and Claude Underwood, hurried about battening everything down.

The sea would have been better in June or July, but we hoped that we could run out to the drop-off in between the weather fronts, work a few days, and hurry back before the next storm came down on us. We had deliberately chosen to go in the dead of winter when the surface water was the coldest. If we had any hopes of taking our specimens back alive, thermal shock had to be minimized. The surface water was down to nearly seventy degrees now, and the bottom was only forty-five degrees F. Bringing the trawls up from those depths would still kill off many species, but hot summer surface temperatures of eighty-five to ninety-five degrees F. were a guarantee that everything that came up would die.

We had gambled on the weather, and now according to the weather radio our bluff was apparently going to be called. A storm was coming through. If it stalled over land, we could work. If it didn't, the expedition would be over.

We turned in, and I lay there most of the night listening to the engines revving up and down, fighting the ever-rising waves. I dozed off, but the surge breaking over the bow got so strong that it sprayed in through a porthole above my head, making the night drag on even more uncomfortably. That old queasy, familiar feeling in my guts returned with each wave. All this blue water business was fascinating and adventurous, but at heart (and stomach) I was a seashore naturalist, one who likes to walk along warm Florida beaches at low tide with buckets in hand, picking up things.

At three in the morning, Frankie was shaking me. "Captain wants to talk to you."

The skipper's mood was somber. "We're at one hundred fathoms," he said solemnly, pointing to the depth device, "and from here on out it starts dropping off pretty quick. In two hours we'll be over two hundred fathoms." The Fathometer's needle was etching a sloping line going down, down, down to the bottom of the page.

"But, Jack, the way these seas have been building, I ain't so sure I'm going to put the rigs overboard. Now it's possible that they'll lay down at daybreak; they usually do. Then we'll make at least one deep-water drag, but after that I ain't promising nothing. If that wind goes to switching around, I don't want to be where it will drown us."

I returned to my bunk. All that planning, and all that work and money, and now it would probably come to nothing. How foolish I was to believe that we could actually go out there, and drag up a big sea roach at the snap of a finger. The odds were too great against us. I popped another pink anti-seasickness pill and tried to get some sleep. There were thousands of square miles of deep ocean out there, rolling on for an eternity. And we, with our two little trawls, dragging a tiny part of it.

Thomas Lee's concerns were real. He had seen big steel-hulled shrimp boats return from the royal red grounds at the edge of the Gulf Loop current with all the pipe rigging torn off, the windows shattered, and the electronics smashed. They were the lucky ones. There were wooden boats that went out and never came back.

At dawn we assembled, yawning, on the deck, gloomily contemplating the red skies and scruffy angry little clouds that hung overhead. They were moving before the wind, traveling ever southward before the cold front. The seas were a vast panorama of gray water frothed with whitecaps and huge rolling waves.

The deckhands, Claude and Frankie, were busy working the rigging, wearing their heavy yellow slickers as the boat pitched from side to side. "All right, we're setting out at one hundred ninety fathoms," Thomas Lee shouted, raising his voice above the winds. "That's the best we can do right now. We'll be dragging on out to two hundred fathoms."

Then with a jerk on the lever he started the winch turning, and the ten-foot-long, five-hundred-pound, iron-clad otter doors were snatched out of their brackets with a loud crash and dangled from the outriggers. Frankie threw the nets overboard, and when the winch brake was released, the two trawls splashed into the sea. The green webbing sank down behind them, and the net started its long journey to the bottom.

The giant drums spun rapidly, spewing out fathom after fathom of strong steel cable. Thomas Lee hurried to the pilothouse to push down the throttle, and the *Norma Yvonne* churned forward, her great spinning cable spools becoming thinner and thinner. When he was sure there was enough cable out, he slowed, and the crew locked the winches. The big steel hull strained ahead, her outriggers stretched wide like the wings of a giant bird as she pulled her heavy trawls over the soft muddy bottom.

Now it was our turn to get busy. There was much to be done before we were ready for the nets to come up. As I gushed seawater into the large waiting styrofoam containers from the deck hose, Joe Halusky made his way up and down the long steel ladder that reached into the giant ice hold, bringing up buckets of ice. Anne scooped the crushed ice into plastic bags and tied them tightly. The ice bags were to be used to chill the seawater temperature down to forty-five degrees F. without allowing any melted fresh water to dilute the seawater. That would be deadly to any living specimens .

Nixon checked our packing manifest. We strung electrical lines and duct tape around the deck and inspected air pumps to see that they were working. If any creature came up alive, the water would have to be aerated.

The deckhand Frankie Nelson watched our activity. His voice was skeptical. "I don't see what y'all rushing so hard about; it'll be three hours before we're ready to take up. 'Sides, you ain't gonna get much to stay alive nohow. Most all the fish I see come up from this deep water got their eyeballs burst out of their heads. This ain't like regular shrimping where everything on deck is a-jumpin' and a-floppin'. "

Three hours dragged on, and we waited with anticipation.

By midmorning we entered the Gulf Loop current. Suddenly the waters turned a deep transparent blue and the air was almost balmy. Off in the distance, a blue marlin, an enormous thing with a long pointed bill, leaped high out of the water and landed with a great splash. All around us the waves rose like blue hills crested with patches of golden brown sargassum weed.

It was wonderful being in the Gulf Stream again. We took off our heavy jackets and walked around the deck in sweaters, and for a while the cold winter weather almost disappeared. But high overhead, clouds continued to move ominously across the sky, pushed by the impending arctic front. Finally, Thomas Lee started reeling in the nets. It was thirty minutes or more before we could see the two otter doors on the starboard side ascending rapidly toward the surface, coming together and closing the mouth of the net. The heavy wooden doors broke from the sea with a splash and dangled from the outrigger, dripping into that blue, blue sea. Then the other set of doors rose and hung from the other outrigger.

Frankie grabbed a long bamboo pole and deftly hooked the lazy line that connected the doors to the end of the trawl bag. The fifty-foot-long starboard net came up first. The young crewman wrapped it around the cathead and started bringing in the webbing.

With creaking groans the rope hoisted the green-webbed bag higher and higher until it dangled from the boom above the deck, showering water, gorged with life. I tried to peer through the covering of brightly colored, red, yellow, and white chafing gear, but all I could see were blotches of pale color, of red scales and white bodies and shrimp antennae.

The skipper went forward and snatched the release ropes that kept the trawl bag closed. Suddenly a few fish started spilling on the deck, then an avalanche of little orange shrimp, along with every imaginable creature. "My Lord, will you look at the shrimp!" declared Joe loudly.

The captain and crew didn't seem impressed. "There ain't no shrimp, very few that's royal reds. Most of them's peewee *megalops*, and there ain't much of a sale for them! They're too damn little."

I surveyed the pile, dumbfounded. With more than fifteen years of collecting in the shallows of that very same Gulf of Mexico, I expected that I would know some of the creatures piled on the deck before me. But I couldn't classify a single one. There were long flat eels with wicked-looking teeth, huge horny-plated prehistoric gooseneck barnacles in twelve-inch-long clusters. The deck bounced with big leathery-skinned white sea anemones, and scattered everywhere were moon snails whose shells glowed with brilliant iridescent and opalescent col-

Nearly all the fish, including the red armored sea robin shown here, were dead on the deck because of the abrupt chnge of temperature and pressure.

ors. But they were the exceptions. The deep-water creatures lacked the shallows' diversity of color, most of them were either jet black, pale orange, or pasty white.

We were dragging at the very edge of the Gulf's continental shelf where the bottom begins its sharp plunge to the abyssal plains. The animals that live on this frontier are more closely related to the bizarre, spindly, spiny forms of life that dwell on the ocean floor three miles deep than they are to the familiar shallow-water species. But what they lack in color, they make up for in diversity of form, texture, and shape.

Nearly all the fish, the speckled stargazers, the red armored sea robins, and the toothy brown goosefishes, were dead on deck, their mouths sprung open, their tongues protruding, their dead eyes popping grotesquely out of their heads. All of these casualties had swim bladders, gas-filled sacs used to regulate their buoyancy. At two hundred fathoms they existed under a pressure of 550 pounds per square inch. As the net rapidly ascended, the pressure decreased, and the gases rapidly expanded, blowing up the swim bladders like balloons and tearing the fish apart. Some of the crustaceans and fish that lacked the swim bladders were still alive, although others had gone into shock from the abrupt temperature change.

Our eyes peered over the near-lifeless pile for any kind of movement, looking especially for the big, segmented, armored *Bathynomus giganteus*. But it was nowhere to be found.

Before the second net was dumped on deck, Anne cried excitedly, "Hey! Look at this! It's a chimaera, and it's alive!"

As she pulled it out of the pile, Nixon jumped up with excitement. "That's a rattail fish; I've only seen pictures of them in books. We've got to get that back alive. That will make the expedition even if we never catch a *Bathynomus*."

In Greek mythology the Chimera was a fire-breathing she-monster. This creature had a soft, bulbous nose; its skin was soft, almost mushy like the squids on deck; and its elongated coal-black body tapered to a point. A wicked spine protruded from its back, and the network of lateral lines was prominently marked over its soft, clammy, scaleless body. But most impressive of all were its huge bright-green luminous eyes. They were like two big crystal balls, so big you could look into them and see the world.

But when Anne hurried her specimen over to the waiting styrofoam box and gently eased it in, it began to swim beautifully. Its fan-shaped pectoral fins spread out like an angelfish's, and it hovered gracefully in the water. Suddenly it became beautiful, more beautiful than any fish I had ever seen.

When the second net was opened, more creatures piled out and there were more chimaera. There were also intricately striped, tan, chain-dogfish sharks with black markings and slanted green eyes. They were alive and healthy. Sharks and their kin, which include rays, skates, sawfishes, and chimaera, have no swim bladders and can withstand the rapid decrease in pressure. But unhappily many of the cigar-shaped bioluminescent green dogfish sharks, sexually mature at nine inches long and lacking a dorsal fin, had perished from the abrupt temperature shock.

Before long, our boxes were filling up with every imaginable creature, small spindly orange lobsters, hermit crabs living inside red sea anemones, delicate creatures with long flexing legs. We worked rapidly, raking through the catch. Time is critical on a shrimp trawler, especially with a thousand pounds of gasping creatures dumped on deck. If you don't get the animals into life-giving water within a few minutes, most perish.

Even with the two big piles of life, it didn't take long for the crew to cull it off. In thirty minutes, they had four baskets heaped high with the fluffy bright royal red shrimp.

The crew shoveled all the other creatures overboard, including three or four hundred pounds of the small orange shrimp, *Peniopsis megalops*.

"Yeah, I know it's a waste," the skipper said, "but until they get some way to machine-process them, they ain't worth fooling with. They're just too small and too fragile."

Like many of the Gulf species, *Peniopsis megalops* was an untapped resource. Yet Thomas Lee spoke of seeing Russian and Japanese trawlers working out in the deep water, saving almost everything that came aboard. Even with the two-hundred-mile limit, foreign exploitation would probably continue. According to international treaty, if we didn't utilize the tasty little shrimp and other unexploited species, they were fair game for other countries that would.

Thomas Lee looked over the three and a half baskets of royal reds. "We ain't gonna get rich this way." But he looked pleased.

"Hey, Jack," Nixon called, "come look at the chimaera. I'm afraid they're dying."

The fish were now belly up, or lying flat on the bottom. I blasted pure oxygen into the water, hoping to revive them, but I knew it was hopeless. Their delicate bodies had undergone too much of a shock. Moments later I sadly lifted them out of the tank and put them into a plastic bag to preserve later.

"Skipper, we need to make another tow," I said. "We didn't get the sea roach, and we lost our other little monsters."

Joe had been in the wheelhouse, studying the loran readings and his charts. He was excited. "Look, the way I figure it, we were dragging just a little bit too shallow to catch *Bathynomus*. We were at one hundred ninety fathoms most of the time, and they're just a few fathoms deeper. I'll bet if we put over in two hundred and fifty fathoms we'll catch one."

"That's about an hour's running," said the skipper, rubbing his unshaven chin. "Hell, we'll try it. The seas ain't picking up any worse, and they always say that if you're catching those little red *megalops* shrimp, step off into deeper water, and you'll hit the royal reds. Last year about this time we hauled the nets up and caught six thousand pounds!" Shrimping fever was getting to him.

Now that the nets were out of water, the *Norma Yvonne* churned ahead, straight into the big rolling swells. Her twin diesels strained, as the boat began to beat loudly. It was misery on deck: we watched the creatures slopping back and forth in the styrofoam boxes. Nixon puffed his cigarette, looking ashen and pale. Before long I felt that all-too-familiar weakness.

But we had to keep on working. The water had to be changed periodically, replaced with new prechilled seawater, when the old became slimy from the mucous secretions of the sea creatures. Anne wasn't much help. "You know," she said cheerfully, "I heard about one oceanographer who used to go out and get seasick every time. When he'd have his students out on deck, he would start lecturing, stop to throw up over the side, and then go right back to teaching his classes."

"Such dedication," muttered Nixon, taking yet another puff on his cigarette. Joe, on the other hand, was hurrying about, taking pictures of all the living and dead creatures in our boxes before their colors faded.

As I watched the hard round sea anemones sloshing back and forth in the boxes, I wondered how they were reacting to this unfamiliar wave action. Down where the chimaera glide like fairy creatures over the bottom, and giant sea roaches tunnel through the soft ooze, there is no wave action. Yet royal red fishermen spoke of tremendous undersea currents that were so strong they could catch the nets and nearly flip a shrimp boat over.

The ecology of the depths is little understood. The bottom is often formed from the nearly microscopic shells of billions upon billions of single-celled organisms that have died and sunk down into the depths over millions of years. So stable are the bottom temperature, salinity, and other environmental conditions that the shells never deteriorate. Consequently they cover the seafloor with many feet of fine sediments.

We were now at latitude twenty-nine degrees, twenty-three minutes North, longitude eighty-seven degrees, twenty-five minutes West, dragging the nets in 280 fathoms of water. Three more hours had passed, and it was time for the net to surface again. It was getting cold: the vanguard of the front had come through, and the winds were starting to swing around to the north just as the captain had feared. Those puffy gray skies were now hard on the move, pushed along by the wind, leaving a cold empty sky behind.

By the time Thomas Lee said, "All right, let's get her," we were wearing heavy jackets beneath our foul-weather gear. Then once again, we waited and watched the winch spools growing fatter as the incoming cable coiled endlessly around them. Finally the otter doors rose from the surface and dangled from the davits with their usual loud noisy crash. The net followed lightly behind, and for just an instant we saw a shark follow it. The crew hoisted up the bag, and it fairly whipped out of the sea it was so light. "God damn!" Thomas Lee snorted and began a stream of angry cussing. "We made a water haul!"

Thomas Lee opened the flaccid bag, and roughly fifty spiny sea robins poured out onto the deck, every one of them dead. The second net also had dead sea robins.

"What happened?" asked Nixon, stooping down to examine the fish.

"Shoot, we weren't even on the bottom; that's what happened. I'll bet we caught those fish in midwater when we were hauling it in. We didn't even tiptoe out here. Damn, I hate that!" He stared up over his shoulder. "This front is coming right along. We've got to go in."

Everyone looked depressed. All that anticipation, all that waiting for nothing. The skipper was embarrassed—he had underestimated the amount of cable to put out—and we were waiting in silence as he cursed and muttered. "All right, I'll tell you what. We'll make one more tow. This time she'll damn sure be on the bottom, I promise you. But the way these seas are building, it's gonna be miserable. If you can take it, that's fine with me. Frankie," he said, turning to the young deckhand, "tie the bags. Let's go fishing. You all watch you don't get washed overboard, you hear me?" he warned unnecessarily, and as he started back to the wheelhouse, he declared for all to hear, "I ain't got no damn sense. We ought to be heading in before we get drowned."

Hours later, the sun was beginning to set, a cold, orange ball sinking into the horizon, when the nets were once again on their way up. This time, as they came out of the depths, there was a heavy solid look about them. The very angle of the trawls pulling solidly down into the water foretold that it was gorged with creatures. Then, suddenly, there was trouble.

"Sharks! Goddamn it, there's sharks all over," yelled Frankie. "They're eating the nets up!" All the dead fish we had culled overboard hours before, all the slime, had attracted them. Suddenly the sea was boiling with sharks, big ones, long sleek grayish-blue bodies whipping in just under the waves and attacking the nets.

Thomas Lee hurried to the pilothouse, shoved down the throttle, and tried to outrun them. But there was no way to buck those twelve- and fifteen-foot waves. Even as the two gorged bags were pulled to the surface in the foaming white wake of the churning boat, we could see the sharks lunging in, biting out mouthfuls of the brightly colored chafing gear that protected the webbing, and violently shaking their bodies to and fro. Fish were spilling out.

"Hold it!" Frankie shouted to the skipper. "We've got to get these nets on deck before they eat the webbing down to the hanging fines."

Desperately the crew began to hoist up the heavy bags, but even as they did so, the sharks streaked in for more. As the first bag lifted clear of the water, fish began spilling out into the sea, and the sharks greedily rammed in and gulped them down. A moment later, the second net was lifted clear and dumped heavily on the deck, riddled with gaping holes. Another minute or two and only shredded webbing would have remained.

The sharks hung back, trailing behind the trawler now, waiting. Frankie put three wraps of rope around the revolving brass cathead and the big teardrop-shaped net was hoisted up to the lifting boom, where it dangled like an enormous webbed sock. Fish and shrimp began spilling out of the holes, but then they compressed, plugging the leaks. The heavy polyethylene rope groaned under the tremendous weight and stretched taut.

But all that weight didn't prevent the net from swinging back and forth with the ever-increasing rocking motion of the fifty-ton steel trawler. With each wave bigger than the last, the bag went wild, gyrating like a huge punching bag. Thomas Lee stepped forward like a wrestler about to tackle his opponent with a grim expression. The big man grabbed the two release ropes that hung beneath the swollen bag and tried jerking them open. The net crashed into him, knocking him down.

Joe and I started forward to help him. "Get back," he shouted. "This damn thing will knock you overboard. Get back!"

He rose once again and tried to grab onto the ropes, but they were snatched from his hand. For a moment the giant bag went wild. "Let off on it," he shouted to Frankie, who let the gorged bag crash to the deck with a loud plop. I shuddered to think what that was doing to the specimens; then I glanced at the other shark-torn net bag, also on the deck waiting to be opened with all those fish out of water. If we didn't open the nets and get those creatures into cold seawater soon, what life remained was bound to perish.

"All right, bring it up," said the captain between gritted teeth. This time when it was hoisted back up to the mast, Thomas Lee lunged in, braced himself with all his might, his muscles bulging, and snatched at the trawler knot. The first bit of pressure eased off the constriction, and

We were staring at an enormous sea roach. It was as if the Norma
Yvonne *had dropped her nets back into time and brought a creature
of the Eocene directly into the present.*

shrimp and fish began spilling out from the bottom. And suddenly,
right in front of us, we were staring at an enormous sea roach on the
white deck. It couldn't be confused with anything else in the world, not
those slowly flexing, long, needly pointed legs, or that flattened pur-
plish-white segmented body, and those huge triangular eyes and small
pointed antennae. I stared at it for an instant, unable to move. It was as
if the *Norma Yvonne* had dropped her nets back into time and brought
a creature of the Eocene directly into the present.

I rushed over to grab it before it got buried, but the skipper bellowed, "Goddamn it, Jack! Stay the hell clear of them nets, you hear me?
I don't want nobody getting killed!"

In a flash our precious *Bathynomus* disappeared beneath the living
avalanche. But then, as my eyes took in all those diverse lifeforms, those

confused flapping or inert creatures with their red, black, or white pale colors, two more prehistoric sea roaches emerged and slid across the deck. Anne grabbed one and we began hollering, "Ya-hoo! We got 'em, we got 'em!"

Nixon had been hanging desperately onto the railing, fighting the rolling seas. He suddenly strode forward and picked up the other one. He was grinning for the first time in hours. An electrical charge went through us at the excitement of discovery. Even the skipper and crew crowded in looking at these creatures. They were strangely beautiful and horrendous at the same time. Their antennae flexed almost mechanically; their segmented bodies, rolled up like armadillos, opened a circular mouth surrounded with cutting plates and spat out a strange brown fluid.

When we dropped them into the waiting boxes of water, they began to swim. I dived back into the pile and dug out yet another *Bathynomus*. By this time the other net was opened and we found three more. The pitching boat and blustering winds made it hard even to squat down now and glean through the catch without falling face-first into the midst of it. But our excitement banished our discomfort. There were more treasures there, sculpins, spiny deep-water crabs, more rattails, large flat skates and gray dogfish sharks with giant green strobelike eyes. Something great and exciting had just happened aboard the *Norma Yvonne*. The crew was nimbly moving about, shoveling the trash to the sharks, culling out the royal reds, and helping us pick out anything alive.

Suddenly our skipper, Thomas Lee Mills, the man who had come on this trip only because he wasn't catching any shrimp inshore, was in there with us. His perpetual scowl and doubt were gone. There he was, with his own Brownie camera, cube flashbulbs and all, taking pictures like crazy.

"You know," he declared loudly, "I ain't never paid no attention to this stuff before. I hate to think of all those tons of critters I've shoveled overboard and never bothered to even look at. But damned if there ain't something special about all this. I want pictures so I can show my youn-guns."

In moments, our boxes were crowded. Then Frankie tossed a mack-erellike fish into the box with the largest *Bathynomus*, the one that measured a big muscular twenty-four inches long.

"Good Lord," he said, his eyes wide, "will you look at that!"

The fish lay gasping limply on the bottom of the box as the giant sea roach crawled forward and grasped the hapless creature with its needly hooks. Then it abruptly spun the fish around, its plated round mouth opened, and it clamped down on its tail. Using its ten pairs of claws, before our eyes, it began to shove the entire creature into its mouth. It was almost like seeing a snake swallow a rat, except that the jaws were so powerful that they rapidly sheared away muscle and bone. In no more than a minute the fish was chewed down to bits, leaving only the head and the gnawed-down backbone. Here a creature had come up from fifteen hundred feet of pressure and darkness, up through the warm thermoclines, had been hoisted out of the water, and its first action was to start eating ravenously as if nothing had occurred.

We finished culling under the glare of the deck lights, surrounded by darkness and a star-studded sky. And when the last of the trash was shoveled overboard and the five baskets of royal red shrimp were stashed down below, the crew busied themselves getting the boat ready for the return voyage. Frankie crawled out on the outrigger, hanging above the rolling black seas, clutching the steel ladder, and looped a rope around the heavy otter doors so they could be hauled up on deck. All it would take was one slip, and we knew these rolling swells of darkness would swallow him up. Even without the sharks, there would be no saving him. But there was no problem. In a moment he was back safely on the boat, manipulating the steel-framed doors back into their brackets.

Then the grueling voyage back to port began. As those twenty-five-foot seas slammed over the bow of the big steel trawler, the sea foamed around the wheelhouse and flooded the rear decks. Periodically we would get up from our exhausted sleep, clutching the railings, and check on our specimens, keeping the heavy, weighted styrofoam boxes from being swept overboard as we crept back slowly toward shore. We were making scant headway. Soon fifteen hours had passed, then twenty, and still no sight of land. It had only taken ten hours to get out.

It was late in the afternoon before we managed to inch our way back into Mobile Bay. At the dock we worked frantically, repacking the styrofoam chests, hurrying to meet a six o'clock flight to New York out of the Pensacola airport. Once again darkness fell, only this time Nixon and I were now twenty thousand feet up, watching the lights of the cities down below, the long strings of bioluminescence of the highways.

The full impact of it was beginning to sink in. We had done it: we had captured the monstrous sea roach. Soon many thousands of people would be peering at the deep-water creatures through the glass walls of the aquarium, newly aware, as we had just become, of the incredible diversity and enormity of life in the deeps.

It was eleven o'clock the next morning, and the public relations department of the New York Zoological Society was insistent. "Hurry up, you've got to get down to the Aquarium right away. The press is coming."

Before the blazing lights of television cameras, leathery skinned, prehistoric gooseneck barnacles expanded their scarlet feathery legs. Tan-and-black-striped chain-dogfish sharks glided effortlessly along the bottom. Reporters gazed upon luminous moon snails and deep-sea lobsters. And six *Bathynomus* peered out from behind the glass walls of their new home with their huge triangular eyes, looking more like something from another galaxy rather than creatures of the deep. Nixon Griffis happily held one up for the reporters to see, keeping his fingers well clear of those terrible mandibles. Later viewers across the country awoke to see our giant sea roaches swimming across their television screens on "Good Morning America."

Crowds flocked to the New York Aquarium, even in the dead of winter. The sea roaches had indeed proved to be a monster hit.

Afterword:
Monsters of the Mind

Who can say why the giant sea roach made such an uproar with the press, why viewers all over the country watched it swim across their television screens, or why *The New York Times* and the *Daily News* carried pictures of it on their front page? Obviously we had struck a nerve, and were still getting clippings from France, West Germany, and Japan.

But at last the fanfare subsided, and once again we found ourselves wading through the fields of needlerush marsh that glowed radiant in the setting sun. Our goal was still unchanged: to find the lost mineral springs. It was something we did casually, during slack periods, or when we wanted to get away for rest and relaxation.

But my mind was still on sea monsters, and why people were so attracted to them. John Steinbeck wrote in *The Log from the Sea of Cortez:*

> When sometime a true sea-serpent, complete and undecayed, is found or caught, a shout of triumph will go through the world. "There, you see," men will say, "I knew they were there all the time. I just had a feeling they were there." Men really need sea-monsters in their personal oceans.

Periodically someone calls me up, introduces himself, and begins in a hesitant voice to tell me about his encounter with a sea serpent. Usually it happened years ago; he was sitting on the bank of the Intracoastal Waterway, or on a river, and suddenly a huge thing rears up, sometimes twenty or thirty feet out of the water, and goes back down, and swims off with undulating humps momentarily showing, typical of the Loch Ness monster. Sometimes it throws a wake, sometimes it just sinks out of sight. It's something the observer sees only once in a lifetime, and

Periodically someone calls me up and tells me about his encounter with a sea serpent. A huge thing rears up out of the water, goes back down, and swims off with undulating humps momentarily showing. It's seen for only a few seconds, but the impression is etched forever in his memory.

only for a few seconds. But the impression is always etched forever into his memory. And sooner or later he contacts me, because of my books. I am among the few who will take the time to listen and write down what the person has seen. Most of them are credible people, and I believe they really saw something. On the other hand, a fledgling newspaper wanted to boost its circulation in Tallahassee, and caused a great stir when it reported a huge serpent popping up in one of the local sinkholes in 1970. The account described how it raised its head, undulated about, and then disappeared before the horrified eyes of the people picnicking on the shore. It was thirteen years later that one of the sighters admitted to me no such thing ever happened; it was done only to boost sagging circulation. The newspaper went out of business anyhow.

I was disappointed but I wasn't going to stop hoping. Not far from where we were hiking were two of the largest springs in the world, Wakulla Springs and Spring Creek. It was in Spring Creek, which gushes out two thousand cubic feet per second per day into a marsh creek, that old man Willie Spears, a fishing guide, found an enormous skeleton of what he thought was a sea serpent.

He hired a crew of men to dig the bones out of the mud far up in a tidal creek, reassembled it in a room of his fish house, and charged people a quarter to look. It was back in the 1920s, and the old-timers said he got rich at it.

Eventually the novelty wore off, and he locked it away behind fish boxes and nets. He never would let me in to see it, but a few years ago a friend, Dr. Donald Hazelwood of the University of Missouri, managed to look at it and declared it to be the skeleton of a baleen whale. So much for monsters!

Some of those enormous springs would be a good place for monsters to live. Standing on the banks of the Suwannee or Aucilla river, watching water roar down immense sinkholes in great swirling vortices, carrying sticks, leaves, and debris into the very bowels of the earth, I can't help wondering if there might be some subterranean creature of great size hiding in the vast underground networks of caverns below.

The spring we were seeking was only a tiny porthole of the Floridan Aquifer. As we hiked toward the distant tree hammock where the spring was alleged to be, hordes of brightly colored fiddler crabs scurried through the grasses. Probably they were as close to monsters as we were ever going to get.

Years ago I discovered that we really had dragons and sea serpents all about us. It was just a matter of size. To create the strangest, most ominous creatures, all we had to do was place common small invertebrates like a fiddler crab or a mantis shrimp in a clear dish and project its image on the wall with an overhead projector. And behold the apparition, a six-inch clam worm was blown up to a six-foot shadowy horror, dancing and writhing before us on the screen, undulating its snaky bottom, moving its hundreds of tiny legs.

I carried my little invertebrates to classrooms and lecture halls and always found the audience gasping in awe at the projected monsters before them. Yet the same creatures spread out in dishes on laboratory tables produced only mild interest. We, like the simple organisms about us, respond to size. The back of our brain says, if the thing before us is as large as we are, we had better pay close attention to it.

"Do you suppose we'll ever find a real monster?" I mused, as we approached the border of a creek, watching a blue crab dart off the edge and bury up.

"Yes, and there it is," said Anne, pointing to a bump perched on top of the water. It was an alligator, which cruised slowly along until it spotted us and then abruptly sank. "After what just happened, I'm not sure I feel so safe out here." I looked up with a start; alligators were strong in our minds these days.

Only twenty miles from where we were hiking, a young man had just been killed by an eleven-foot alligator at Wakulla Springs. Over the objections of lifeguards, he swam away from the cordoned-off swimming area and snorkeled downriver where dozens of immense 'gators lay sunning. An hour later tourists aboard the jungle-cruise boats spotted an enormous 'gator dragging something through the water, and then saw the grisly sight of the young man's head and torso lifted up in its jaws.

The Game Commission had the alligator shot, and for weeks the newspapers were filled with stories and interviews. The same papers had the usual run of back-page stories of fatal car wrecks, drownings, plane crashes, war, and so on, but as usual no one paid any attention to them. The alligator-caused death was striking. Perhaps it's an atavism that causes us to react so strongly to a wild animal taking a human life. Over the past 2 million years man has had a lot of monsters to deal with. Even though we've just about eliminated them all, the saber-toothed tigers live in our minds. Yet we stand a far greater chance of being struck by lightning than being eaten by an alligator.

We waded across the creek without seeing anything else of our reptilian friend, and continued on following the animal trails through the marshlands. Far off in the distance we heard a roaring, vibrating sound that jarred across the wilderness. "Bulldozers," I growled, "they're clearing more land over by Spring Creek for another subdivision. The County Commission just gave them permission."

"Those are the real monsters at work," said my wife, wiping the sweat from her forehead, "the mechanical dinosaurs devouring the land. How much longer do you suppose the Panhandle will remain a wilderness?"

It was a race between the developers and the conservationists. While the state of Florida had one of the best land acquisition programs in the country and, along with the Nature Conservancy, was doing its best to buy up large stretches of west Florida's coastal forests, marshes, and freshwater swamps, 6 million people a year were moving into the state. Houses and condominiums were being built in hurricane-prone zones, as the Farmer's Home Administration was gleefully squandering money on giant sewer systems in the Panhandle. It was being done in the name of cleaning up the environment, but developers were the strongest backers of the new sewer lines because they would help proliferate housing subdivisions and development in previously undeveloped swampy land.

If the politicians and developers prevailed, then all the wildlife refuges and acquired endangered lands would simply be turned into more city parks, surrounded by carscapes and urban sprawl. And if storm-water runoff with its pollutants, pesticides, and heavy metals didn't poison the waters too badly, the only escape would be by boat, out into the underwater wilderness and the tideflats.

We forged on, these gloomy thoughts heightened by the sound of the bulldozers and tree choppers. But abruptly the focus of our attention changed, for suddenly the grass ended and before us was a great round pool in the middle of the marsh. It looked as if a meteorite had been hurled down from the heavens and blasted a hole in the earth. From the air, flying over the coast, you could see places where a number of such holes were scattered throughout the marsh. They weren't meteorite depressions but sinkholes.

Most of the west Florida shelf is made up of quartz or carbonate sand that overlies a limestone rock platform which is honeycombed with underground channels and caverns. From time to time an underground cavern roof collapses and the ground caves in. Sometimes houses, roads, and schools go with them. Often dry, sometimes filled with water, the result is a sinkhole, a window into the underworld.

The one we found didn't appear to be a deep sinkhole; it just sort of sagged down into the mud. It was about a hundred feet across, and we could see the sloping silty bottom. "This is certainly one of the places we want to show the class," Anne said happily. "I wonder if there're any interesting animals in it."

There didn't appear to be anything unusual: fiddler crabs made their burrows at the edge; killifish browsed around the green *Spartina* stalks that fringed the water. I took an experimental step in and found the bottom soggy.

I lurched back out of the mud not wishing to sink out of sight, backed up, and began prying my empty boots out with my muddy hands. This made the air really reek of sulfur, much stronger than normally. I looked down and noticed that the bottom was stirring as if there were little volcanoes erupting. Liquified white sand was coming out of the ground; mysterious clear water was jetting up through the turbid layer I had just stirred up.

"The spring! The spring! I found the spring!"

Anne took off her boots and waded out to me. "Hey, it is!" She cupped some water, tasted it, nodded, and made a face. "It's sulfur water all right, and fresh. But who would want to drink that?"

"The old-timers who lived here didn't have any choice, besides it's supposed to be good for you. Cures whatever ails you, just like the other springs around Panacea are supposed to do."

"What do you suppose you'd find if you could go three or four hundred feet straight down, where the water is bubbling up?" I mused, studying the little boiling volcanoes of springwater.

"I don't know, a few freshwater fish and eels. Maybe some of those blind white cave salamanders with the orange blood, or that blind white crayfish. But no monsters, if that's what you're thinking about."

"I don't know, I've seen some pretty big river eels in the sinkholes. I know someone who went two hundred feet down into Wakulla Springs and saw a six-foot *Anguilla*. "They've caught them all the way up in Georgia, and they're born a thousand miles out in the Gulf Stream.

"Well, if they weren't so mundane we should go catch some of them, instead of trying to bring back a giant snake eel. It would be much easier."

We were planning another expedition with Nixon Griffis to catch a sea serpent, or as close to one as you could get. Living out at the edge of the continental shelf, we learned, was a giant eel, *Ophichthys rex*, that grew to ten feet long, and weighed over a hundred pounds. So ferocious it was, with its slimy body and recurving teeth, that most deep-water snapper fishermen preferred to cut them loose or shoot them before bringing them up on deck. It was said that when boated, they slithered across the deck with great furor and with tremendously powerful muscles raised up one-third of their bodies, their wicked cobralike teeth latching onto anything in their path.

One deckhand was so severely mauled by one that he had to be airlifted by the Coast Guard to a hospital in Pensacola. It was the stuff that monster stories are made of.

The giant eel wasn't big enough to be a real full-blown monster, but it was as close to a sea serpent as we would probably get. And yet I knew when it was all said and done, and we hauled it back to the New York

Aquarium, it would probably sit there with its mouth gaping, opening and closing its gills, and looking like any other eel. Right now it was better talking about them, and letting them grow as monsters in our minds.

"We'd better get back. We've got to get busy and start building eel boxes," I said. "Those snake eels are supposed to produce copious amounts of slime that will probably suffocate them in regular plastic bags. We'll have to use some sort of filtering device."

"And what about the logistics of shipping one, they'll weigh a thousand pounds by the time we put water in the boxes," my wife added. "Do you suppose we can get a cargo flight out of Mobile..."

Acknowledgments

Many people have been involved in the creation and production of *The Wilderness Coast*. Anne Rudloe co-authored many of the original articles that appeared in popular magazines, collaborated on others, and later assisted in turning them into chapters. Her long hours of reading, rereading, editing, and criticizing the manuscript made it change from an idea into a reality.

Mary Ellen Chastain, my office manager at Gulf Specimen, gave it the pragmatic readings and criticisms that can only come from fifteen years of close association. But without Cynthia Brown, faithfully typing and retyping the drafts, progress would have been far slower in a busy world with competing responsibilities.

I want to thank Cindy Phipps and Jim Keeler, who helped with the assembly and collection of photographs, and William H. Herrnkind for reading the manuscript and suggesting certain revisions. Mike Shambora was invaluable in crash editing sessions, and other friends like Jack Van Doran, Ron McElderry, Roland Ting, and E. Stuart Gregg III were there to listen sympathetically when I needed them.

Larry Ogren of the National Marine Fisheries Service helped update marine turtle information, and many others provided tidbits of natural history in the text.

But there were many who gave indirect support, financial and moral, that made this writing possible, like Nixon Griffis, Robert H. Johnson, and Robert Truland. Douglas Gleeson, my chief collector, Jim Loftin, and Mark McClanahan made it possible for me to stay at the typewriter while they assumed my responsibilities of collecting in the field, and Diane Keith gave domestic and logistical support. Also the tireless environmental community that has fought so hard to keep the "wilderness coast" green deserves thanks.

But I especially want to acknowledge my editor and publisher, Truman "Mac" Talley, for his patience, persistence, and many helpful suggestions. Above all, I must express my gratitude to Turtle Mother, the goddess of electric rays and mysid shrimp and all the powers that continue to make the sea bring forth.

Index

Index

Index

Index

Index

Index